3

The Wayward Pressman

Books by A. J. Liebling

THE WAYWARD PRESSMAN

THE REPUBLIC OF SILENCE
(with French Resistance Writers)

LA RÉPUBLIQUE DU SILENCE
(with E. J. Sheffer)

THE ROAD BACK TO PARIS

THE TELEPHONE BOOTH INDIAN

BACK WHERE I CAME FROM

A. J. LIEBLING

Joseph Liebling

The Wayward Pressman

DOUBLEDAY & COMPANY, INC.

GARDEN CITY, N. Y.   1948

To the Foundation of a School for Publishers,

Failing Which,

No School of Journalism Can Have Meaning.

"As newspapers only serve to excite the masses to subvert the present order of things and the editors concerned are composed of the dregs of the literary classes, no good can be served by the continuation of such dangerous instruments, and we hereby command the entire suppression and sealing up of all newspapers published within the Empire, while the editors connected with them are to be arrested and punished with the utmost rigor of the law."

The Empress Dowager of China, 1898

(From Pearl Buck's prize essay, written at Cornell in 1925: "China and the West." Unpublished.)

Acknowledgment is made to *The New Yorker*, in which "The Wayward Press" articles on pages 119 to 129 and from 134 to 259 originally appeared; and to the *Dartmouth Alumni Magazine*, in which the article on page 265 was first published.

Contents

WHO TOLD ME?

THE WAYWARD PRESS

WHAT ARE CHANCES?

READING LIST

Who Told Me?

The Big Question

Once when I was working for the *Evening Bulletin* in Providence, R.I., about twenty years ago, a local epidemic of influenza so decimated the city staff that I was called in from dalliance with the less than onerous feature assignments that I habitually thought up for myself and placed on the drastically reduced copy desk. We read all the stories and wrote all the headlines that went into that large, fat newspaper. As I remember, there were four of us on the desk at the worst of it, and only Mallace, the man in the slot, was a hardened copyreader. One of my colleagues on the outer rim of the desk was a young man one year out of Brown who was reputed to think well of himself, having been a campus literary light. The other was a baseball writer named Eddie Doherty, very little older, who had been drafted for the desk because midwinter was a slack season in his specialty.

One morning the literary chap was missing until twelve o'clock noon, when he appeared, tossed his black cloak over the back of a chair, and sat down to the mountain of copy that had piled up in front of us. I remember one of the things going on was that Ruth Snyder was due to be electrocuted if Alfred E. Smith didn't commute her sentence. Nobody knew whether he would or not. It made a difference whether we sent down the last edition with a headline reading "Ruth Snyder to Die Tonight" or "Smith Saves Ruth from Chair." There were a great many other things to worry about too.

Doherty said genially: "Where the hell have you been?"

The even younger chap said, "Up at Brown, giving a lecture to an English class. I was telling them all about newspaper work."

Doherty said: "Who told you?"

That is a question that is always likely to be asked of a man writing about the press, and I have tried in the following few pages to set down something of my life with newspapers, which began long before I first worked on one, in 1925.

The Sapulpa Giant

The first thing I remember reading was a newspaper story about a fighter called Carl Morris, the Sapulpa (Okla.) Giant. I have calculated, for reasons that I shall furnish later, that this must have been in September, 1911. I had read before, of course, but I cannot remember what. Probably this was not even my first experiment in reading newspapers, for I must have attempted to decipher the words printed within the balloons outside the mouths of comic-strip characters. I had been attending Public School 9 at West End Avenue and Eighty-second Street since September, 1910.

The Morris story was illustrated with a picture of the biggest man I had ever seen, and it long seemed to me in retrospect the whitest, but when I attempt to analyze this recollection I do not see how he could have been any whiter than any other patch of paper. The memory of whiteness must relate to the term White Hope, which was used in the story. Carl Morris, it said, was the White Hope who would surely make trouble for Jack Johnson, the heavyweight champion of the world. He was the largest, strongest man in pugilistic history, standing six feet six inches and weighing 250 pounds, and the paralyzing power of the fists propelled by his mighty arms would pulverize anybody foolhardy enough to climb into the ring with him.

The newspaper must have been the *Evening Mail*, which my father brought home on his return from business every night, for no reason that I can recall except that it contained Rube Goldberg's cartoons. Frank Munsey bought and killed it in the early twenties. I read the story about Morris by electric light and in bed, which would indicate that I sneaked a read while my par-

ents thought I was asleep. I can date it so precisely now because
an old copy of Tom Andrews' record book I forgot to return to
Philadelphia Jack O'Brien shows that on September 15, 1911,
Morris fought Jim Flynn, the Pueblo (Col.) Fireman, at the old
Madison Square Garden, and that up to that time he had
knocked out all his opponents in places like Sapulpa and Bartles-
ville, Okla. This story must have been part of advance publicity,
because after September 15 nobody would have written of Morris
in such terms.

The sequel of it was that Flynn, a fighter of ordinary dimen-
sions and accomplishments, gave Morris a beating.

"There is no pugilistic 'white hope,' " the World said on the
day after the fight (my researching alter ego has not been able to
find the files of the Mail). "Morris's chief asset was his courage.
He proved game to the core. But as a fighter he was a joke."

And so, while I was a newspaper reader from the beginning of
my reading career, I learned ab initio not to believe everything I
read in the papers.

For all that I loved them. I would spread them on the floor
and lie down on my belly on them, or take them to bed with me,
or into the bathroom. There were in the New York evening field
then, besides the Mail, the Globe, the Telegram, the Evening
World, the Journal, the Post, and the Evening Sun. I didn't become aware of all of them at once. The Post had no funnies, and
the Evening Sun was my grandfather's habitual paper, which I
associated with him like elastic boots and chin whiskers. The
Journal was about the best, from my point of view, because it
published a full page of comics, including a strip by Harry Hersh-
field about two characters called Desperate Desmond and Daunt-
less Durham of the U.S.A., and another by McNamara about a
bunch of kids named Skinny Shaner and Shrimp Flynn and
Eaglebeak Spruder, who ran a baseball league of teams like the
Starfish Giants and the Hinky Dinks. Krazy Kat was on this
page too. But I had to sneak out and buy the Journal for myself
and then read it surreptitiously. My mother, who had grown up
in San Francisco, said it was a yellow sheet and would corrupt
me.

She feels the same way about it now. Once, a couple of years
ago, she asked me if Westbrook Pegler had died. I said no, why?

and she said she had not seen any of his stuff in the *World-Telegram* for a long time. Of course she never would have known, unless I had told her, that he had gone over to the *Journal-American*, because she had been taught that a respectable woman never looks at a Hearst paper.

I continued to believe the *Journal* was fine, even after my interest had extended beyond the funnies, which was soon. It seemed there was nothing I wanted to do, at that particular period of my life, except read and eat. Newspapers were the most alluring and omnipresent sources of reading material. Their smell and texture had the same sensual immediacy for me as the taste of the cookies I ate while reading them. In the summer of 1912 the gambler Herman Rosenthal was killed in front of the Metropole Hotel on West Forty-third Street, and the *Journal* carried diagrams of the hypothetical course of the Murder Car, a new instrument in American assassination. The diagrams were illustrated with drawings, from the artist's fancy, of the gunmen shooting and of Rosenthal falling off the curb clutching his belly. When it developed that the men who did the shooting had nicknames like Lefty Louie, Gyp the Blood, and Dago Frank, my imagination was stirred more deeply than by anything else I had read up to that time. My mother's attempt that same summer to get me interested in "Uncle Remus" was a pathetic failure. In fact if some sports writer had not nicknamed Sam Langford the Boston Tar Baby, I would not remember a single incident from "Uncle Remus" today.

I took little interest, at first, in morning papers. My father would monopolize the New York *Times* at breakfast and then carry it off to read on the subway on his way to the fur district. There must have been room in the subway then. But I knew from my experience with the *Times* on Sundays, when it remained at home, that it was not worth regretting. It seemed horribly dull then and continued to seem so until World War I broke out, when I began lapping up the communiqués.

I can still remember my sorrow when my father stopped taking the *Herald* on Sundays and ordered the *Times* instead. The *Herald* had a colored comic section including Little Nemo, the beautiful boy who had fantastic dreams. Abandonment of the *Herald* in favor of the *Times* at approximately the same time by thousands of other comfortable families like ours was a turning point in the history of New York newspapers. It was to lead to the final abandonment in Frank Munsey's lap of the paper the first James Gordon Bennett had founded, which had started as the poor man's champion and wound up as the well-to-do woman's shopping guide. Munsey in turn was to sell name and goodwill to Ogden Reid, whence the first barrel of the *Herald Tribune's* name. But I was not yet interested in the rise and fall of empires. All I knew was that I had lost Little Nemo.

It is impossible for me to estimate how many of my early impressions of the world, correct and the opposite, came to me through newspapers. Homicide, adultery, no-hit pitching, and Balkanism were concepts that, left to my own devices, I would have encountered much later in life. Reading about Verdun, I formed Francophile attitudes that were to become automatic by 1939. Seeing newspaper pictures of Irene Castle, I formed convictions about feminine good looks that were not to be shaken by subsequent changes in fashion. (My father, whose tastes had been fixed in the early Lillian Russell era, could never understand my views.)

Through newspapers I acquired a vicarious knowledge, or perhaps more accurately an illusion of knowledge, of just about everything in the world from polar exploration to the mores of choir singers and the names of the ten greatest novels ever written. The novels were chosen by a vote of experts selected by the New York *Times* Book Review in the summer of 1915.

I have often wondered how fellows raised in lesser places, where there were no dailies or only a few, have ever been able to make up the educational handicap they were under when they came up to New York and tried to compete with me.

Even now I read five or six papers a day and try to figure out from them what's happening, in the way a fellow would buy five or six tip sheets at the entrance to a race track and try to put them together to get himself a winner. Newspaper readers, like bettors and lovers, are hard to discourage.

Professor Kills Santa Claus

A newspaper gives the reader the impression of being closer to life than a book, and he is likely to confuse what he has read in it with actual experiences he has not had.

"You should have seen Charlie White," a middle-aged bore may say to me in a bar. "*He* had a left hook."

I too know White had a left hook, because I read about it so often, but it is no more or less likely that the fellow talking saw him than that I saw Ty Cobb, about whose base-running I talk with the same knowing ease. I don't think I ever did see Cobb, personally, but I do know I saw Hans Wagner and Christy Mathewson in a game between the Pirates and Giants when I was small, and I can't remember what either of them looked like on that particular day or what he did. What I *know* about them, like what I know about Cobb, is simply the cumulative product of newspaper stories and newspaper photographs, and in that way I know as much about Cobb as I do about either.

In the same way, the first President I actually saw was Warren Gamaliel Harding, but he is a paler memory to me than the first Roosevelt, or Taft or Wilson. And it is incredible to me even now that I never saw Franklin D. Roosevelt, who was nearly as much of a personal experience as my own father.

I cite these examples of the suggestive power of newsprint because the principle applies also to ideas. You read a thesis set forth as a fact in the newspapers a certain number of times and you begin to think you have figured it out for yourself or at least had it at first hand from what the press would call an authoritative source.

A book has a less treacherous effect. Even its least wary reader is strongly conscious that there is a man at the other end of the process, telling him something. The studied impersonality of the newspaper, its simulation of photography in words, all soften the outline of the printed phrase as it blurs against the background of reality.

So when I went up to Dartmouth in the fall of 1920, lacking a month of being sixteen, I took it for granted that William Jennings Bryan was a crackpot and Nicholas Murray Butler a profound scholar, that the Reds in Europe were ravening beasts and Socialists here a bit touched in the head. I believed that all Allied failures in the then recent war had been well-conceived and ably conducted enterprises, doomed by circumstances beyond human control, and that the country would be forever prosperous if we let prosperous-looking people run it. All these notions I erroneously thought were the result of my own ratiocinations.

During the two years that followed the war, newspapers had begun to exert another sort of attraction upon me, one of which I was more conscious. I had become an admirer of the more literate columnists of the day, Don Marquis of the *Sun*, Christopher Morley of the *Post*, and Baird Leonard, a witty woman who wrote for the *Morning Telegraph*, which then was less exclusively a racing sheet than it has since become. The family continued to take the *Times* in the morning. The *Telegraph* in my teens was what the *Journal* had been in my years of dawning literacy, a secret, extramural indulgence. It gave me a glimpse, vicarious but convincing, into a world not even the Hearst papers covered, in which theatre people and horse trainers seemed as casually real as the fur merchants, lawyers, general agents for insurance companies, and cotton converters who formed the most numerous element in my parents' milieu.

I had arrived at the point in my own aesthetic development when I thought that Miss Leonard and Marquis and Morley were not only gay but important, and perhaps they were. Nobody writes stuff like theirs in newspapers today, and I sometimes wonder whether this marks a decline in the public's level of taste or the publishers'. It may denote a universal change in the type of thing people like to read about, or, it seems more likely to me, the quest for the common denominator which goes along with the consolidation of newspapers. There were more newspapers in the New York of 1920 than there are now, and they had more individualized clienteles for a writer to aim at. Nor was the mark of a columnist's eminence then his suitability for syndication to the back country. Syndicates have perhaps raised the reading standards of the provinces. San Francisco, for example, can now enjoy George Sokolsky and Robert Ruark day and date with New York, instead of having to put up with some local chump like Ambrose Bierce. But the syndicates have taken the publishers' minds off the highly literate column hand-tailored for the New York trade.

There is not, in fact, in these days even a New York paper that *is* a New York paper. The biggest of the lot are either national institutions, like the *Times* and *Herald Tribune*, or show windows for national chains, like the *Daily News, Mirror, Journal-American,* and *World-Telegram*. The *Sun* is a suburban paper published on the island of Manhattan.

Most of my 623 classmates at Dartmouth were older than I, but I never heard one of them make any criticism of newspapers except that the Boston ones devoted a disproportionate amount of space to Harvard and Boston College football. The college was liberal; there was an exemplary freedom of thought and speech, but we never bothered to think or say anything more that "Hi" or "Howdy." Professor John Moffatt Mecklin told one of his classes that they were intellectual flappers, they had more freedom than they knew what to do with.

We weren't reactionary; the word wasn't even part of the current vocabulary. We were just indifferent. A certain number of students had served in the war, but they must have been convinced of its episodic quality. That was the autumn of Harding's presidential campaign for a "return to normalcy," and the concept seemed reasonable to our parents and us, although the English department sneered at the bastard word. We had not yet even arrived at the era of the campus aesthete, which was to be followed by that of the campus radical. F. Scott Fitzgerald, who had just published "This Side of Paradise," was the most heterodox prophet we listened to. If I go into this seemingly superfluous detail it is because I want to reconstruct for myself as well as for you the portrait of the paragon of news-paper readers I then was. I was as avid, unquestioning, and respectable as a piece of blotting paper with the name of the Guaranty Trust Company printed on the reverse side.

It was Professor Mecklin who continued the journalistic education that Carl Morris's downfall had begun. Professor Mecklin's arrival at Hanover had coincided with that of the class of 1924, to which I belonged. Journalism was not his sub-ject; as I shall illustrate later, a course in journalism is the last place in which to look for journalistic education. Mecklin, who was then fifty years old, had left the chair of philosophy at the University of Pittsburgh as a fairly direct consequence of his senti-ments and speeches in the great steel strike of 1919. He had come to Dartmouth as a professor of sociology. I didn't know anything about him or his past when, in the week between the Penn and Brown games—that was the way we measured time—I was sum-moned along with all my class to a lecture he was to deliver. This lecture was part of a survey and orientation course in the social sciences, which all freshmen had to take. I cannot remem-ber anything else that happened in any other session of this course. This is an example of the charming grab-bag quality of a liberal-arts college education—the items that will prove of subsequent value turn up in the most unexpected places. The lecture was a great event in Mecklin's life as well as mine, al-though I didn't learn this until much later, when I read the old man's autobiography, "My Quest for Freedom," published in 1945.

"Soon after my arrival at Dartmouth in 1920 I was asked to address the freshman class on the great steel strike," he wrote. "The question at once arose in my mind as to whether I could tell the bald truth. I was assured, however, that I could talk frankly. I faced several hundred freshmen who had already been lectured into a state of incipient revolt. They were restless and noisy, but I had provided a map of the steel mills and as I began to state frankly the treatment of the workers by the "Cossacks" they began to listen. Within thirty minues I had close attention. At the end, to make things concrete, I drew a parallel between the military methods of the steel barons and the militarism of Germany and stated that the strike was merely a crude effort by the strikers to do for the steel industry what Wilson sought to do in his struggle to 'make the world safe for democracy.' At the close a dozen or more rushed to the platform and insisted that I was talking 'socialism.' One boy with a white and tense face said that his father was in the steel business and he knew that what I said was false.

"This incident was to me more or less of an acid test of Dartmouth liberalism. So far as I could see it did not affect in the least my standing on the campus." Professor Mecklin stayed at Hanover the rest of his life, retiring as professor of philosophy and social ethics.

The part of Professor Mecklin's test-case talk that affected me most was not about the company police, whom he called Cossacks. It concerned newspapers. He has written, "The press in particular became utterly untrustworthy. We had to get the news as to what was going on in Pittsburgh from the Philadelphia and New York papers." But what he said was that of even the New York papers, the *World* was the only one that told the truth about the strike. After I heard him there was only one paper in the country I would have considered working on. That was the *World.*

The impact of the Mecklin lecture on me, which I am able to measure only after all these years, must have been directly connected with the nature of the man himself, although I never sought out his acquaintance afterward. I started reading "My Quest for Freedom" only when I began to write this book; my primary reason was to check on my recollection of the lecture and of the circumstances under which he left Pittsburgh. But it is evident from his autobiography that he must have been an impressive man in 1920. He had begun his life with a struggle against the Calvinism in which he had been reared as the son of a backwoods Presbyterian clergyman in Mississippi. Educated for the ministry himself, he had quit it after one year of self-torment in a small town in Georgia. He had made his definite break with Calvin after a controversy with the president of Lafayette College which had resulted in the resignation of both of them, in 1913, when Mecklin was forty-four. The Pittsburgh episode had followed. He had been a man all his life desperately trying to live at peace with authority, first spiritual and then temporal. But he had always been impelled in the end to speak out by the terrible Calvinist conscience he had inherited along with the God Who oppressed him. He was a most reluctant rebel, and I think this is what made him so convincing.

How to Learn Nothing

An honored friend of mine named Eugene Campbell, a student of the classics, lawyer, and steeplechase rider until the age of thirty, and from then until nearly seventy a newspaperman, once began to write a history of the American press under the title of "The Iron Ball." "I conceive the iron ball as the supreme force in American journalism," he wrote. "Of course there is no actual, or ponderable, ball duly concocted of heavy metal. It is merely a *figmentum mentis*, once aboard a newspaper, no one is ever laid off, or let out, or just plain fired. He is 'hit by the iron ball.'"

Mr. Campbell approves enthusiastically of schools of journalism.

"In these days of diminishing, and of tabloid newspapers, and of newspapers linked overnight into coast-to-coast chains to save money, increase in the number of colleges of journalism goes nevertheless forward and on," he said early in the course of a work which has so far found no publisher, possibly because it is written in the English of an educated man and makes sense.

"There were 77 of them in the United States as of the year of this country's entrance into global war, lending their strong color of justification to the inference that, apparently, every able-bodied American wants to be a newspaperman once himself. A distinguished foreign publicist did a monograph on this a few years ago, going deeply into the question of supply and demand as it addressed the naked eye, and inquiring specially whether the men currently employed on American newspapers rejoiced in all this plethora of academics in journalism or were allergic to it.

"Nobody vouchsafed him an answer, so here it is now.

"It is that American news writers perceive the schools as a blessing and a bulwark. They would like to see more of them, with much bigger buildings and much more munificent endowments, uprearing wherever there still remains room to squeeze another on a campus. For colleges of journalism must have faculties, and deans and librarians and furnace-room and coatroom men. And every place on every pay roll, as the news staffs envisage the potentialities, is a spot for some working newspaperman who has been hit by the iron ball."

My long, lean friend Gene, with his fine, thin-lipped gammoning face based on a long pointy jaw, came as an adult into a game where men stay children. His recollections of the Golden Age of Park Row seem to me in sharper focus than the blurred evocations of the officially licensed reminiscers, those professional mourners over a glory that never was. Perhaps that is why he is not even today dean of a school of journalism.

The newspaper world is full of alumni of schools of journalism, but they seldom admit it until their interrogator thrusts hot needles under their fingernails. I got to be one primarily because I was thrown out of Dartmouth twice for absenting myself from chapel on cold mornings. Every morning from October to May is cold in New Hampshire. I could not believe, even after I had been set down for one semester, that the college could be serious about maintaining such an absurd vestige of its missionary days. It was easy to make up the points lost during a semester by attendance at summer school, and I returned to college and stayed away from chapel some more. So they threw me out definitively. Dartmouth, realizing its loss, or so I have surmised without being told in so many words, abolished compulsory chapel a couple of years later. Professor Mecklin records: "The abolition of required chapel was received with great satisfaction." But then it was too late.

Like Stephen Burroughs, another great misunderstood Dartmouth man who found himself in a similar situation in 1784, "I began to look about me, to see what was to be done in my situation, to what business I could turn my attention." Burroughs temporarily solved his difficulty by hiring out as a minister, having thoughtfully stolen a set of his father's old sermons as a provision against such an emergency. He later became a counterfeiter. My misfortune determined me to become a newspaperman, a decision which I might have reached in due course anyway, but which I would have postponed as long as possible, like every other I have ever had to make. In deciding to go to the Pulitzer School of Journalism at Columbia, I was influenced equally by my reluctance to go straight to work and by a feeling that to attend another undergraduate school after Dartmouth would be anticlimactic. The name of Joseph Pulitzer of the *World* may have had some slight influence upon me too.

The inspiration of Dr. Mecklin's lecture had been reinforced by the assurances of all my English teachers except one obvious fool that I was a hell of a writer. My secret plan was to write fiction combining the macabre qualities of Bierce with the naturalism of the Ecole de Medan, but I did not feel ready to fulfill myself. I had told a Barnard girl during the summer holidays of 1922 that I did not think I would write anything great until I was twenty-five. In the meantime I determined to conquer journalism.

There is an underestimation of the potentialities of the journalistic medium inherent in this attitude, but I am convinced that it has brought into the current newspaper game whatever writing talent is at present engaged in it. Thousands of youngsters going into journalism dream of writing the great American novel, but few think of building a great American newspaper. You don't need to have ten million dollars to start a novel.

I found my classmates at Pulitzer divided into a number of categories. There were:

1. Men and women who wanted to do "creative" writing, but couldn't conceive of anybody making a living that way, and who were attracted to a trade that involved putting down words on paper; they thought that there must be some sort of a relationship.

2. A couple of fellows who expected to inherit or buy country papers and were under the illusion they might learn something useful.

3. Men who had worked a couple of years on small city news-

papers for thirty dollars a week and noticed that school-of-jour-
nalism graduates got thirty-five dollars for the same jobs.

4. Women with time to kill who thought journalism sounded
fascinating.

5. A brilliant Armenian, my dear friend to this day, who was
in the country on a student's permit from the Department of
Labor, and had rightly estimated that a school of journalism was
the least demanding place to be a student in.

The faculty was liberally studded with old boys of the type
Campbell believes schools of journalism were designed to provide jobs for, but it also included a number of able-bodied young
people who seemed to me to be taking advantage of the situation. Although the school bore the name of a fighting editor-
publisher, there was nothing in the instruction to suggest that
a newspaper ought to take a definite position in any controversy.
The pattern held up to us was Adolph Ochs's colorless, odorless,
and especially tasteless *Times* of 1923, a political hermaphrodite
capable of intercourse with conservatives of both parties at the
same time. We were constantly assured that all publishers were
righteous. The clinching argument was always that they "could
not be influenced by advertisers." (Why should they be? They
are on the advertisers' side anyway. The problem is to make
them feel the influence of the far more numerous and less pecu-
nious non-advertisers.) We were enjoined to be sober and in-
dustrious, because the day of the drinking newspaperman was
past. And we were given paragraphs from newspapers to recom-
pose, as an exercise in "newswriting." It had all the intellectual
status of a training school for future employees of the A & P.

My queerest disillusion came in a course in just straight writing. I was excused from it, on the ground that I could already
write "well enough." I have often thought back on that "well
enough" with wonderment; well enough for what? The aim of
a serious professional school should have been to teach every
journalist to write as well as Tom Paine or William Cobbett.

I never heard Cobbett's name during my two years at Pulitzer,
incidentally. Nor were we urged to read the great polemic editorials of Greeley and Garrison and Bryant, nor the courtroom
reporting of James Fenimore Cooper, whose coverage of the case
of Lieutenant Commander Alexander Slidell Mackenzie stands

with the best Zola ever did on the Dreyfus trial. We were allowed
to infer that things were being done rather better in 1923.

If I dwell on this lack of attention to writing—and by this I
don't mean fancy writing, which is a different thing—it is because
I think it reflected the attitude of the prospective employers,
and so stemmed from the same source as other newspaper weak-
nesses even more important.

Cobbett and Greeley, Bryant and Garrison, were the bosses
of their own papers. The paper's success depended on their
writing, and they exercised the standards of accomplished writers
in judging the work of their subordinates. I can hardly imagine
a less promising experiment than a standard newspaper page
written by a team of their successors, Reids, Sulzbergers, Hearsts,
and McCormicks. Kent Cooper, chairman of the board of the
Associated Press, who distributes more words to more papers
than anybody else in the world, has furnished the public with
a sample of how a press lord writes, in a queer so-called historical
novel called "Anna Zenger":

"Impetuously he felt he would like to possess her. There was
to him liquid passion in her every feature. No such thoughts
had come to him years ago when she was a girl. Now her body
having thrived upon the satisfaction that comes to a married
woman when her husband does his office competently, she was
tantalizing. For once a woman had penetrated the resistance he
had built up against such a temptation as he now faced."

Fancy trying to write for a boss like that.

My exclusion from the writing course resulted happily for
me. I was allowed to choose another course from the university
catalogue, and picked Old French, under Raymond Weeks,
Virginia gentleman and medievalist who occupied the chair of
Romance philology. This proves that, if the way to learn about
journalism is in a class in sociology, the way to learn about Tris-
tan and Iseult is to attend a school of journalism.

Some of my classmates at Pulitzer have turned out well. Vic-
tor Bernstein of *PM* is a first-rate foreign correspondent; another
chap is a nocturnal news editor and a third a fast rewrite man.
Still another teaches philosophy at Antioch College in Yellow
Springs, Ohio, one makes photographs of cats, and one fellow,
supporting himself meanwhile by filing clippings in the *Times*

morgue, has written several Broadway plays. A particularly high-ranking student is editor of a corporation house organ, and a number of the girls have got married. One chap joined successive splinter groups of Marxists until he ran out of wood, and is now working for Henry Luce. Another is assistant to a president of a university, in charge of publications. My Armenian, the best man in the class, has helped sell rugs, taught English in an orphanage in western France, established the largest advertising agency in Bucharest and lost it when the Nazis moved in, served most usefully throughout the war on the British Political Warfare Board, and is now investigating the possibilities of the Middle East for an American advertising firm.

"Till the war, when hazard and circumstances put me in such close contact with the high and mighty," he recently wrote to me, "I always thought that those in the know had at least as much sense as I have. Alas, I do not have that comforting belief any more."

The member of the class who was the school's prize exhibit until recently—so high an executive of the Associated Press that he was breathing on the soles of Cooper's feet—is now a public-relations man in Honolulu.

Dr. Frank Luther Mott, the popular historian of American journalism, himself the dean of the School of Journalism at the University of Iowa, has set down without recorded emotion that such schools annually turned out twelve hundred graduates before the war "of whom about half entered newspaper work and the others went into advertising, magazines and trade papers, radio, publishing, and other lines of work." It would be hard to imagine 50 per cent of graduates of medical schools going into podiatry, permanent waving, massage, and the compounding of toothpaste.

The committee headed by Robert Maynard Hutchins, which published a report called "A Free and Responsible Press," noted:

"Ideals and attitudes in the professions of law, medicine, and divinity are cultivated by the professional schools of those disciplines. They act as independent centres of criticism. The better they are, the more independent and critical they are. The schools of journalism have not yet accepted this obligation. With few exceptions they fall short of professional standards.

Most of them devote themselves to vocational training, and even here they are not so effective as they should be. The kind of training a journalist needs most today is not training in the tricks and machinery of the trade. If he is to be a competent judge of public affairs, he needs the broadest and most liberal education."

What he will do with this education, when the judgment of public affairs will be exercised primarily by his employer, the report does not specify. For journalism is the sole civilian "profession" that can be exercised only as the employee of somebody else. A young Philadelphian entering the law may join one of a thousand firms, or, failing that, hang out his own shingle and wait for clients. A young Philadelphian entering journalism today has three possible employers, the *Inquirer*, the *Bulletin*, and the tabloid *Daily News*. The *News* is a pygmy compared to the other two. If he works for any of these papers his judgment of public affairs had better be conservative Republican.

Even the student at West Point, preparing for a calling that emphasizes obedience, has one chance in many of arriving at command. He doesn't have to buy the Army in order to be Chief of Staff.

See What I Mean?

I had just finished writing this chapter when I picked up a copy of the New York *Enquirer*, dated Monday, May 12. The *Enquirer* is a phenomenon local to New York City. It appears only on Sunday afternoons, but carries a Monday date line so that it will be eligible to carry legal notices—announcements of sheriffs' sales and the like. Its publisher, William Griffin, is a Hearst protégé who has navigated the journalistic seas in the fashion of the *remorae*, those sucker fishes which attach themselves to a larger host. I read the *Enquirer* every Sunday afternoon, principally because it is the only paper published between Sunday morning and Sunday night, a proof of my insane addiction.

The lead editorial in the May 12, 1947, issue was a eulogy of William A. Curley, editor-in-chief of the New York *Journal-American*. It was headed "Curley—A Great Editor" and said, most importantly:

"A further analysis of Mr. Curley's success reveals that he is and always has been a 100-per-cent supporter of the policies of William Randolph Hearst. Mr. Curley never questioned these because he knew from his own knowledge and experience that Mr. Hearst's wisdom was such that in a matter of policy Mr. Hearst would be right. He therefore enthusiastically embraced these policies, followed them through, and in so doing has become one of America's most noted editors."

Max and the Corpse

There is always a temptation to attribute to one-self in retrospect attitudes quite recently acquired. In my first year at the school of journalism I hadn't worked out or learned from experience any particular reason why newspapers weren't as good as I thought they should be. I simply thought that the examples set before us were uninspiring (the negative qualities of the *Times*), the future unattractive (stodginess without afflu-ence), and the amount of hypocrisy necessary to simulate en-thusiasm for such a calling exorbitant.

In my second year there I developed such a liking for one kind of newspaper work that I could not imagine what I would do if I did not get a newspaper job on graduation. I had a desperate aversion from the formal instruction in a course in "reporting" at the school. The students, equipped with little cards saying they represented the Columbia School of Journalism, were sent to interview people in the news. There were two ways to get such interviews, by impersonating a real reporter or by throwing yourself on the mercy of the victim and implying you would flunk if he didn't talk to you. The whole business seemed to me an imposition on the subject. One of the professors in the course, a dull, handsome old man whose reputation was principally based on a two-volume biography of a Baltimore cardinal, had the same effect on me as a glass of warm water and mustard. I spoke my mind to C. P. Cooper, the other professor, an old boy with a voice like a foghorn who had been managing editor of the *Evening Sun* in the nineties, when it was a bright, tough news-paper. He had been, as I later was to learn, an extraordinary master of profanity and the most accurate tobacco-spitter on Park Row.

Coop cautiously sympathized with me, and made me a proposition: he would make me a permanent Police Headquarters man; all I would have to do was go down to the newspaper shacks on Centre Market Place behind Police Headquarters for two days a week, hang around there, and bring in a couple of police items. Coop would see that I got a passing grade in reporting.

"You'll like it down there," he said benignantly, and mumbled something about Jake Riis. "Just ask for Max Fischel of the *Evening World*," he said, "and tell him I sent you."

Police Headquarters was and is a flat-footed, square-shouldered building fronting on Centre Street. Behind the broad back of it runs Centre Market Place, cold as a glacial crevasse in winter, hot as a fat man's breech in summer.

Two industries exist in this canyon, the sale of police supplies and the gathering of police news. In those days the newspapers and news services hired flats in the tenement buildings across from Headquarters; you might have another newspaper or a Neapolitan family of nine people as your neighbor across the hall. These offices in tenements were called shacks, perhaps because in the prehistoric era when Police Headquarters was on Mulberry Street police reporters had utilized actual shacks. Now all the newspaper offices are centralized in one renovated building that has a smart brick front and no families in residence. But they are still called shacks.

Fischel, a plump, gray man with a round face and a psittacine nose, was sixty then. He liked to call himself "the dean of the corpse" of police reporters; he had been legman for Jacob Riis in the early nineties, when that Danish-born *Sun* reporter had made slum clearance a national issue. The slums were still there, but Jake had left a great name. There were others around who seemed as old as Max, but they did not dispute his claim to seniority; he had come there at an earlier age than any of them.

Max knew the East Side so well that despite his advancing years and short legs he could beat almost anybody to the scene of a story when he really wanted to. He knew the roof pattern of every block by heart, for one thing, and by traveling across roofs he could often arrive at an upper-floor tenement before less resourceful reporters had reached the street door. He didn't like to go racing out more often than he had to, however. He had as partner another former *Sun* man named Frank Roth, who had worked for Cooper and was still going strong. Roth, an angular, knobby-browed gent, had a book on rhetoric that he studied constantly, with the intention of improving his writing. "This is no game for a man who can't write," he told me soon after I had begun to hang out in the shack. "A man who can't write is likely to stay at Headquarters for his whole life." He had already been there thirty years, but still had hopes.

Max also had a couple of younger subordinates, Basil Gallagher and Milt Lewin, and a "slip boy" named Arthur, whose function I will presently explain.

In the basement of Police Headquarters there was (and is) a tiny door, like that of a dumbwaiter. This door conceals the mouth of a tube, and out of the tube come penciled slips of paper, each the record of a misadventure.

Arthur's job was to cross the street every couple of minutes, look for new slips, and copy their contents (it was forbidden to remove them). Names, street numbers, precinct specifications, notation of time, and then the nature of the mishap: lacerations of left hand, or fractured right leg and internal injuries, or perhaps "asphyxiation, D.O.A." "D.O.A." meant "dead on arrival" (of the officer). If the D.O.A.'s description and address were uninteresting, Max would ask me to run over and check on the circumstances. "There always might be something," he would say. It hurt his conscience to let anything go unchecked, but he wanted to reserve his *World* men for the more promising break that might come. He knew I liked to go. I never got him more than the makings of a few lines, but I began to learn my way around.

There was a tight combination at Headquarters in those days. The men working for competing newspapers swapped news. This was a tactical necessity, for otherwise, while all the papers were competitively covering the same fairly good story, a real story might break and find the shacks stripped of reporters. One day a paper might have needed seven men to cover Headquarters properly, and another there wouldn't have been work for one. The city desks, set, as always, on keeping pay rolls low, tacitly connived in the practice. So my excursions furnished a form of insurance for everybody. That is to say, that going over to North Moore Street, near the water front, to check on a D.O.A. sailor who had done the Dutch act (committed suicide) in a lodginghouse, I was representing the entire press of New York City. If the sailor had turned out to be the Prince of Wales incognito, I would have telephoned the news to Max, who would have been honor-bound to inform all the others. I never discounted this possibility.

Then there were fires. Almost any fire on the East Side has potentialities of a "10 Trapped By Fire In Tenement Tragedy," so somebody went to each of them. We would be sitting around playing poker, nickel and dime, usually, and an electric bell would ring. One of the men would count the number of strokes: for example, Nine, Eight, One—981. He would look up the number in a huge book that gave the number of every fire-alarm box in the city. "Foot of West Houston, might be a dock fire," he would say. "Want to go down there with me, Lieb?" If there was a chance of a dock fire they would not want to send me alone, but I was always welcome as company.

The other fellow and I would head north through the little canyon of cops and copy, walking with the long, straining stride downtown children recognized, and as we went Mike Finnegan of the old *Telegram* or Willie Keegin of the *Bronx Home News* would call out to us: "Give us a ring if there's anything doing!" I was proud that the children would think I was a real reporter.

Three quarters of an hour later we would be back with an item about a fire of no particular consequence.

"We met the engines coming back!" we would yell.

Last summer I was walking through Centre Market Place, and Keegin, who is on the *Post* now, was sitting in front of the shacks as if nothing had changed. "Hello, Joe," he said. "Was it much of a fire?"

It would have been great roadwork for a fighter.

The men themselves fascinated me. By external index they fell into two classes, those who were married and shabby and those who were unmarried and dressed like Mississippi steamboat gamblers.

Red Gallagher was my beau ideal. He was only five years older than I but he knew everything. He wore a derby hat on the side of his head and a chesterfield overcoat with a velvet collar; a colored man had slashed one side of his face in a clip-joint brawl, he had a crush on a woman who had been divorced five times, with bigger headlines over each reprise. She was twenty years older than Red, and some of the other fellows said he hardly knew her, but the scar of the Negro's knife was tangible. Nobody could say he was making that up. Red was killed in an airplane crash in Guiana during the war, the same one, I believe, in which Eric Knight, the Yorkshire author, lost his life. Coming to work, Red would see one of the shabby married types standing in front of the shacks. He would do a Charleston step, feint a left jab at his colleague, and ask:

"Whatsa dope, Bob?"

Bob would turn sad, gentle eyes on him and say in a sad, gentle tone:

"Not a thing, Red. There hasn't been a murder or a stickup all this week. I never saw the town so dead." He would be worrying about the iron ball. Editors had a custom of cutting down on departments where news was slow.

Then the shabby man would go out into the street to play ball with the Italian children, while Red would try to make up a bridge game inside. It was always harder to get four for bridge than seven for poker.

The real old-timers, like Fischel and Roth and Bob Patterson of the *Sun*, played less cards than the others, except that Max was always trying to find a sucker for two-handed pinochle, in which he was invincible. Patterson had a white mustache and a high, rusty derby that was as Victorian as Gallagher's was dashing. They would often get talking, and for once in my life I was content to listen. I am, in fact, still a good listener when working at my trade. I talk too much only in private.

They would tell of murders by perverts, then of rats eating babies, and how old Dan Peabody used to beat more information out of stool pigeons than the new cops would ever learn how to get in a police college. If Jack Brophy of the *News* was there he would always talk about his dog. Brophy, a baby-faced man, was a great lover of animals. He was always pulling mangy dogs from under the wheels of crosstown cars and installing them in his shack, where they would howl and keep his number-two man

from sleeping. The particular dog he had at home, according to
him, was very intelligent. Brophy, working on a morning paper,
would rise late. While he was still in bed, he said, he would send
the dog downstairs for the newspapers—he lived up in the re-
mote Bronx, in a house. "Bring me the *Tribune*," he would say,
and the dog would. "Bring me the *Times*," Brophy would say,
and the dog would. "Bring me the *Herald*"—and so on. "When
the *Herald* and *Tribune* merged," Jack told us, "the dog nearly
went crazy. 'Fetch me the *Herald*,' I would say, to tease him;
God forgive me I shouldn't have. He got so ashamed not being
able to find either one of them it broke his spirit and he refused
to eat. Ten days later he was dead."

Not many readers feel that badly about merged papers. They
are less sensitive, apparently. And still I guess a few of us have
passed up meals after looking for the old *World* in the *World-
Telegram*.

Some of the men could barely decipher captions in the tabloids they worked for. They admitted they had never written a
story. Police reporters, particularly on afternoon papers, turn in
most of their stuff by telephone no matter how literate they are.
There was a fellow from the *Staats-Zeitung* who had a Ph.D. in
anthropology from a German university. He wasn't much of a
reporter. Another German, whom we all called the Count, really
was a count, according to the regulars. The Count reveled in
crime. He had a nose for it. He joked about it.

Once a Pole stuffed his sweetheart into a burning furnace.

"You ought to have seen her," said the Count, who had
viewed the funeral baked meat. "The legs, just busting with fat,
like nice broiled sausages."

The Count was a lobster man on the *Journal*, Hearst's evening
paper, working from two until nine in the morning. Promptly at
the conclusion of his day's work he would get drunk and hang
around the shacks until evening. He slept, usually, in the *Journal*
shack, from after dinner until time to go to work again. He had
the most extensive collection of obscene postcards I had until
that time seen. I was to see nothing to equal it until I was shown
some taken from German prisoners in Tunisia nineteen years
later.

One day the Count impersonated the police commissioner, who was, naturally, an Irishman, making a speech in French while decorating the recipients of the Police Medal. This was surrealistic creative mimicry; the commissioner didn't speak French, but the Count made it seem more like the commissioner than the old ex-harness bull himself.

It was a hot day. A patrol wagon was parked at the curb. A curly-haired reporter named Davidson, a Negro detective, and I sat on the low stoop of one of the tenement houses.

Between the stoop and the patrol wagon the Count staggered back and forth, like a pendulum or a sloop tacking against the wind. Wonderfully, he never touched either boundary marker.

"*Mes chers confrères*," he would begin, and then search in his pockets for the *figmentum mentis* medal. "*Mes chers confrères*," and then politely, as a girl passed, "You like music, madame?"

The girl did not answer.

"Listen," said the Count, replacing his black derby. It was in July. With the air of a prestidigitator producing a rabbit from inside a thermos bottle, he bent gracefully over the seat of the patrol wagon and sounded the electric horn.

"There, you got music," he said.

The girl was already half a block away.

"*Mes chers confrères*," the Count resumed, "*mes chers confrères*——" and sitting down on the rear step of the patrol wagon, he began to weep.

One morning in Centre Market Place I was introduced to a detective named Kelly who had caught a crook on Abraham Lincoln's shirt stud. Men who obtain money under false pretenses look at it to see it isn't marked. But Kelly, posing as the sucker, had given this particular confidence man a five-dollar bill on which he had previously decorated with a discreet, inky stud the white bosom of the shirt in Lincoln's portrait. Afterward he had arrested the fellow—"a regular artist," Kelly said. During the trip to Headquarters in a taxi, Kelly said, the prisoner "had sang so sweet, it brought tears to my eyes. He used to be a ballad singer in a dive on Chatham Square."

There was a day when we had a story from St. Barnabas, the Episcopal Church home for women on Mulberry Street a few blocks uptown. An unmarried mother was to be handed over to the police for vagrancy, being without visible means of support seventeen days after the birth of her baby. The estimable institution had accepted the mother and the baby on their discharge from the Bellevue maternity ward the week before, but had been under the impression that the woman was Episcopalian and married.

Now that the nead matron had learned the truth, it had seemed obvious to her that a child, even seventeen days old, should not be left under the "depraving influence" of its own mother. It was the charity worker's own phrase. But as St. Barnabas did not keep unaccompanied babies, it would be necessary to send this one back to Bellevue alone. We in the shacks did not think highly of the baby's chances of survival at Bellevue. The mother was raising hell, and the matron had had to call in a policeman and have her arrested. A couple of fellows from the combination got to St. Barnabas ahead of the patrol wagon and said that the broad had scratched the cop's face and raised a monumental row, but the charity people had gotten the kid away from her safely. Then the wagon came and took the broad away.

I wrote little stories about Lincoln's shirt stud and the unruly mother and handed them in as classwork at Columbia. The old raspberry-sherbet-faced biographer of cardinals said that neither would be worthy of inclusion in the *Times*. The *Times* sustained his judgment by not mentioning either item, but Joe Van Raalte, a columnist for the *Morning Telegraph*, confirmed mine by writing a long indignant piece about the woman at St. Barnabas. Van Raalte said the girl would have "received better treatment in any hook shop." The *Telegraph*, I suppose, had little Episcopalian circulation. Hook shop, by the way, is a term I used once before in a book and it got printed hock shop, which is quite a different thing. A hook shop is an old term for what our British cousins call a knockin' shop.

I liked to pound up tenement stairs and burst in on families disarranged by sudden misfortune. It gave me a chance to make contact with people I would never otherwise have met, and I learned almost immediately what every reporter knows, that most people are eager to talk about their troubles and are rather flattered by the arrival of the *World* or the *Journal*. Women, in particular, are never so friendly as when something has happened to their husbands. Petronius' story of The Widow of Ephesus should be assigned reading in any practical course on reporting.

I liked even the sociable smells of the East Side. It was something of a return to the manor for me. My father had spent his boyhood there, although by the time he married he had got five miles uptown and even further away economically. Yet he had often told me stories of this vivid world in which all his adventures, according to him, had been personal triumphs. My mother professed to find these stories boresome, and I don't think I had ever been sure, before I got down to Headquarters, that he hadn't made most of them up.

I remember the first time I saw a dead man who had not died in bed. There was a police slip about a wrecker's workman who had fallen from a building, a long walk east of headquarters— Pitt or Cannon Street, I think. Langdon Post, a Harvard man who had decided to enter newspaper work at thirty, had been sent to Max at the *Evening World* shack to break in. We started out together on the story of the fallen workman. Both of us were in good condition, and I think we broke all records for walking through an obstacle course of children and pushcarts. We did not consider it sporting to run. By the time we reached the knot of curious people on the sidewalk in front of a half-demolished wall we had almost forgotten the nature of the thing we were racing to. Each of us had been concentrating on walking so fast the other fellow would have to run a couple of steps to keep up.

The crowd opened up before our evident urgency and the police cards we wore in our hats, and there the man lay on his back. He was gray with cement dust and there was no blood on his face. There was no blood in sight. Under his short white nails there was mortar; falling, he had tried to hold onto the top of the wall by his fingers. He must have lost his balance as he heaved to loosen a stone. The bloody old building had revenged itself. Many an immigrant must have died in it, and even going down, it was taking another European to the grave.

. A cop standing by had the man's name already; the boss of the wrecking gang had furnished it. None of us knew how to pronounce the name, but Post and I copied it out of the cop's notebook. It was Polish, or Ukrainian, or Lithuanian, I forget.

The cop said: "Nobody but a Polack would take a job like that."

The first money I ever earned from a newspaper came to me from the treasury of the *Evening World* in the early spring of 1925. Max Fischel and Lindsay Denison, a renowned *Evening World* rewrite man, had been relieved from their regular routine for a few weeks to write a series of articles on the different colonies of foreign-born Americans in New York. Denison, who seldom got out of the city room during his ordinary working hours, used to come to the shacks during this collaboration. I regarded him with awe.

He was a red-faced man, not nimble, who reminded me for some reason of Dr. Johnson. He wore an old porkpie hat which at that time was an archaic affectation in dress, recalling college fashions at the century's turn. The porkpie style was to be resurrected, but much later. Denison was Yale '95, and had been at his peak when Irvin S. Cobb and Richard Harding Davis and Frank Ward O'Malley were at theirs. He was supposed to be marvelously fast and fluent, literary qualities for which my early training had given me no esteem, but of which I was now learning the pre-eminent newspaper importance.

Max had acquired from one of his Italian friends a book about the history of the Italian immigration to America, which contained good background material for the series, but it was in Italian. A reporter for an Italian paper tried to translate parts of it for Max and Denison, but his English was insufficient. So I read the book, made a précis of it, and translated the chapters they wanted, all for fifteen dollars. They gave me a voucher on the treasurer of the *World* for that amount, and it was a proud day when I cashed it.

The World of Sport

A police reporter sees more than he can set down; a feature writer sets down more than he possibly can have seen. I was eager to get a job as a police reporter after I took my degree. As a maraschino cherry on the sundae of academic absurdity, the degree was entitled Bachelor of Literature, although what literature had to do with rewriting the Times paragraphs I never found out. I went swimming on commencement day.

There were no police jobs going; in fact for a while there seemed to be no jobs going at all for beginners. The assistant city editor—I seldom got as far as the city editor himself—would ask me if I had had experience in Denver or Texas. They seemed to think it cheeky for a New Yorker to ask for a job. Translating the Italian book for Max and Denison, I had read a lot about the immigrant custom of getting a job in a firm and then bringing on all one's paesani, peasants from the same village in Apulia or Lucania. It seemed to be an old custom in New York newspaper offices too, except that the paesani came from places like Binghamton and East St. Louis.

I have always thought that a dozen young men fresh out of the top third of the senior class in the liberal-arts course at Columbia, N.Y.U., C.C.N.Y., or Brooklyn College would make a more valuable reinforcement for a newspaper staff than the same number of men freshly arrived from the bush with ten years' small-city experience apiece. The New York boys would be more mature emotionally and more literate. They would have a local news background acquired from reading New York newspapers all their lives. Also they would romanticize themselves less. I have known out-of-towners on newspapers whose

primary urge toward journalism had been a consuming desire to
escape from Iowa.

I know this a controversial subject, and I seem to be the
only one on my side of the controversy, due to the continuous
rumble of logs being rolled for one another by the staunch
Hoosier-Sooners and Razor-backed Rocky Mountain Boys, but I
am sure I've got something.

I looked about for a job for portions of six weeks. It was summer, and the beach at Far Rockaway diverted me from job-
hunting pretty often. Then a copyreader named Laurence J.
Spiker in the sports department of the *Times* called Professor
Cooper one day and asked the old boy if he had an ex-student
with the makings of a copyreader. By this, I presume, he meant
a broad bottom and a captious disposition. Coop recommended
me, and I went unromantically to work sitting down. In the
back of my mind was the thought that after a tour of sedentary
duty I might convince some editor I had experience enough to
use my legs. This was a faulty line of thought, for trained copyreaders are usually harder to find than reporters, and few editors
will turn an experienced copyreader into an inexperienced outside man. It often, but not always, works the other way—when
a fellow's legs give out he comes inside, providing he can read
and write.

In addition to the frustrated reporters who know exactly how
a story should be covered because they have never covered one,
and the superannuated reporters who are just resting their feet,
there are in every newspaper office the congenital, aboriginal, in-
tramurals. They are to be distinguished from the frustrates because they have never even wanted to see the world outside.
They come to newspapers like monks to cloisters or worms to
apples. They are the dedicated. All of them are fated to be
editors except the ones that get killed off by the lunches they
eat at their desks until even the most drastic purgatives lose all
effect upon them. The survivors of gastric disorders rise to
minor executive jobs and then major ones, and the reign of these
non-writers makes our newspapers read like the food in the New
York *Times* cafeteria tastes. It is as if, in football, only bad
players were allowed to become coaches. Indifference to language thus becomes hierarchized. The proprietor wouldn't know

decent writing if he saw it; the managing editor wouldn't know decent writing if he saw it. No one who even aspires to be a managing editor will admit knowing anything about writing if he knows what is good for him.

At any rate, I went to work. It was arranged that I was to receive eight dollars a day, six days a week. My pay was on a daily basis so that, if the *Times* found my work inadequate, it would not feel obliged to give me a week's notice. It was a paper with sensibilities. After I had worked there five months I was raised to fifty dollars a week. My parents moved back to Manhattan from Long Island in the fall of 1925, and since they insisted that I live rent-free with them in an apartment hotel near Central Park, I found my salary more than adequate. This gave me a less than realistic first impression of the economic aspect of newspaper work.

I spent eight months on the *Times*, and they gave me my first and, I am thankful, only sample of what must be the common experience of the great majority of workers—a clean, painless job without any intrinsic interest. Sports copyreading is as easy to learn as how to play a fair game of anagrams. You check on scores: for example, you make sure, in basketball, that the field goals and foul goals do not add up to more or less than the final score. If they don't check, you give some player a couple of extra points, or maybe deprive him of one or two. This goes for baseball, football, and any other game you can think of. We never did have a copyreader who could fathom a cricket score, so that copy always went to type just as it was brought in, handwritten, by a long-haired British gentleman who attended the matches, most of which, I think, were held on Staten Island. Reader interest was nil, but Major Thomson, the sports editor, thought cricket high class. The cricket correspondent also covered chess matches. There was a copyreader, John Drebinger, who understood what the chess reports were about, and he would sometimes protest at the small size of the headline he was ordered to put over a chess story. "That's a hot match!" he would complain. "Lasker held to a draw in 63 moves!" We called him Bogglejobble, after the Russian chessmaster, Bogoljubow, one of his favorites.

Drebinger, incidentally, is one of the few confirmed copy-

readers ever to escape into the outside world. A few years later
he became the *Times* correspondent with the New York Giants.
I think Drebinger effected his release by pretending to be a
bourgeois type, extremely contented with his life on the copy
desk. This so irritated the higher powers, used to copyreaders'
continual complaints, that they decided to make Drebinger un-
happy too, and kicked him into exactly the place he wanted to
get.

Having verified, or at least rectified, the statistical matter
which forms the real meat of the story, and "cleared it"—that is,
sent it up to the composing room to be set in agate type—the
sports copyreader takes a cursory look at the sports writer's text.
He quickly learns not to try to improve it, as sports writers are a
temperamental lot and like to get maximum mileage out of the
used adjectives they lease from the Merriam-Webster Dictionary
Company at the beginning of every season. The copyreader is,
however, allowed to sneer.

"Old Dick Vidmer has moved the slough of despond over to
Pittsburgh," he may whisper roguishly to the colleague sitting at
his right. "Yesterday he had the Dodgers in the slough of despond in Cincinnati and last Friday they were in it in Chicago.
Must be part of their traveling equipment, like a bat bag." All
sports copyreaders feel that sports writers are overpaid and over-
rated windbags who spend their time sleeping off drunks in the
open air while the copyreaders have to sleep off their drunks at
home and in the daytime, which is a great hardship.

Once the text has been cleared, the sports copyreader has a
chance for his nearest approach to creative effort: the composition of a headline. This is a form of art, like the Japanese nō
poem or writing on the head of a pin, which must be exercised
within extremely exiguous limits. One form of head I remember
called for two lines of 16½ spaces maximum (16 was prefer-
able) with a dozen words falling away under them in an
inverted pyramid called a bank. A space is a unit used in headline writing, roughly equivalent to the space a letter takes up.
However, M and W count 1½ spaces, and I counts only ½. The
interval between two words is counted a ½ space. So a fellow
can write "Giants Beat (or defeat, stop, topple, batter) Reds,"
but just "Giants Trip Pirates," because Pirates is 2½ spaces

longer than Reds. "Giants Trip Pirates" would not look quite so
crowded. In the second line you can elaborate "2–1 as Ott
Homers," perhaps. Of course not many ballplayers have names
as easy to fit in a headline as Ott. You'd be surprised how
quickly an evening passes amid big intellectual problems like
that.

To top is probably the most useful headline synonym for to
beat, defeat. It occupies only *three* spaces instead of four. The
trouble with it is that sometimes all the copyreaders on a desk
start to use it simultaneously and every baseball headline has
somebody "topping" somebody else. Then the man in the slot
gets stuffy and accuses his subordinates, the men on the rim, of
a certain lack of originality.

On the *Times* I used to come to work at seven in the evening,
six o'clock on Saturdays, which was the busy day, and get
through at about one-thirty in the morning. There was no lunch
period, but at about midnight a boy brought us a cup of bad
tepid coffee at the desk, or else we went up in couples to the
cafeteria in the Times Building, to drink the equally bad but
warmer coffee available there. After one-thirty the gayer elements of the group—"of whom I was," to borrow a phrase from
a Russian colonel I once knew—went out to have a few glasses
of beer needled with alcohol in the speakeasies around Times
Square before going home. We slept late.

It must be like that in a lot of industries. When you come to
work all you think of is what you are going to do when it is over.
It was no use trying to throw yourself heart and soul into
making "Giants" fit into 4½ spaces, because you couldn't anyway. And there are a lot of other jobs in the world with
limitations just as rigid.

There was, however, for a man of twenty-one, as I was, a fascinating sense of being a dashing chap just because one was in the
newspaper game. A fellow named John Muldowney, who had
been the youngest copyreader until my advent, was my most
frequent companion on the speakeasy circuit, but other copyreaders often came along. And once we got our flat feet on the
brass rail and the twenty-five-cent needle beer in front of us, we
felt the social and professional equals of Frank Ward O'Malley
or any other sonofabitch we wanted to tell lies about.

There was, in truth, more of interest outside the *Times* sports department than inside it, so that no man in his right senses could have made the work his main preoccupation. Social intercourse among newspapermen, and for that matter among all kinds of people then, was not restricted by any difference of ideologies. The touchstone of liberalism was opposition to the liquor laws and we were all liberals. Anybody you met in a speakeasy had to be a liberal too, or he wouldn't be there. Our idea of a great liberal statesman was Al Smith, because he came right out and told the farmers, knowing in advance that they weren't going to vote for him anyway, exactly where he stood. He stood on the same side of the bar we did. This bond of liberal faith predisposed us favorably toward anybody we encountered in a saloon and made for quick friendships. We felt there had to be some good about anybody that resisted tyranny.

It made us feel a responsibility for drunks that I happily feel no longer. I remember one bleak January night Muldowney and I found a young fellow lying in the snow on Forty-fifth Street between Sixth and Seventh and we decided it would be wrong to let him freeze to death. We barked lightheartedly, doubtless a matter of allusion to St. Bernard dogs, and picked him up. He was rigid, more probably with liquor than cold, but he felt as if he weighed not more than fifteen pounds. Either he was a levitationist or it was good alcohol they put in the beer at Canavan's. "Where do you live?" Mul asked the impersonation of a corpse, and it murmured, "United States." With an intuition born of liquor we understood that he meant the Hotel America, on Forty-seventh Street, so we carried him up there.

"What's your name?" Mul asked him when we arrived at the hotel, and the corpse said, "Johnny." "Johnny what?" "Ask m'brother." "Ah," I said, "he has a brother in the hotel." So we entered and carried him through the lobby to the elevator. "Where does this man's brother room?" I asked the night elevator man (it was the kind of hotel where the night elevator man sometimes had to distribute people to their rooms). He gave us the number and we carried Johnny to the door and knocked. "Who the hell is it?" somebody shouted gratefully, and we said: "It's your brother." The door swung open, although no light went on, and the same voice shouted: "Throw the bastard in!" Mul and I threw him in and the door slammed shut. We went on our way knowing we had done a good action. If I saw a man lying in the snow like that now, I would just jump over him and leave him for dead.

There were eight or nine sports copyreaders, besides two or three reporters who joined us Saturday nights, when there was a big sports section, to earn an extra eight dollars reading copy. Prices were not low in 1925, and my senior colleagues were not affluent, but the whole scale of pay was much higher than it was in the shacks at Police Headquarters. In 1934, when the *World-Telegram* unit of the American Newspaper Guild won a minimum wage of thirty-five dollars for experienced reporters, an old-time police reporter whom I knew down there said that the contract would bring him *a higher wage than he had ever had in his life*. This man, in 1925, must have been getting around twenty-five dollars.

The rewards of office in the sports department did not seem to me particularly brilliant, but they were sufficient to motivate a tangle of political intrigue. Once I had learned to compose headlines I became bored with the whole business. It wasn't that I disliked sports; the fact was that I had never in my life, since the age of six years, had so little contact with sports. Nineteen twenty-five was the first football season since 1917 when I didn't see a single college game. I had to be in the office early Saturdays. I saw no boxing because I worked evenings, and no horse racing or baseball because it seemed a shame to pay admission when I worked in a sports department, even though I was so junior that I never got any of the office passes. I used to go down to Police Headquarters sometime in the afternoons just to make sure that the world was still going on. On these occasions I was pleased to note that I was accepted by my former overlords as a real newspaperman because I was making fifty dollars a week.

Winter was a quieter season for sporting news then than it is now. Professional ice hockey had just come to New York, and had not yet been built up into something almost as much publicized as baseball. Basketball was still played only in college and

school gymnasiums, and winter horse racing didn't amount to
much. So we used to fiddle around a lot with such picayune
matters as scholastic basketball, pocket-billiard matches—the
head of the sports copy desk did publicity for a manufacturer of
billiard equipment—and Class B chess tournaments. At about
half-past ten dozens of schoolboys with changing voices would
begin to call up to tell how St. Ambrosius had defeated Sodom
Academy, or the High School of Sales Management had won an
uphill battle with the Letchworth Village School for Feeble-
minded Children. Major Thomson had an idea that we ought to
get the names of all the dashing adolescents and how many bas-
kets they had scored. He had heard that the more names you got
into a paper the more people would read it. This accounts for
the high reader interest of the telephone directory. Also he was
in a race with the *Herald Tribune* to see who could publish
more schoolboy scores. This competition in inclusiveness had
started during the football season, centering first, however, on
college football scores. After we had compiled our list of College
Games each Saturday we would wait until the copy boy brought
in the first copies of the *Herald Tribune* and eagerly count to see
whether they had any we didn't. It was by keeping this list of
results (a chore that always devolved upon the newest copyreader) that I acquired a repertory of names of American colleges unmatched except by textbook salesmen. If the *Tribune*
had the score of the Muskingum-Baldwin-Wallace game and we
didn't, Major Thomson was inconsolable, even though we might
have scooped them on two other games, Upsala-Rider College of
Trenton, N.J., and Cornell (Ia.)-Columbia (Ia.) perhaps. Sometimes he even suspected the *Tribune* of ringing in a couple of
colleges that didn't exist.

Early in November the struggle seemed fated to end in a
deadlock. A conviction began to dawn that both papers were
publishing the scores of every game on earth. Then we got a new
correspondent in a Southern state who sent us the scores of
dozens of games the *Tribune* didn't carry, games played by teams
with names like Lincoln and Virginia State. It wasn't until the
following week that Thomson learned that all these teams were
colored. The question then was whether he should keep them all
out of the next issue, since the *Tribune* apparently disdained

them, or strike a simultaneous blow for liberalism and the prestige of the *Times* sports section by keeping them in, so we would have the longest list of college football results in the city. Thomson was tempted by the second alternative, but it was too radical for him. He threw the colored colleges out and finished in a dead heat with the opposition.

This Thomson was an extraordinary sort for a sports editor. He was a Canadian of the type that plays British, and had been a captain in the first World War, but he seemed more like an old trouper than an old trooper. He was a tall man with a purplish face and black hair parted in the middle. He liked to wear colored silk shirts, white flannel pants, and white buckskin shoes in summer. He walked with long, determined strides, as if he were continually on his way to do something important (but what?), and he acknowledged a profound dislike for sports of all kinds. Frederick P. Birchall, the managing editor of the *Times*, was British and choleric and walked the same way. I am not in a position to say that the sports editor patterned his manner on Birchall's, since I had known neither before their conjuncture on the *Times*, but I have noticed a mimetic tendency among executives on other papers. It is a constant of the newspaper business.

The very existence of the *Times* sports section marked a concession to frivolity on the part of Adolph Ochs, the great merchandiser of stodginess, but the old man had determined that if he had to have a sports page at all, it would be as uninteresting as possible. Thomson was an ideal choice to keep it that way.

One night some boy with pimples in his voice called up from Brooklyn to tell the *Times* about a particularly unfascinating contest between two Catholic-school fives. I took the call and noted down all the drear details until I got to who was the referee. "Who was he?" I asked. "I don't know," the kid said, "and anyway I ain't got any more nickels." So he hung up. We couldn't use a basketball score in the *Times* without the name of the referee. So I wrote in "Ignoto," which means "unknown" in Italian. Nobody caught on, and after a while I had Ignoto refereeing a lot of basketball games, all around town. Then I began bragging about it, and after a short while my feeble jest came to the ears of Thomson.

"God knows what you will do next, young man," he told me

after the first edition had gone to press on a bitter night in March. "You are irresponsible. Not a *Times* type. Go."

So I lost my first newspaper job.[1]

[1]The story of the referee, Ignoto, reminded a friend of mine of the Norwegian industrialist, Ikke, whom he had interviewed aboard the Kungsholm in the late thirties. The Kungsholm had a singularly uninteresting passenger list that trip, but the ship newsmen spotted near the bottom of the column the notation in capital letters "IKKE OMBORD." The list ended with a couple more commonplace names. My friend decided Mr. Ikke must be somebody of importance and went looking for him. Failing to find him, he noted, anyway, that "A Mr. Ikke, Norwegian mystery man, partner of the late Ivar Kreuger, was on board the Kungsholm when she docked yesterday, but got through Customs and sped away to his hotel before ship newsmen could question him." Ikke means "not" in Norwegian, and "ikke ombord" referred to the nonentities at the bottom of the page, who had canceled their passages late.

I Put Me on the Road

Getting fired from the *Times* impressed me deeply with my own worthlessness. This was in March, 1926, and I had only recently been made a member of the Artists and Writers Club, an institution that had begun its illustrious career in October of 1925. I went over to the club, which was then masked behind a blind loft in the front section of its present licensed premises, and sought consolation. I believed that I was thus conforming to tradition, and besides I would have ordered the same kind of consolation even if I had not been fired. I found, however, that being fired was considered in the same light as a first sexual misfortune, not a disgrace but an indication of manhood. It enhanced my standing among the older patrons of the place, mostly *Herald Tribune* men, and I think that W. O. McGeehan, the great sports writer, said "Hello" to me for the first and only time. I have a recollection that Jack Bleeck, the proprietor, even offered to lend me money, but this seems so wildly improbable in the light of subsequent experience with Mr. Bleeck that I can only conclude I was intoxicated.

There was a writing desk, with free stationery, in the Artists and Writers Club. The desk and a suit of armor that Bleeck had acquired at an auction sale gave the place an air of luxury and permanence unusual in those times, and the success of the enterprise, which has lasted twenty-two years, is proof that an elaborate installation pays off. I went over to the desk and wrote a long letter to a woman I knew then, telling her not to depend on my making a living for her, because I was a ne'er-do-well. She had not been depending on me up to that time, being supported by a department-store owner in a Southwestern state, but I

thought I would give her warning. I had cherished a project of
rescuing her from what I considered her equivocal status. I then
wrote another letter to Vic Bernstein, who was working on a
paper called the *News*, in Providence, R.I., and confessed that I
was at liberty. I felt that it was hopeless to look for a job in New
York, but hoped that word of my irresponsibility had not yet
reached New England.

I refrained from telling my parents of what had happened,
because it only would have pained my mother and confirmed my
father in his expressed belief that he would have to support me
for the rest of his life.

Within a couple of days I received a letter from Vic saying
that Claude Jagger, who had been a classmate at the School of
Journalism but had had sense enough to leave after the first year,
was now city editor of the Providence *Evening Bulletin*. Claude
is the fellow who is now doing publicity in Hawaii. Vic had
spoken to Jagger, Jagger had spoken to the managing editor, and
Providence was eager to welcome an experienced New York
newspaperman. Next day I had a letter from David Patten, managing editor of the *Bulletin*, confirming this intelligence and
offering me forty dollars a week to do general assignments in the
capital and largest city of Rhode Island. I hastened to accept. It
gave me a chance to tell my parents that I had succeeded at last
in getting the kind of work that interested me, even though it
meant leaving the *Times* without notice. "They can get along
without me," I assured my mother, who apparently expected the
Times to come out with several blank columns on the sports
page next morning. "It's a dirty trick," my father said. "They'll
never hire you back."

The rail approaches to the Union Station at Providence, R.I.,
are uninspiring even to a casual traveler, and I found them singularly depressing on the afternoon of my first journey there. But
my misgivings were unfounded. I liked the place from the start,
and they printed my stories in the paper.

The Providence Journal Company, which publishes the *Journal* (mornings) and the *Evening Bulletin*, now enjoys a monopoly in Providence. Even then it had what pretty nearly amounted
to one. There were two feeble opposition evening papers, the
News, which was supported by Democratic United States Sena-

tor Peter Goelet Gerry so that the party would have one organ in the state, and the *Tribune*. The latter was an anachronistic survival of family journalism, owned, edited, written, and, I think, printed by a tribe called Barry. The *Tribune* had a circulation of only a few thousand, and the *News* not very many more. The *Journal* papers were big and prosperous. They were also sober and literate, and they paid better money than the *News*. Bernstein had landed me a forty-dollar job, but he got only thirty-five, which included a new five-dollar raise.

Providence is a good place to observe the processes of American government, for it is not only a sizable city, with a population of a quarter of a million, but a county seat, a state capital, and the site of a United States District Court. Moreover it controls two seats in the United States Senate, since most of the state's population is concentrated in the Providence metropolitan district. Every local political move therefore has a bearing on the next senatorial election. When I went there Gerry's colleague in the Senate was Jesse H. Metcalf, a director of the Journal Company. The Metcalf brothers, Stephen O. and Jesse, owned a majority of the shares. They were, and are, extremely wealthy textile men, as conservative as Lady Astor. Gerry, the Democratic senator and owner of the *News*, was a multimillionaire with interests principally outside the state who had a fine home at Warwick Neck. There were plenty of potential Democratic votes in Rhode Island, an industrial state, but few Democratic bank rolls. Gerry was the angel of the party, and the Metcalfs resented him as a "colonist." Rhode Island Republicans said that Gerry had moved into the state because his wife liked Washington society. They thought there was something fishy about a rich man being a Democrat anyway, even though Gerry was the antithesis of a radical.

The city and state went along on a pretty even economic keel, but at low speed. The New England textile industry was pretty sick even then, three and a half years before the official depression, and there was no feverish prosperity among the manufacturing jewelers or machine-tool people. But the city's industry was so variegated that somebody always seemed to be doing a little business somewhere. The port, which had been a great haven in colonial times, was somnolent except for numerous tankers from Texas. But there was a Fabre Line boat from Mediterranean ports about once every two weeks. The Fabre boats touched at Providence before going on to New York. Once they had brought throngs of immigrants direct to New England, but now they carried mostly naturalized Americans returning from visits to their relatives in the old countries. There were also occasional chartered tramp steamers with lumber from Russia for the A. C. Dutton Company. Ships were sufficiently rare to be news, and yet there were enough of them to provide a fairly steady supply of feature stories.

The Coolidge boom was manifest only in the number of branch brokerage offices which nestled in every cranny of the downtown business buildings. Everybody in town, it seemed, had a little bet on a stock every day, just as everybody there now has a bet on a horse at Narragansett Park. Horse racing was not legalized there in my time, and I suspect it was brought in to fill the gap left in daily life when the bottom dropped out of the Republican form of gambling. The rich men of Rhode Island sat on their money or invested it in operations outside the state that had more glamour than the highly unionized Rhode Island textile industry. There was no overexpansion, but a kind of shabby comfort that I found relaxing. The Chamber of Commerce, abetted by the Journal Company, fought a sort of perennial sham battle with the New York, New Haven & Hartford Railroad, the only one that came into town. This ceremonial dance began every spring with a story that somebody was going to revive the project to build a Grand Trunk Railroad from Canada to Narragansett Bay. The completion of the Grand Trunk would jump Providence over Boston's head in four and a half years and New York's in five and three quarters, one of our editorials would point out. This, of course, would have made life a perfect hell for the quiet old Rhode Islanders who enjoyed living in the place and feeling they owned it, and who also owned the paper and a lot of stock in the New Haven, so old hands on the *Journal* staff never took the campaign seriously. It was usually farmed out to the latest arrival from some other city. I think I was Mr. Grand Trunk of 1926, or perhaps of 1928, after I came back from Europe—I forget which. The Grand Trunk was an annual event, like Jacobs Hill Hunt Club Horse Show.

Doing it gave a new man a chance to get acquainted with the local notables, each of whom kept a stock of prepared statements on the subject in his desk, ready to be handed out to reporters.

A survival, in an attenuated form, of the New England conscience impelled the rulers of this tight little grand duchy to a certain amount of gratuitous self-criticism. For example, in about 1926 they hired a professor at M.I.T. to make an industrial, political, and economic survey of the state. His conclusions, made available in 1928–29, were unflattering, but they paid him for them. Of course they never did anything about his recommendations. The survey showed that even in 1926 annual earnings of most individuals in the state were low. They seemed to me startlingly low, ranging, as I remember, from seven hundred dollars to thirteen hundred dollars a year in the textile industries. This was during a period now frequently endowed with a reminiscent halo of prosperity. Nearly all the plants were handicapped by superannuated machinery which had repaid its original cost many times, and the owners declined to install new machines, preferring to transfer their capital to the less completely unionized South, where they built fine modern mills. The Gastonia, N.C., textile strikes in 1929 were represented in the Providence papers as a reprise of the War of Secession. But anybody except a mill baron would have known that once they got the mills built Southern labor would unionize.

The survey reported that Rhode Island politics were almost honest, but so niggardly that less got done for the public than in many of the graft-ridden cities of other regions. This is a topic to which I shall return presently.

Within this framework Providence was a lovely place to work in. There was nothing you could do about anything, but then nothing was so bad that you felt a burning urge to do anything about it. The city has Brown, a good university, and a lot of people who read books and talk about them. There was more good liquor always available than I had money to buy it with; scotch was run right into Narragansett Bay; bootleggers with automobiles brought ale and rye from Canada, which is not too distant. The best liquor was to be had of a bootlegger who had a flat in a frame building behind the State House. He felt a responsibility for the quality of legislation that got passed under its influence.

The girls seemed to me remarkably pretty. I have always found the New England accent endearing in women. There is a suggestion of primness about it that is as aphrodisiac as a starched gingham dress.

Bernstein and I rented a room and a bathtub on Park Street, on the State House hill. The bathtub was in a closet with a folding bed, so you could use it only when the bed was down. Our establishment did not include what people usually mean when they ask for the bathroom, but we figured that the tub took it out of the furnished-room class and justified us in referring to it as an "apartment." Besides the bed there was a couch, on which Bernstein slept, and a gas plate. We both worked days for the first couple of weeks I was in Providence, and our quarters then seemed a bit crowded, but after this fortnight I was transferred from the *Bulletin* to a bastard shift on the *Journal*—three in the afternoon until eleven at night. That solved our domestic traffic problem. When I came home at one or two in the morning Vic would be asleep, and when I awoke he would be gone.

We were together on Tuesday evenings, when I was off. Vic used to write the advance blurbs for the burlesque shows that played the old Empire Theatre, so he got two free tickets every week, and our Tuesday-night routine was always the same. We would go to an Italian speakeasy for dollar dinners and a dollar bottle of homemade wine. Then we would attend the Empire. We never went backstage, and if you had seen those dames you would know why. The burlesque troupes were always in a bad humor when they played Providence anyway, because of a solemn cop named Lieutenant Cowan who acted as a theatrical censor. Cowan made all the girls wear long stockings. He later stopped Eugene O'Neill's "Strange Interlude" from playing at the Providence Opera House. This is an example of why it is important never to give censorship a foothold. One of the greatest liabilities of civilized man is his tendency to laugh at people like Cowan instead of squelching them at once.

I tried hard to make good in my new environment, and I did not find it too difficult.

The first day I went to work for the *Bulletin* they had a hot local story, the kind with a lot of "angles" to be covered simultaneously, so that the desk assigns several men to track them down and then communicate by telephone with a rewrite man who puts his story together out of the accumulating fragments. This artist usually tries to change his lead and make it sound like a new story for each edition. A real-estate speculator of some prominence had gotten himself into a jam some time before my arrival in town, and had recently been convicted of a good-sized swindle. Placed in the state prison at Howard, R.I., whether to await sentence or to begin serving time I forget, the man had succeeded in hanging himself. I was rushed out to the prison to ask the warden how it had happened. The warden was most apologetic. When I called in with my report from prison I was ordered to find the man's widow and ask her what she thought of the situation. This was the kind of assignment that, if I had not had my experience at Police Headquarters, would have caused me to throw up my job then and go home. But I remembered how welcome ghouls usually were in such circumstances and set out with equanimity. The widow wasn't home, of course, but I tracked her down at a relative's. They were all glad to see me, because they wanted to say that the dead man had been double-crossed, framed, and crucified, and they hoped the same thing would happen to the whited sepulchre of a banker who had put him on the spot. There is almost no circumstance under which an American doesn't like to be interviewed, an observation which I have had a chance to verify in cracks in the Tunisian rocks, under mortar fire. We are an articulate people, pleased by attention, covetous of being singled out.

I think the quotes from the family got within three paragraphs of the lead in the noon edition and stayed on the front page until the Wall Street closing, when it went into the first column of runover on the inside page. This first slight success encouraged me.

It wasn't until a couple of weeks later, however, that I really hit my stride. I had been sent over to the Federal Building to substitute for Jerry Price, who covered that beat regularly. There was a long hearing before a United States Commissioner in a prohibition case. It was about a German in Cranston, the dormitory city next to Providence, who had had a still in his basement. He had been chopping down a tree in his front yard when the prohibition agents arrested him. When they asked him about the still, he said he had not known it was there. I said that he had been chopping down a tree, but he was no George Washington, and everybody who read the story agreed that I had a humorous touch. My superiors decided that I was primarily a writer, and I was therefore transferred to the *Journal*, where there was more space for the leisurely deployment of my talent. Patten swapped me to the *Journal* for a recently married nightsider who was now anxious to work days so he could be with his bride in the evenings. It suited me fine, as I hate to get up before noon. I had the double satisfaction of getting what I wanted and feeling that I had helped preserve the domestic felicity of a man I had never met.

I then oozed prose over every aspect of Rhode Island life. I wasn't supercilious about it. I was in there trying. I wrote about the crews of two tiny Newfoundland schooners lost in a tornado, who were rescued and brought into port by a Fabre liner; about a Portuguese banquet for a newly appointed vice-consul; about the ghost of the Grand Trunk; the Jacobs Hill Horse Show, and a society charity drive; about a collision between two passenger trains in which there were only a couple of fatalities. I got a first-page yarn, which we sent out on the Associated Press wires, out of the inauguration of Rhode Island's State Boxing Commission. At that time there was a lot of blather going on about a heavyweight championship fight between Jack Dempsey and Harry Wills, the Brown Panther. The New York State Athletic Commission had said it would never permit such a match. I asked the new Rhode Island commissioners if they would sanction it in Rhode Island (where no fight had ever drawn more than $15,000) and they said sure. Of course there was no chance of it coming there, but it sounded important. (Dempsey's handlers didn't want the match under any circumstances. He took on Gene Tunney instead and blew the title. Then Wills lost to Jack Sharkey, and nobody has thought of the great controversy since.) One Sunday I went out to see the superintendent of the Rhode Island State Police about a recent stickup of a country bank. He said there was nothing new in the case, so I didn't

write any story. A couple of weeks later he called the *Journal*
one evening and asked for me personally. He said that since I
had "preserved his confidence" he was going to reward me by
giving me an exclusive story: a dangerous lunatic named
Weeden had escaped from the State Hospital for Mental Diseases. The man had been committed to the asylum thirty years
before after an attempted homicide, and he had escaped a number of times since. He usually escaped for the summer and came
back to the hospital when it got cold. During these excursions
he had never harmed anybody, but he was officially "dangerous,"
so each escape had been treated with outward respect in the
Journal, like the revivals of the Grand Trunk. I decided to take
a new line; it was obviously a funny story. I called up the superintendent of the hospital, who said Weeden was a nice old dodo.
I quoted him. A couple of years later Weeden came back and
blew off the head of the superintendent's successor with a shotgun.

I also did one long, hard job of rewrite. There was a big fire in
Fall River, Mass. We had an office there, but the two or three
men who staffed it were not nearly enough to cover the story.
So most of the night staff of the *Journal* was sent down to the
fire, and I remained in the office to write the running story as
they telephoned it in. I did at least five thousand words that
night. It taught me how few synonyms there are for fire—just
blaze, flames, and conflagration, and conflagration is lousy. I
must have used each about four hundred times. Some fellows
that age would have weakened and used "holocaust," but I
didn't, and it is one of the few things in my journalistic career
of which I am justly proud.

This is the kind of thing that newspapers in all times and
cities are largely made up of, and I've nothing against it, but I
can't see that it means very much. Within a couple of months I
was sure I could do it as well as anybody anywhere, and better
than most. This was a pleasant thought in one way, but in others
less so. How would it feel, I wondered, to be doing the same
thing at forty or fifty? And how could a man of forty or fifty,
with dignity and responsibilities, make a living at it, when there
would always be kids of twenty-one able and willing to do the
same job for peanuts? The run of news is repetitious: the luna-

tic's escape, the embezzler's suicide, the conflagration, the rescue
are prototypes of continually recurrent stories. In times when
great things are happening, young men have to cover earth-
shaking events. In ordinary grubby times the city editor can find
no more important assignment for the most sapient reporter in
the shop than the opening of a new wing in the municipal art
museum.

This did not disturb me unduly, because I was having a fine
time. Every day, awaking at about eleven, I would breakfast on
three soft-boiled eggs, three cups of coffee, and three oranges,
read awhile, and then stroll down to the YMCA where I would
jog a few miles and swim in the pool. I had the gymnasium
almost to myself at that hour, but sometimes I would find a
fellow to box with. At three I would show up at the office and
draw an assignment. Then I would go off to see somebody,
usually a person I had never met before, and this constant passage across other people's lives entranced me. A newspaperman
gets to know nothing thoroughly, but everybody very well. Life
is his spectator sport. After eleven at night I would go to a
Waldorf Lunch to drink coffee with a couple of other fellows
who got through at the same time. We were generally still there,
talking, at midnight and at one, when we would be joined by
men getting through on succeeding shifts, and then still later we
would sometimes go for long walks up College Hill and over to
the little Seekonk River. I made a lot of good friends there.
Most of them were as uncertain about life and as outwardly shy
and inwardly conceited and inordinately curious about other
people as I was.

After I had worked in Providence a few months my father
evidently began to miss the steady drain upon his finances to
which he had been accustomed. One day, while I was home visiting, he said: "You always used to talk about going to Europe
to study, and I have always thought that a man should." He
himself had quit grade school at the age of ten, but he was a
remarkable old bird. "If you don't go now, you never will," he
said. "You will get a good job and then you won't want to give
it up, or you will get mixed up with a girl." "As a matter of fact,"
I said, not wanting him to weaken on his idea, "I was thinking
of asking a woman to marry me. She's fifteen years older than I

am, and she isn't Jewish, and she hasn't any money, and she has been divorced four times and has a child by each of the four husbands, but I am sure Mother and you will like her."

Within a month I was on my way to France.

But I had the best kind of assurance that I was a good newspaperman. Sevellon Brown, the over-editor of both the *Journal* and *Bulletin*, asked me how much money I wanted to stay and said there would always be a job if I wanted to come back. Patten of the *Bulletin* and George Carpenter of the *Journal* said the same thing.

And somehow I knew I would be back on a newspaper some day. What Max Fischel called the taint was on me.

What I did in France had nothing to do with newspapers, but when in the spring of 1927, in a sixth-floor room in Paris, I began to write my version of the great American novel (148 typewritten pages, unfinished) it was about a newspaperman. He wanted to cover Police Headquarters but had to make his living writing feature stories.

The Kurdled Kurd

I returned to Providence in the fall of 1927 as a passenger on board the Patria, one of the Fabre boats that I had occasionally boarded in 1926 as a reporter. My father had declined to stake me to any more European culture. I think now that his decision coincided with a decline in real-estate values, beginning several years before the official crash, that had affected what was by then his principal source of income. He had made two comfortable fortunes in his life, losing one in 1914 and recouping by about 1920; he had now retired from the fur business and was husbanding the second accumulation.

I had looked forward with no pleasure to a quest for a job in New York, so I had written to Sevellon Brown that I would be pleased to hold him to his old offer, and I had in my pocket an answer asking me to call in and see him. A reporter from the *Journal* met the ship, and with his assistance I landed three bottles of cognac and two of champagne. This triumph over an idiotic law once again vindicated my liberalism. The reporter, whose name was Ralph Harber, got one bottle. I then went up to see Brown and was hired for sixty dollars a week, which as I knew put me up in the top brackets of Rhode Island journalism. I mention, with what may seem undue regularity, the salaries I received at each stage of my newspaper work, but this is done consciously. I think that from the curve of a single newspaperman's earnings some general conclusions may be drawn about the economic status of members of the "profession" in general, particularly in the years preceding the formation of the American Newspaper Guild. Sixty dollars a week for a man twenty-three years old, even in 1927, a year of high prices, was not bad pay at all. I had only myself to support and amuse.

When I resumed my work I began thinking up feature assignments for myself, as well as taking them from the desk. Straight news might have taken precedence over such stuff if there had been straight news to cover. But newspapers in those somnolent days (while the train rushed toward the open switch of October, 1929) had turned increasingly toward the exploitation of the inconsequential, since advertisers insisted upon a certain minimum ratio of editorial to advertising matter and people had to read something while they ate breakfast. In some cities crime and scandal provided a substitute for anything more important, but Providence had few spectacular shootings, and the *Journal* papers were not prurient. The best we got, in a criminal way, was an occasional shooting match down on the Narragansett Bay shoreline, between Federal agents and rumrunners who tried to land their stuff without making the usual payments. There were disasters from time to time, like Bay steamboat explosions and the losses of the submarines S-4 and S-51. But you couldn't count on them.

Newspapers all over the country, however, played silly stuff in a way that would seem incredible to the generation that started its newspaper reading under Franklin D. Roosevelt. For example, a promoter of dance marathons imported from Turkey a Kurd named Zaro Agha who was heralded as the oldest man in the world—157 years old. Zaro was to make personal appearances as a special added attraction at the dance marathon. There were, as every editor in the country knew, no vital statistics in eighteenth-century Turkey; Zaro's age could be only a press agent's claim. But when the Fabre liner bringing the old man to New York from Istanbul called at Providence, four of the top-notch reporters of the nation, two male and two female, came up to go aboard the ship and meet him before the regular ship newsmen could get a crack at him in New York. That was early in 1930, when the depression was supposed to be only a temporary lull and boomtime patterns in journalism persisted. Alva Johnston of the *Herald Tribune* and Harold Denny of the *Times* were the New York men, and Dorothy Dayton of the *Sun* and Lorena Hickok of the Associated Press were their distaff-side competitors, claiming no sex allowance. I myself was to cover the event for the North American Newspaper Alliance as well as the *Journal*, and also to file a six-hundred-word special story for the New York *Evening Post*, at that point in its hand-to-hand history a branch of Curtis Publications.

The pack was accompanied by a press agent named Calvin Harris, a phenomenal character whose most cherished regular account was the Australian prison ship that used to dock in the Hudson River every summer. Harris would invariably manage to get somebody locked up in the ship's black hole in manacles and then lose the key and notify the police emergency squad. Zaro had a Turkish attendant with him who spoke a smattering of English, and Harris tried to channelize the "interviews" through him. But I found a Turkish doctor aboard ship who spoke French, and I asked my questions through the doctor. About all Zaro said for himself was that he was probably very old because he felt very old. The doctor said that people of the laborious class in Turkey usually looked older than they were because they had very hard lives. "Since he looks like a man of ninety," he said, "I would say he is about sixty-five." I mention the doctor only to indicate how hard I worked when I was young. Johnston and Denny simply assumed the old boy was a phony, which was right, and went on from there. Miss Dayton, I think, wrote a story about how the old fellow still had an eye for the girls, and Miss Hickok's yarn touched on plural marriage as a revitalizer. I, naturally, thought that my three stories were remarkably funny. I rather pitied the *Post* for having to make do with only six hundred words. I gave the *Journal* a couple of thousand.

That was the best editors could find for men like Johnston and Denny to do then. Both were just over forty. Johnston quit the newspaper business shortly afterward and has devoted most of his time since to writing about characters like Samuel Goldwyn and Beardsley Ruml. I got to know him well years later, on the *New Yorker*, when we used to have furious arguments in the hallway just outside the men's room, which would sometimes last from there to the water cooler at the other end of the hall. Alva bet on Landon in 1936. He always used to say that what the country needed was a mediocre president, so that big businessmen, whom he venerates, could run it. He attributed the prosperity of the United States in the twenties to the low I.Q.s of three successive incumbents of the White House. I often wonder what he has to kick about now.

Denny stuck, and in time got stories that were big enough for Thucydides. He wasn't a Thucydides, but he made an honest try. I was with him often in Normandy, in 1944. He used to blame me for luring him into St.-Lô on the day the Twenty-ninth Division took the ruins of that city. "I was going to stay out," he used to say, "until I saw the *New Yorker* walking in." It was a big mistake. We were both glad to get out a few minutes later, and for a few hours thereafter we were incredulous about our survival. I remember him standing on the end of a diving board at Bagnoles-de-l'Orne later in the campaign. That was the last stop of the press before Paris. Charlie Collingwood of CBS (twenty-five years old) and Bill Walton of *Time* (thirty-five but very fit) had just done dives, and Denny (fifty-five) felt their agility a challenge. He made a very good dive, too, back jackknife, I think.

The day we went into Paris I saw him get the worst break a newspaperman could experience. I came into Paris in an automobile driven by a young lieutenant named Jack Roach, with a reporter for *Stars & Stripes* named Alan Morrison, whom we had picked up out of a crowd at Chartres. When we got to the Boulevard de Montparnasse there was shooting in some streets but not in others, so we stopped to ask for directions. The French First Armored Division, Leclerc's, had set up a headquarters in the Gare de Montparnasse, and we went in there to look at a situation map. Denny and Paul Gallico and Dick Tregaskis were there for the same reason. It soon developed that we had all walked in on something. Leclerc and a couple of American generals, Gerow of the Fifth Corps and Barton of the Fourth Division, were in the station awaiting the arrival of the German Commander of Paris, Von Cholltitz, and his staff. He was to sign the formal surrender of the city, and they to acknowledge it. General de Gaulle was also scheduled to appear. It was a fine eyewitness story to run into, on a day when all the United States was presumably avid for stories of the liberation of Paris. Denny and Tregaskis unlimbered their typewriters. It was no good for me, of course, since I was writing for a weekly, and still less for Gallico, who was representing some monthly with a hundred-day deadline.

The Germans appeared, looking and acting like exaggerated caricatures of themselves, as they always did. Von Cholltitz signed, after a moving and indignant oration by his chief of staff, who, it seems, had been kicked in the pants by a Frenchman after the surrender. I think he wanted Leclerc to go out and start firing into the crowd.

Denny and Tregaskis banged away at their portable typewriters, and then they asked me to let them have Roach and the car, so he could take their despatch to a communications centre that the Public Relations section of the Army had promised to set up in the Hotel Scribe on the other side of town. Of course I wasn't going to be a dog in the manger, and that is how I lost that particular car. Roach took the despatches and started off, and in time, by circuitous routes, he got to the Scribe. There were islands of resistance throughout Paris, but they were signing off as official word of the surrender got to them, conveyed by teams of paired French and German officers. So Jack didn't get shot, and he did hand over the copy for censorship and forwarding to the United States. The copy never got there. Some Public Relations genius, probably a colonel who subsequently got the Bronze Star and the Legion of Merit for having breathed the air of France, simply mislaid it. Denny went to bed that night thinking he had a hell of a story in the paper, and learned a couple of days later that the *Times* had had to lead the front page with a cut-and-dried Associated Press despatch because nothing had arrived from him. It made him ill for days.

In January, 1945, after I had returned to the United States, I used to read his despatches in the *Times* from First Army—that was a thing we never had a chance to do when we were together in the field—and I thought they were almost the only ones that let a reader who had been out there know how things were going on. His heart went bad and he died suddenly after returning to this country later in 1945.

Zaro Agha's tour, incidentally, was not a success. He got in just too late to cash in on the era of wonderful nonsense.

"He should have come over here when he was a kid of 155," Harris said to me afterward, "and he would have hit the sucker market right on the button."

The Indian Pathologist

When I had been home awhile, Brown decided that there was a serious side to my genius and that I had the makings of an investigator. He put me on a story that has remained a marker in my memory, like the Mecklin speech. While I was doing it I formulated a few ideas about reporting, and since they happened to work out I acquired a certain amount of confidence in myself as a serious operator. I also ran across the pitiful raw material of a novel—one that could be written only by the author of "A Passage to India." If E. M. Forster should see this, and feel like returning to the mood of his early masterpiece, I will not charge him one rupee for the material. But the chief significance of the story for me was the light it shed on the form of graft in favor of the well-heeled which is generally referred to by their apologists as "rigorous economy" in government.

At the time I returned from Europe there was a muted factional war within the Republican Party organization in Rhode Island. Senator Metcalf, the most cautious man in the United States (he spent two terms in the United States Senate without making a speech, and habitually refused to be quoted in his own newspaper), headed the liberal wing of the party. This will give you an idea of what the tories were like. Fred S. Peck, the Republican National Committeeman and state boss, was another rich old man who lived in the town of Barrington, in Bristol County. He had a cardiac hemorrhage every time the tax rate rose one mil. The Republicans had a permanent grip on the State Legislature because of a rotten borough system, which gave a disproportionate representation to the little rural communities. The Democrats had managed to elect a governor in 1922, but the Republicans, profiting by the Coolidge landslide of 1924, had regained the governorship, and still held it in 1928. The governor was a benevolent old Frenchman from the northern corner of the state named Aram J. Pothier, whose interest in his duties was restrained. Metcalf's strength within the party derived from his control of United States patronage.

Early in 1928 conditions at the State Hospital for Mental Diseases, which like the prison is at Howard, R.I., caused much disquiet among the good Providence doctors. Rhode Island is so small that everything that happens there is virtually within earshot of the entire population. The hospital at Howard was the only state psychiatric hospital, with about twenty-five hundred patients. The old superintendent, a strong-willed, decent old man who through the years had become a state character, had been forced out by the Public Welfare Commission appointed by Peck. The boss considered him "extravagant." A new man, of no distinction, had been brought in with the apparent object of making the free hospital self-supporting. He had reduced the per capita cost of maintaining patients to an unbelievably low figure. To do this, according to the Providence psychiatristy he had developed "occupational therapy" to a point where the state hospital was rapidly turning into a labor camp. There was a strong suspicion that if a good plumber happened to be committed to Howard he was lost to the world forever, no matter how sane he subsequently became. The superintendent just kept him plumbing.

Providence has Butler Hospital, an endowed psychiatric institution of considerable repute, and there were good, conscientious psychiatrists in town who felt sick about what was happening in the much larger public hospital. Medical and psychiatric treatment, even under the old superintendent, had been no better than in most state hospitals. But it had deteriorated since, as one after another members of the staff had been forced out and replaced, in every case, by physicians obtained at even lower salaries. This was not a period of low earning, and competent men did not come cheap.

The Providence doctors were socially acceptable, some of them even being members of the Hope Club. So they were able to approach the proprietors of the Journal Company directly. They appealed to the spot of New England conscience which the proprietors kept precariously alive, like the slices of chicken heart that Dr. Alexis Carrel used to preserve immortal in a test tube. The *Journal* decided that the thing really was too bad, and besides, it was a good chance to show up Fred Peck. I was put to work on the story.

My first sources were doctors in Providence, who told me what to look for. I then went out to Howard to see the new superintendent, saying I wanted to do ordinary Sunday stories. He was leery of me. My real purpose was to establish contact with a couple of members of his staff, survivors of the old regime, who hated his guts. Having done this, I used to go on two kinds of conducted tours of the wards and storerooms. There was the officially sponsored kind, with a guide chosen by the superintendent, usually from among the attendants. And there was the unofficial sort, under the guidance of the dissident doctors. I had a most unfavorable impression of the place, but for weeks —and weeks then seemed to me very long—I couldn't find anything to base an effective series of stories on.

There wasn't an extravagant amount of brutality at Howard. At least they didn't kill many patients. You have to have deaths to convince the public that there is excessive bruality in an institution. Every newspaper reader has heard or read somewhere that psychiatric patients have a "persecution complex," so complaints of inmates or ex-inmates are discounted in advance. If this is true when the subject is brutality, it is doubly so when the complaints are of inadequate food or overwork.

Howard wasn't too dirty. The "occupational therapy" with scrubbing brushes and mops took care of that. Even if I had smuggled a photographer in with me we couldn't have brought out horror pictures like those with which Albert Deutsch enlivens his *PM* exposés. And there wasn't any graft of the sort every newspaper likes to denounce—somebody knocking down a couple of bucks. It is not illegal to starve a poor devil or to leave him without therapy. Sensible people, if they read a story based on such flimsy complaints, would ask why public charges should be pampered.

A reporter working on this kind of a story gets his leads from people who have grudges, and one such passes him on to another. But just because his informants are angry, he must check every lead with double care. When I checked, the individual stories were never quite good enough to go to bat on. I myself could think of a line of defense against each charge. Still the sheer number of the complaints, and the partial truth I could see behind many of them, convinced me. Insufficiency, rather than inefficiency, was the trouble at Howard. This is not a spectacular condition.

One character who recurred frequently in the complaints of doctors, discharged attendants, and former patients was the pathologist, an Indian doctor who had been brought up to Howard by the new administration. This man received only twenty-two hundred dollars a year, with living quarters for himself and wife and child. His being an Indian predisposed me in his favor; I could conceive that he found it hard to work up a practice in the United States. His acceptance of a low salary therefore did not seem to me conclusive evidence of his incompetence. Nor could I feel much sympathy for the former patients who said that "that black man" terrified them, or for attendants who said they wouldn't take orders from a colored man. I was rather more impressed by the testimony of doctors that he seemed unaccustomed to standard procedures—for instance, that in taking Wassermann tests he broke off an uncommon number of needles in patients' spines.

A Providence doctor, not one of the Hope Club set, but an aggressive little West Sider, had under the old regime been retained as pathologist on a part-time basis. He had received about thirty-five hundred dollars a year. It had taken up about half his working time; during the rest he had maintained his practice in Providence. The medical dignitaries assured me that in spite of his plebeian ways he was an able fellow. He was, not unnaturally, angry at having been dropped, but he was even angrier at what he heard about the new man. I had introduced myself to the Indian out at Howard, and had found him cautious and apparently frightened, although patients and attendants had accused him of arrogance. He seemed a stranger and so alone. He told me he had studied at the University of Calcutta. I found out from the superintendent that he had engaged the

Indian doctor through a medical employment agency in New York—"one of the best-known in the United States."

When I had worked for four or five weeks on the hospital story without cracking it I began to feel homesick for my old feature job. But I told Brown that before chucking the Howard story altogether I wanted to go down to New York and check on the Indian's past. Incidentally, I was constantly in search of pretexts for trips to New York at the *Journal's* expense. I wasn't very hopeful about this last thrust. At most, I thought, I might meet some former colleague who would say the man wasn't a very good doctor. That wouldn't be enough.

I called in at the agency in New York and was told by a young woman there that the Indian client had listed as references the superintendents of the Coney Island and Cumberland Hospitals, both municipal hospitals in Brooklyn, and a prominent homeopathic physician uptown. I asked her what they had said about the man and she said, with apparent astonishment at my question, "Oh, we didn't get in touch with them. We take it for granted that if a doctor gives a reference it wouldn't be somebody who didn't know him."

I had an evening's fun, and next day drove out to the Coney Island Hospital and asked for the superintendent. I introduced myself and asked if he knew the Indian doctor. "Doctor!" the superintendent yelled. "Why, he wasn't even a good laboratory technician. He used to feed the guinea pigs in the pathology lab." He did indeed know the Indian, who had worked for him for two years, but he had let him go. Just like that a story breaks. A reporter must never make the mistake of attributing to his subject his own mental processes. I would never have thought of attempting a fraud which could be so easily discovered; neither, naturally, would the conventional young lady at the medical agency. So she had accepted the Indian as what he said he was. I hadn't really believed he was a fraud either. But I had gone one step further than she: I had gone through the routine motion of verifying his story. This had paid off.

From Coney Island I went to Cumberland. I wasn't overlooking any bets now. The Cumberland superintendent, a Dr. Jacobs, now at Bellevue, had an almost identical tale. The Indian had fed his guinea pigs too. And the homeopath's story checked with the other two. All three were, naturally, pretty indignant at the thought of a non-medic doing the tests and autopsies for an institution with twenty-five hundred beds, and all gave me the written statements I wanted. I have often thought of the terror in which the Indian and his wife must have lived, among the psychopaths and the hostile American colleagues, conscious that the deceit might be discovered at any moment.

From a tactical, reporting point of view, the story also proved that appearances are not so deceptive as we sometimes assume. There is in the human mind a pull to reconcile all phenomena with the normal and friendly. It was exemplified in the wartime cry, "It's all right, boys, she's one of ours!" A reporter should lean backwards not to give a potential subject the best of it.

This was just the kind of story that a newspaper can use with political effect. Any reader can understand that an administration is less than bright if it engages a man as a doctor and he turns out not to be a doctor. I am sorry to confess that the man's nationality and color helped the story. The reaction to the word "Hindu" in a free association test is quite likely to be "sinister." The real fault of the Welfare Commission was deeper than the failure to check the Indian's credentials. It consisted in the immoral parsimony that impelled the members to seek the cheapest doctor obtainable. If they had hired some doddering old fool who happened to be provided with a proper diploma, they would have been just as much at fault, but their offense would have been hard to dramatize.

Naturally I hung all the rest of my unfavorable findings about Howard onto the story about the pathologist. But his story, I am sure, was the only part of the denunciation that stuck. It broke the Welfare Commission, all right. A couple of the commissioners resigned, and new ones with a more progressive reputation were appointed. The governor appointed a special committee of inquiry into the administration of the state hospitals, which blistered the Peck policy. The new superintendent did not resign; the Peck faction fought stubbornly to represent him as a public servant being crucified by the *Journal*. But that summer my old vicarious acquaintance, the lunatic Weeden, came back from one of his many escapes and killed the superintendent. After that the state, on the recommendation of the committee, which represented the views of the Providence doctors, brought in a good, modern-minded psychiatrist from Colorado to be superintendent at Howard. Things there improved considerably for a time. But the appeal to the taxpayer of "rigorous economy" is inexorable. The Democrats have run the state for fifteen years now. They have tried conscientiously to be even more economical than their predecessors. After all, the big contributors to *their* campaign funds are taxpayers too. I was talking to a Providence psychiatrist last fall and happened to ask him about the state hospital. "The treatment is sub-standard," he said. "They don't want to spend any money."

If the wife of a man like Fred Peck fell ill he would send her to some place like Butler or the Hartford Retreat or Chestnut Lodge. This is cheaper, for a large taxpayer, than paying a proportionate share of the upkeep of an adequate hospital system.

The public-school system in any city, whether Providence or New York, has to combat the same form of negative larceny. The man of property sends his kid to a private day school when young, to a preparatory school and an endowed but expensive college later. His only interest in the public schools is to see that as little money as possible is spent on them. Schools never fare worse than during a "reform" adminstation.

My wife, not a particularly rugged woman herself, took a Red Cross Grey Lady course a dozen years ago and was sent to Bellevue to do volunteer nursing. She came home one evening and said she had been on a ward where there were fifty-four chronically ill, bedridden women—and one professional nurse. With my customary arithmetical magic, I calculated in time that this meant that if the nurse worked eight hours without a break for lunch or once sitting down to rest her legs, she could devote less than nine minutes to each patient. She would of course have to arrange that no two patients should need her at the same time. A mere matter of organization.

It wouldn't matter very much on a ward like that if the nurse were 100-per-cent efficient or just 95, or 60. She couldn't really do a damn thing for that many patients anyway, and the same is true of a public-school teacher with a class of fifty or sixty children. When people barely in the economic middle class become ill their families send them to voluntary hospitals, just like the wealthy. This is not cheaper for *them* than it would be to pay a pro-rate share of a higher tax rate, which would provide decently maintained public hospitals, but they have no alternative. The rigorous economy grafters, and the newspapers that are their mouthpieces, have shoved the level of public education and public hospitals so low that the poor little white-collar gulls have to shun them too. Then, since the public schools and hospitals are no good to them, these invertebrates dissociate themselves from the fate of public institutions. And the economy hogs let things run down some more.

I often wonder what would have happened if all men of military age hadn't been compelled to go into the same public armed services during the most recent war, and if there had been a nice private auxiliary army available for the sons of large taxpayers. I believe that rations, clothing, medical attention, and pay would have been lousy in the ranks of the public army. To compensate for these drawbacks, discipline would have been much more severe, and the newspapers would have been full of editorials against coddling public soldiers.

There was no attempt to run war on that system, and I sometimes doubt that we should run peace that way.

A Reprise

The city, as I write this (June 1, 1947), is witnessing a mass demonstration of the rigorous economy applesauce, presented, as usual, as the highest type of public service. The *World-Telegram, Sun, Journal-American,* and the *News* have been carrying on a "crusade" against pampering of relief recipients by the New York City Department of Public Welfare. A *World-Telegram* reporter "discovered" a few relief families living in hotels at the expense of the city. I put quotes around the verb discover because a disgruntled politician had told the Scripps-Howard Columbus where to go. These were families for which the Public Welfare people had been able to find no apartments, and the hotels were of the humblest sort. I remember one of them as a squalid little joint twenty-five years ago, and it certainly hasn't improved in the interim. One family, the *World-Telegram* announced with horror, was receiving six hundred dollars a month in relief. It was a family of nine people. Try living in New York on less than one ninth of six hundred dollars. The *Times* and *Herald Tribune* tagged along in the early days of the crusade, like little boys of nice family tailing along with a gang of toughs. But when Rhatigan, the Welfare Commissioner, Mayor O'Dwyer, and all the organized charity workers of New York put on a counter-offensive backed with statistics, the nice little boys ran away home, leaving the ragamuffins to take the rap.

The most interesting result of the crusade (a medieval word meaning a wanton expedition of intolerant people) was the incidental revelation that the number of persons on relief had increased threefold in a few months. The attack evidently meant, therefore, that the *World-Telegram* and *Sun,* anticipating a large-scale relief problem in the near future, were determined to set patterns of sub-standard treatment for future applicants.

Both papers are read largely by suburban people who in many cases pay New York City taxes as the owners of New York property, but as they see it derive no benefits from the care of the city's poor. This shucking of civic responsibility by the mere expedient of moving across a boundary line is a problem of almost every great American city, according to Robert S. Allen's interesting symposium, "Our Fair City." The suburban argument runs that Greenwich, Conn., and Roslyn, L.I., inhabited by people who make their money in New York and in many cases own New York property, can take care of their own poor (anybody making less than twenty-five thousand dollars a year). So why should New York City have a problem that necessitates high tax rates? Naturally the *World-Telegram* and *Sun* are the organs of predilection of the large real-estate owners.

That the *Journal-American* and *Daily News*, papers with rich owners and poor readers, also advocate low standards of public service is simply an indication of their contempt for the people who buy them.

Farewell to Providence

The end of my Providence experience was less idyllic than the beginning. Beginning early in the spring of 1928, I lived in a rowdy nest on Benefit Street, near the corner of Benevolent, just across the street from the First Congregational Church, a gracious building erected in 1815. Bernstein had left Providence before I returned to Europe; he went out to California, worked on a couple of papers there, and then made a trip around the world as a sailor. I roomed first with a Catholic mystic who went on the wagon and moved out, and then with a lean and quizzical Cape Codder known as Chip, who had worked his way up through the New England newspaper circuit—Brockton, New Bedford, Springfield, and Providence. He had skipped Worcester, usually an intermediate stop after Springfield.

Chip was a good newspaperman and a remarkably indefatigable convive. He still is a good newspaperman, in Boston where there are no good papers. In the summer of 1929 and the throes of a particularly bad hangover he too turned to Christ and moved to a lodginghouse where drunks would be less likely to climb through his windows at odd hours of the night. The Benefit Street place was on the first floor. It was a furnished apartment, three great rooms with peeling wallpaper and vast fireplaces. We used to stoke the fireplaces with cut lumber we stole from the site where the new Superior Courthouse was building. If we had not had so many fireplaces the courthouse might have been completed sooner. I wanted to stay in the apartment, but the rent was too much for one man to carry (sixty-five dollars ill-furnished and ill-kept). Two Brown seniors lived in a small basement apartment in the same building while Chip and

I roomed together. We were good friends. After graduation one of the Brown boys went down to New York to study law. The other thought he would like to be a newspaperman. So I got him a job on the *Journal* and he moved into the wood-eating apartment with me, paying one third of the rent. He got twenty-five dollars a week from the *Journal*. Luckily, he was a frugal fellow.

Lou was an Italian who had come to this country when he was already seventeen years old, had finished high school in Woonsocket, and then come up to Brown. He wrote English distrustfully, but correctly. He was a conscientious legman, and his command of Italian and French made him particularly useful on many Rhode Island stories. He was very proud of being a newspaperman.

After he had worked for a little over a year, and shortly after he had been raised to thirty dollars, the *Journal* let him go, for no given reason except that he wasn't a brilliant performer (for thirty dollars!) and the management wanted to cut the staff. At the same time, however, they took on a youngster whose father was an officer of a large local utility company. I got mad as hell and went down to Sevellon Brown's office and asked for my pay.

Several morals may be drawn from this incident.

One is that if I had been a married man and the head of a family I could not have afforded the luxury of such a gesture.

Another is that if there had been an American Newspaper Guild at that time, and if it had had a contract with the *Journal*, Lou would not have been laid off without specific cause. Even if he had been laid off for economy, the management would have had to hire him back before taking on a new man in the same category. Incidentally, the fellow hired in Lou's place stayed on the paper a very short time, during which he evinced no talent of any kind, and is probably now helping his old man clip coupons.

A third is that if I had not been fed up with my own job on the *Journal* by that time I would not have exploded.

My salary, during three years of journalistic success, had attained the figure of sixty-three dollars a week, but that was not what worried me. I had only one Morris Plan note and a couple of unpaid charge accounts, so that I was one of the most solvent journalists in Rhode Island. The seasonal repetitiousness of assignments had begun to get me down about a year after my return. I felt that I was ripe for the big time. We used to love to use expressions like "big time" around the table at the Waldorf Lunch, as if we were important persons like baseball pitchers. So I had made repeated efforts to land another New York job.

Once I had written to Stanley Walker, then the youthful city editor of the *Herald Tribune*:

"I have been informed that you are looking for a good reporter. I am one."

Stanley wrote back:

"You have been misinformed."

I made the brief correspondence serve as an introduction and called in to see him whenever I got down to New York. He was always affable, and never failed to ask me to keep in touch. I got to know him very well later, and a couple of years ago he said that he would have liked to hire me, but that the Providence *Journal* had been paying higher salaries than the *Herald Tribune*.

My main effort, however, was directed toward getting on the *World*, which I still idolized. So did every newspaperman I worked with in those days. Maybe it really wasn't so red-hot, but it seemed fresh and decent compared to the rest. Also it had more talented writers than all the other New York papers put together—F.P.A., Lippmann, William Bolitho, Deems Taylor and then Chotzinoff doing music, Laurence Stallings and then Harry Hansen on books, Frank Sullivan, James M. Cain, Milt Gross (on Sundays), and cartoonists like Rollin Kirby and Denys Wortman. I got to be a regular caller on James W. Barrett, the *World* city editor. Generally I called on him at Racky's, a beer joint across Frankfort Street from the *World*, where he was less harassed than at his desk.

Somehow, I never seem to get a job while I have a job.

When I left the *Journal* I knew I would have to find one.

Bread-and-Butter Note

Sevellon Brown and I are very good friends now. I see him almost every time I go up to Providence, which is fairly often, and we talk about every subject in the world except how I left the *Journal*.

Brown is one of the many newspapermen who think that there is room for improvement in American newspapers, which sets him off quite a way from the Robert McLean-Kent Cooper-Wilbur Forrest type of hurrah-for-us boy, but his approach to the problem is incestuous. He has been a leader in setting up a thing called the American Press Institute at Columbia, where workers in various departments of newspapering—reporters, city editors, editorial writers—come together for three-week resident sessions of mutual exhortation to more towering efforts. Prominent practitioners like Reuben Maury[1] of the *Daily News* in the editorial-writing field and Frederick Woltman[2] of the *World-Telegram* among reporters address their humbler colleagues. Once a Scripps-Howard publisher from Cleveland got up and told his enthralled auditors how to get out a good paper.

As Eddie Doherty might say, who told him?

Anyway, I like Rhode Island.

[1] *If you want to know why this is ridiculous, read the three-part New Yorker profile of Maury called Editorial Writer, by John Bainbridge (New Yorkers of May 24, May 31, and June 7, 1947).*

[2] *If you want to know why this is ridiculous, read the* World-Telegram.

My Name in Big Letters

In September, 1930, when I left the *Journal*, it was apparent that Mr. Hoover had laid his egg. But I had a plan to get a job. I had thought of it so often that I didn't see how it could fail.

I went down to New York with Lou and another fellow named Charlie Layer, not a newspaperman. They had decided to seek their fortune in Argentina, why I don't know. Anyway they went, and returned a year later no worse off than when they sailed. I am sure that they look back on their detour with pleasure.

As soon as we got to New York I looked in the classified telephone directory for a sign painter. I found one with a shop fairly near the Grand Central Station and ordered a sign to be carried by a sandwichman. The sign was to say, front and rear: "Hire Joe Liebling." The sign painter, a Hungarian who liked to use bright colors, advised an orange job with blue lettering. It cost eleven dollars, fully rigged. I gave him a five-dollar deposit. He promised he would have it ready next day.

I then went down to Battery Park, where there always were sandwichmen advertising passport photographers. The passport bureau was at the Custom House then; there was none at Radio City because Radio City hadn't been built. I addressed myself to a man who was carrying a sign that said "6 Photos for 75 cents," and asked him if he knew any sandwichman at liberty who would consider an engagement for just a couple of days. He said sure, there were lots of colleagues laying off, because the volume of display advertising had fallen off drastically. He lived in a rooming house on Greenwich Street, under the elevated rail-

way, that was largely patronized by sandwichmen. He promised
to find a good reliable practitioner for me. The regular tariff, he
said, was two dollars a day. I said I would want the man only
from early noon to sundown. Jim Barrett, the city editor of the
World, was the man I wanted to see the sign, and Barrett wasn't
at the office mornings. I guess I wasn't interested in a job on
the Evening World. I gave my sandwichman friend the sign
painter's address and told him to have his candidate meet me
there at noon next day.

The man who reported to me on the morrow was a superannuated Norwegian seaman named, with startling originality,
Larsen. He wore a full beard. I considered this an extra attention-
getter which made him a bargain at the two-dollar rate. I gave
him his sign and his instructions. He was to walk up and down
Park Row in front of the entrance to the Pulitzer Building, and
not talk to anybody unless they asked him what the sign meant.
If that happened he was to say he didn't know. But he would
report to me at six each evening in front of a cafeteria on the
west side of City Hall Park, to describe the people who had
asked him questions. We then rode downtown together on the
subway and I told him to go to work.

I watched him for a while from a bench in City Hall Park.
Seeing my name on the sign made me feel self-conscious and
furtive, as if the people around me knew who I was. Larsen was
a good, experienced sandwichman. I could tell from the way he
slid his feet over the sidewalk. It must be extremely difficult to
walk that slow without standing still. After I time I got tired
of seeing my name in big letters and went away for a walk of
my own without getting paid for it.

At six I kept my rendezvous with Larsen and bought him a
dinner at the cafeteria. As we ate I asked him about his day.
Nobody had spoken to him whose description at all resembled
Barrett's. It had been my hope, of course, that Barrett would
see him. It would hit Barrett right on the funny bone and he
would see what a resourceful young fellow I was. When I
walked in, perfectly deadpan, and sent in my name to him he
would start laughing again and ask me to come in and choose
a job. I arranged with the boss of the cafeteria to leave the sign
in his basement overnight so Larsen could get it next afternoon.

Again I went to the park to watch him, and again I met him at the cafeteria at six. People by now had accepted his presence, it seemed, and weren't asking questions. Maybe they thought Joe Liebling was another passport photographer. After the third day I figured Barrett must have at least heard of the gag, so I paid Larsen off for the last time and stowed the sign away in a friend's apartment, where for all I know it still is.

On the fourth afternoon I went to see Barrett. He greeted me cordially but without any unusual emotion. "I hadn't any idea you were in town," he said. "Thought you were still up in Providence." I didn't know whether or not he was kidding me, but I weakened. "Haven't you seen my sign?" I asked pitifully.

He said no, he hadn't. When I told him about it he said that he always used the rear entrance to the building, on William Street, so that it was no wonder he hadn't seen a sandwichman walking on Park Row. He thought it was a funny story, but it hadn't proved to him that I was very resourceful. I should have either learned Barrett's route in advance or made the old sailorman circumnavigate the building instead of just working one door. Barrett said the *World* wasn't hiring—nobody was. The panic was on.

I eventually recovered the capital I had invested in the sandwichman deal.

I sold the story of the misadventure to the Sunday *World* Metropolitan section, at space rates, for twelve-fifty, late that year, and in January sold it again to *Editor & Publisher*, the newspaper trade magazine, for seven-fifty. As I had paid out only eleven dollars for the sign and six dollars in wages, this left me with a net profit of three dollars if you don't count my time or the meals I bought for Larsen.

The situation now became serious. I had so far refrained from telling my parents of my return to my home town, expecting to be able to walk in on them with the glad news that I had landed on the *World*. Since it was now evident that I would be unemployed for a while, and since I was quite stony, it became necessary for me to admit that I had walked out of my Providence job at a most forbidding time.

I have a granduncle named Kivie Adelson, who is still alive, who ran away to the gold diggings in Colorado when he was seventeen, which was in the late seventies. Out there he went by the name of Steve Allison. Uncle Kivie stayed away for twenty-odd years without writing home. One day in the late nineties, during Klondike gold rush, he called on his sister, my mother's mother, in San Francisco. He had a large gold nugget swung from a watch chain across his waistcoat, and said he had been up North and was going in again. This time, he said, he knew where the gold was and he was going to come out a rich man. That was the last the family heard of him for another fifteen years, and then he turned up in New York, broke. He explained that he had been expecting to write home in a couple of days for thirty-five years, just waiting to strike it rich before he wrote, so nobody would bawl him out. I guess patterns of behavior persist in pioneer families.

I felt small in calling on my parents now, because they no longer had much for themselves. My father's real-estate income, most of which had come from a twelve-story loft building he had built before the last war, had dwindled to almost nothing even before the fatal October of Wall Street. He had never played the stock market, which he had consistently denounced as a sucker's game for as long as I could remember, but in the summer of 1929 he had decided to buy himself a few blue-chip stocks as a hedge against the decline in real estate. He had unfortunately made a bit of quick money, which prompted him to throw in about everything he had. When the crash came it cleaned him out. He had told me all this over a restaurant table in the winter of 1929, and I had never respected him more than when he was telling me about it. He knew how to take a licking. He didn't try to rationalize, he was just angry at himself.

The equity that he retained in his depreciated building was about as thick as a coat of nail polish, and he had become virtually a renting agent for the bank that owned the mortgages on it. He had a talent for that kind of thing. In those days manufacturing tenants had to be nursed like children. My father's biography, which I am not good enough to write, could serve as an anatomy of the free-enterprise system.

And now here I was out of a job, to add to his troubles. I felt pretty irresponsible, even though my departure from Providence had been prompted by high motives.

My parents still had the same apartment in the Hotel Olcott on West Seventy-second Street; they had had a new long lease on it when the knock came. So there was room for me. But I felt like a fool. They were sweet about it, of course.

Eddie Shevlin, who was the boxing coach at Dartmouth when I was there, used to stand by without paying much attention during the first couple of rounds any pair of his pupils worked. "You don't learn anything until you get tired," he used to say. "Then the punches hurt, and you begin to think about protecting yourself. And your arms are tired, so you don't waste punches. You smarten up."

Now that I needed the money I was beginning to learn the essence of newspapering.

This reminds me of the story told by an old Hudson River man I knew. He said that once, when he was a boy, the schooner he was on arrived at the entrance of Eastchester Creek and called for a pilot. An old fellow put out to her in a rowboat, and the schooner captain yelled, "Ever been on the rocks here?" The old fellow yelled back, "Been piloting thirty years and never been on a rock in my life."

"I don't want you then," the captain bellowed. "You don't know where they are."

I will even say that a man who works for newspapers and hasn't been broke is no newspaperman. Of course it is practically impossible to work for a newspaper and not be broke unless your old man owns it.

This was my first serious attack of unemployment. It was not destined to be protracted, but when I looked at the apple-sellers who had begun to make their appearance in the streets I didn't know that. I began, as the saying goes, to make the rounds; but even in 1930, when there were three more New York papers than now (the two *Worlds*, the *American*, and the *Graphic* have disappeared, and *PM* is the only newcomer), you could make them all in a couple of days without hurrying unduly. But I didn't think it would be good policy to call on every city editor every two days. That would be making a nuisance of myself. So I began to spend a lot of time just walking.

A number of authors have written about how bleak and unfriendly New York streets seem when you are pounding them

looking for a job. I found the contrary to be true. The streets
became increasingly alluring, always tempting me to a walk
among interesting people who didn't know I was out of work.
It was the newspaper offices that seemed forbidding, with the
near-certainty of a rebuff in each. Walker and Barrett, just because they were the kindliest editors, were the ones I became
most reluctant to annoy. They always said, "Come around in
another couple of weeks." I began to give them longer respites
than that. Lewis Street, East Broadway, Cherry Street, the streets
around Fulton Fish Market called Slips because they used to
have water in them, Madison Street full of Greek coffeehouses,
and the little streets near the North River south of Canal Street
are most consoling places to walk when you are out of a job. I
found Tompkins Square the park with the ambiance exactly fit-
ting mine, although you might choose a different one.

Walking so much, I found a couple of feature stories. They
were banalities, which had been written many times before, such
as an account of the Fat Man's Shop on Third Avenue. I fortunately didn't know that. I wrote them and took them to the
Sunday Department of the *World*, thinking they might be used
for filler.

A tall young man with an undershot jaw, buckteeth, and yellow hair and mustache, an ensemble which combined with round
eyeglasses to make him look like a good-natured, long-legged
caricature of Teddy Roosevelt, was the person nearest the door
of the Sunday room when I entered. There was no formality
about getting into the Sunday room or any of the other offices
on the twelfth floor of the *World* after you had once been admitted to see Barrett. They all opened off the *Morning World* city
room. I asked the big bucktoothed fellow whom I should see
about some story ideas, and he said "Me." I liked him at first
sight, and I guess that through some peculiarity of taste he liked
me, because he rescued me from walking myself barefoot.

The snips of stories I had with me didn't amount to much,
but I started talking to him about doing a Sunday story on the
Cape Verde Islanders. These Portuguese of mixed blood used to
come across the Atlantic to New England every spring in sailing
schooners of from forty to one hundred tons, spend the summer
working on farms or construction jobs, and then sail back in the

fall to their homes off the coast of Africa, capitalists until next
season. There was no New York angle, but I made it sound interesting. As a matter of fact, the Cape Verdeans had always fascinated me. I used to know some of the schooner captains in
Providence. There were stories that when a Cape Verdean who
had no visa wanted to get into the United States he took passage with a stipulation he should be dropped overboard at a
point three miles offshore. From there he was supposed to swim
in. I still think there's a great story in them, but I don't think
I'll ever write it.

Paul Sifton—that turned out to be the Sunday man's name—
said he would like to have a look at the story, if I would write it.
He didn't think it had enough of a New York angle, but anyway
he would like to see it. And he said he would keep the other
little things, for use on the inside of the Metropolitan section,
a part of the *Sunday World* that has no exact counterpart among
the *World's* survivors.

I came back next day with a two-thousand-word story on the
Cape Verdeans. This bowled Sifton over. He said that people
were constantly coming in to talk over ideas and then going out
and not writing them. A fellow who would go out and write a
smooth story without horsing around was a rarity. He took the
Cape Verdean thing to hold for consideration, and asked me if
I would be interested in doing assignments. The *Sunday World*
was being so starved by then that it had no regular staff men to
send out on ideas cooked up in the office. By the same token it
lacked funds to hire name contributors. So it had to farm out
assignments as best it could. Even mere competence was hard to
find on a piecework basis any time you wanted it. Sifton's
title was Sunday feature editor; he now introduced me to Herman Michelson, the Sunday editor, a rugged type who believed
that nobody should be allowed to operate a typewriter without
passing a test for a license, like an automobile driver. The story
about the Cape Verdeans was never bought. It really wasn't a
New York story. But it landed me what amounted to a job. I
began getting assignments immediately. Rates on the inside
pages were low, but a story on the first page of the Metropolitan
Section would get me from forty to sixty-five dollars. There was
also a Sunday Magazine, the very sick descendant of the slam-

bang pseudo-scientific, gold-and-gore affair which Morrill Goddard had produced for the original Joseph Pulitzer and which
had helped make the paper's fortune. Later Hearst had bought
over Goddard and his entire staff to put out the *American
Weekly*, but by that time the *World* had been able to dispense
with the pictures of dinosaurs eating naked women. Bill Randorf, another good fellow, ran the magazine under Michelson,
and he too provided work for me. I found that by doing only
three or four stories a week I could beat my six-day Providence
earnings easily.

After a week or two Michelson got me a drawing account of
seventy-five dollars a week, to count as an advance against future
stories. Sometimes I beat it by as much as twenty-five dollars.
What I wanted most, however, was to get my drawing account
changed into a regular salary. Then I would be a full-fledged
World man. Mike said he would try to arrange it in a couple
of months. He said the business office was dead against adding
to the staff, but if he could prove that over a considerable stretch
I had been earning more than seventy-five dollars a week they
might be induced to take me on as an economy. There was one
other male member of the feature staff, Phil Stong, who was
writing a weekly piece on radio and banging out an occasional
political satire. Phil hadn't written "State Fair" yet, but he had
produced a staggering number of unpublished novels. Paul, in
collaboration with Clare, his wife, had written a play which had
been accepted for production by the Theatre Guild.

That's the way it goes, sometimes. You plan a flashy gag, and
all it gets you is nothing. Then you go through the routine
motions, give it that old college try, and you maybe get a break.
It's the same thing whether you're investigating a hospital or
looking for a job. Afterward, however, you like to give yourself
credit for being devious.

Rehearsal for 1940

This should have marked a high point in my newspaper life, and, all too briefly, it did. The World of 1930 was not the fighting newspaper that had won Professor Mecklin's admiration by its coverage of the steel strike in 1919. Then it had still been warm with the flame that old Joe Pulitzer had breathed into its body from 1883 until his death in 1911. The men who ran it in 1919 were collaborators chosen and formed by him, like Frank Irving Cobb, the editor-in-chief, who died in 1923. Jim Barrett, who had come aboard in 1916, was later to write:

"We should remember in the first place what kind of newspaper the World was at the death of Joseph Pulitzer. It was more than a newspaper; it was a semi-public institution; it was not the kind of paper to be satisfied with merely printing news, to fulfill its high destiny it must also fight for progress and reform and never be afraid to attack wrong.

"Such an institution, so conceived and so dedicated, could never stand still. It must either advance or perish, sink or swim. If it could not always be fighting for progress and reform, it could never expect to survive by merely printing news like the Times or the Herald Tribune."[1]

The World had undoubtedly softened up, especially after Cobb's death in 1923. It continued to fight, more or less, but its fights became progressively less important, and each was more politely, almost apologetically, waged. Its last bouts were contested with fourteen-ounce gloves and one-minute rounds. It had

[1]James W. Barrett, "The World, the Flesh and Messrs. Pulitzer," The Vanguard Press, 1931. But it certainly could not expect to survive by printing less news than the Times or the Herald Tribune.

changed gradually from a reporter's paper to a writer's paper.
Perhaps this softening had made it more attractive to me, and
to young newspapermen all over the country. When the New
York papers reached the city room of the *Journal* in Providence,
the *World* was always the one that everybody wanted to read
immediately. There never was any struggle over the *Times*. The
brilliance of the writing had become the *World's* chief attraction.

But we also felt that its heart was in the right place. On the
editorial masthead there still appeared the Ten Commandments
that Joseph Pulitzer had placed there. That the *World* should
be:

"An institution that should always fight for progress and reform,

"Never tolerate injustice or corruption,

"Always fight demagogues of all parties,

"Never belong to any party,

"Always oppose privileged classes and public plunderers,

"Never lack sympathy with the poor,

"Always remain devoted to the public welfare,

"Never be satisfied with merely printing news,

"Always be drastically independent,

"Never be afraid to attack wrong, whether by predatory plu-
tocracy or predatory poverty."

They may not have been observed any more fervently after his
death and Cobb's than the decalogue promulgated by another
Jewish gentleman long before Pulitzer's time, but they at least
constituted a fine charter for a newspaper to operate under.
Pulitzer apparently couldn't conceive of people getting predatory
unless they had too much money, so that it became only a sym-
bol of power, or too little to live on, so that they damn well had
to get some more.

Also, the *World* had atmosphere. There were pictures of the
gold dome of the Pulitzer Building in every newspaper office in
the country—on the front cover of the *World Almanac*. Park
Row meant big-time newspaperdom, and the dome had dominated Park Row for thirty years. Everybody wanted to work
under it, if only to be able to say so years afterward, in a bar-
room in Woonsocket, R.I., or Elko, Nev. As it happened, I just

got under the wire. I must be one of the last people who went to work there.

Almost the first time I went out to lunch with Michelson, Sifton, and Stong, I heard that the World was going to suspend publication or be sold in a couple of days. This depressed me until they took pity and said that there had been similar rumors nearly every week since Herbert Bayard Swope had resigned as executive editor at the beginning of 1929. We were now in November, 1930. Nevertheless they half believed the latest report. It was impossible, they said, that a paper should slide continuously downhill without ever bumping bottom. Then I went out on a story and they all went back to the office, and we became so interested in our jobs that we forgot the bad outlook. Nothing happened, and we looked at each other a little sheepishly and smiled, as I was to see people in a London restaurant smile in 1944, when a buzz bomb passed overhead without conking out. Two days, or two weeks, later, there would be another rumor. The last months of the World were an excellent psychological training for war. I was to have much the same emotional experience in Paris in the spring of 1940, when everybody secretly knew that the Germans would get there, but hoped that through some miracle impossible to visualize they wouldn't. In Paris people used to report the Boche at the gate on Mondays, Wednesdays, and Fridays, but still at a reasonable distance on Tuesdays, Thursdays, and Saturdays. On May 16 there was a firm report that the Germans would arrive in a few hours; they arrived on June 14. The main point was that they did get there. So it was with the World.

There are some things that you cannot believe for more than a few seconds at a time anyway. I refused to believe at all that the World would fall. Maybe I thought that the circulation would jump when seven million New Yorkers saw how good I was.

You may remember the Metropolitan section of the Sunday World even though you forget its name, because it was that part of the paper on the front page of which Milt Gross used to produce Nize Baby. Hearst had hired Gross away from the World, but Frank Sullivan and James M. Cain still wrote for the page. Louis Weitzenkorn, another former contributor, had just gone to Hollywood. I did a story for the section about "stooge," a word just moving into colloquial speech. I discussed "stooge" as a noun, as a verb, "to stooge," and principally as an institution. The chief authority I interviewed and cited was Joe Cook, and I remember the interview well because we had a couple of drinks in his dressing room and I undiplomatically said, "I always thought you were funny in vaudeville, but there was a fellow named Fred Sweeney of Duffy and Sweeney who was much funnier." "Would you like to meet Sweeney?" asked Cook. "He's my valet now." Well, Sweeney *was* funnier than Cook was. I also did one about a benefit concert where the music critics played. I took the idea and gagged it laboriously, asking Babe Ruth, for example, what he would think of a benefit baseball game between umpires and baseball writers. "Mister," Mr. Ruth said, "that wouldn't be no benefit to nobody."

The time for frivolity was rapidly passing, however. The best period piece I did for the Met section was a fairly brief talk with an apple-seller in front of "Earl Carroll's Vanities" on a cold night. There were still enough people who were not broke, maybe short sellers on the market, to keep up some of the ostentatious spending of early 1929, and the contrasts between public manifestations of luxury and want were more glaring than in, say, 1932, when practically nobody was spending much. When I had finished my Met-section page-one story for the week I would do a magazine story on something like the new water tunnel cut six hundred feet under the rock. Then I would work up a few inside-page Met stories to bring my space up.

Uncertain as the *World's* existence was, the fellows on the Sunday side paid more attention to the detail of each presentation than I have ever seen expended on any other paper. They battled over the way things were written, in a manner I never saw approached until I came to the *New Yorker*. Sifton and Mike both did a lot to get the superfluous scrollwork out of my writing and make me "pack things tight." This does not mean foregoing the expression of any idea but finding a way to say it completely without dancing all over the place. It's the difference between teaching a young pitcher to cut out his windup and forcing him to cut out his curve.

The poor magazine had got down to such small format and

was printed on such cheap paper that the color printing, the great pride of the art director, Bob Ament, lost most of its effect. Herb Roth, Leo Kober, and Sam Cahen, the artists, knew they were laboring in a lost cause. But layouts and drawing were done with the same care as when the *Sunday World* topped the town. Old Tom Orr, a venerable utility man, used to tell stories about how he had carried rum and advances to O. Henry when that worthy had written for this same magazine. We had no contributors that good in 1931. When I think of that time now, my colleagues remind me of Pompeian lapidaries, putting a careful polish on their last bits of carnelian while the lava bubbled like a rarebit on the threshold.

There were a large number of women about the place, or so it seemed to me. The *Sunday World* had a women's section. The predicament of the paper induced an attitude of respectful gallantry toward every one of them, as on a ship about to be torpedoed. Maybe it was only because of our common situation, but I liked everybody on the *Sunday World*.

I'm certain it wasn't only our plight that made me respect Sifton, Mike, Randorf, and Stong, however. They were the first mature newspapermen of any age I had ever worked with, virile, but not afraid of being labeled leftist or intellectual. Mike and Bill were the furthest to the left; Paul was of about the political shade to make a left-wing New Dealer, which he became later, and Phil was a kind of unorganized skeptic. They gave me a booster shot of what Professor Mecklin had left in my system.

Dome into Ball

The pattern of a newspaperman's life is like the plot of "Black Beauty." Sometimes he finds a kind master who gives him a dry stall and an occasional bran mash in the form of a Christmas bonus, sometimes he falls into the hands of a mean owner who drives him in spite of spavins and expects him to live on potato peelings. The *Sunday World* was a dry-stall interlude in my wanderings (without bran mash), but I was soon to be put between the shafts of the ragman's cart.

So personal a memory of the end of the *World* newspapers may seem as limited as an account by the ship's cat of the sinking of the Titanic. But there were nearly three thousand employees (2,867 was the official count), and each lost his illusions about the validity of the kind-master concept in the newspaper world as abruptly as I did. The total effect, when nearly three thousand workers in a limited field are thrown on the street simultaneously, is much worse than three thousand times one. One newspaper worker out of a job, even in slack times, always has some chance of catching on again. So he has hope. There just aren't enough newspaper jobs in the country to take care of three thousand. So each one knows that the odds are all against him. This three thousand included printers and circulation and advertising personnel, as well as editorial workers. The printers, who were already well organized, did better than the others. They got a couple of days' work a week in the chapels of other newspapers, in accordance with union share-the-work plans, to tide them over until, one by one, full-time jobs opened up. For editorial workers it was a free-for-all scramble, in which we young men had an advantage over the more experienced and

less adaptable seniors, with the higher salaries that they had pain-
fully achieved. A high salary, in a time of newspaper disaster,
operates like too much rank in the Army. It would be indelicate
to offer a general officer a company or battalion, so superfluous
general officers get nothing to do. In the same way, city editors
do not like to offer a high-priced man a low salary, because he
will be discontented.

So scores of skilled journalists like my old preceptors Max
Fischel and Lindsay Denison of the *Evening World* were out
of jobs and stayed out to the end of their lives. They got nice
funerals and long obits in the papers that hadn't hired them after
the *World* went down. Not that there is any harm in good
funerals or obits. The friends who attended the former and
wrote the latter had no power to do anything more.

I had never before been so glad that I had no dependents.

The end of the *Worlds* marked the beginning of realism in
the relation of American newspaper employees to their employers. The employers had been realistic for a long time.

It took the abandonment of an "institution" like the *Worlds*
to drive the lesson home.

There are two good books describing the scuttling while under
way of the *World*, which had been the greatest and was still
one of the leading newspapers in America. I can vouch for
their excellence since I have just reread them after a lapse of
sixteen years. Few events in history have been more vigorously
reported.

One is called "The End of the World" (Harper's, 1931), subtitled "A Post-Mortem by its intangible assets," in which twenty-
seven members of the staff cover each aspect of their common
disaster. The other is Jim Barrett's "The World, the Flesh and
Messrs. Pulitzer" (Vanguard, 1931), in which the city editor,
who led a great impromptu anti-scuttle movement, reviewed the
events leading up to the tragedy. Both must be required reading in schools of journalism if the schools are any good.

So there is no need for me to describe in detail here the legally
sanctioned desertion by Joseph Pulitzer's heirs of the papers he
had forbidden them ever to sell. The heirs had, Barrett points
out, taken out twenty-five million dollars in profits from the
papers subsequent to the founder's death. They had plowed

back nothing into the property—the same story as the New England textile men, except that newspaper publishers like to advertise themselves as more idealistic than mere bag-spinners. The papers had lost three million dollars in their last three years, according to the heirs, who wished to make the deficit sound as impressive as possible. They therefore decided to quit—twenty-two million dollars for them, plus the sale price, and a kick in the pants for the three thousand employees, some of whom had helped the big Pulitzer make the papers.

Barrett again: "I believe they became worried and harassed over money losses and the fear that they might become poor men and really be obliged to work for a living, instead of drawing profits from the estate—to say nothing of salaries totaling more than $200,000 a year."

This would have been less of a shock if any other papers in the United States had been involved.

Back of the city editor's desk on the twelfth floor of the World Building was a bronze tablet subscribed for by members of the *World* staff. Maybe it is still there. It is significant that the tablet was paid for by members of the staff, not their bosses. The legend read:

"In Memory of—Gregory T. Humes—Reporter on the *World* —Mortally Injured in the Stamford Railroad wreck—He thought first of his paper and with indomitable courage sent the news of the disaster—Born April 12, 1878—Died June 13, 1913."

Poor Humes should go down in history as a founding member of the American Newspaper Guild. The contrast of his loyalty to that of his employers had an influence on the mind of every man who had ever worked on the *World*.

The Pulitzer heirs, without any warning of their intention, made public on Tuesday, February 24, their desire to sell the newspapers immediately to Roy Howard for a sum of five million dollars, to be paid in installments by a plan that made the receipt of the last two millions decidedly aleatory. Howard declared his intent to suppress the papers, except "in spirit," combining the name World and some features from the *World* papers with his *Evening Telegram*, a punch-drunk enterprise which had already cost him eight million dollars in four years. Lawyers for the heirs had to go before Surrogate Foley to get permission to break the Pulitzer will and sell, which is probably the only reason the deal became public at all. The procedure the masters preferred would have called for a simple, unannounced lockout, with the pasting of notices on the doors of the Pulitzer Building to greet employees: "This paper closed! Keep Out!" The appearance in court of Max Steuer, a prestigious lawyer of those days, with a competing offer from Paul Block, caused Foley to withhold his decision.

It was then that Barrett started a movement for the employees to take over the papers and run them on a co-operative basis. To do this we would have had to scratch up enough sound financial backing within forty-eight hours to buy the papers (that is if the Pulitzers would have considered such a humbling proposition at all). While Barrett and a few allies battled to raise the money and to delay the sale to Howard, the staffs continued to work as if there were not a possible doubt that the paper would continue to come out until the suns should gild the hills no more. And the last three numbers of the World were good papers. I myself finished a Sunday Metropolitan-section story on the official introduction of the rhumba to New York (at Roseland Ballroom) on the late afternoon of Thursday, February 26, our deadline. I can prove it by a reference on page 95 of "The End of the World," in Hoy Michelson's chapter on "The Hellbox Edition of the Sunday World." The hellbox, in the composing room, is the trough where the printers throw scrambled type. The Sunday World for March 1, 1931, was destined never to appear. There is another minuscular mention of me on page 246, in a story about the art staff of the World by an artist named Leo Kober, a kindly, talented Hungarian émigré. I cite them because for a year after this book appeared I used to look back at the two little notices to prove to myself that I had really been present at the making of history.

The whole staff was behind Barrett. We pledged ourselves to work for practically nothing and buy bonds with the reduced pay we would get. Also the few staff members who had any money offered to buy shares in the co-operative with it. There was a mass meeting at the Hotel Astor on Wednesday evening at which four hundred and fifty of us convinced ourselves that we were going to bring it off. The fellows who were getting out the paper naturally couldn't be there. The turnout, considering this circumstance, was colossal.

I was not again to feel so good about newspaper people in the mass, so sure of their capacity to work things out for themselves on a slightly higher level than traders and diplomats, until January, 1943, in Algiers. Then I was to see the whole corps of correspondents stand up to Robert D. Murphy and block the nearly accomplished murder of American sympathizers by the evil clique around General Giraud.

The effort to establish a co-operative *World* did not succeed. We couldn't raise money or even formulate plausible plans in the few hours the surrogate allowed us. I don't think the Pulitzers would have consented to the deal anyway unless we had outbid Howard by at least one dollar and seventy-five cents. They were gentlemen.

"It is pleasant to think of what might have been," writes John T. Gibbs, one of the authors of "The End of the World." "Calmly judging events in aftertime, one sees the almost insurmountable difficulties in the way of employee ownership of a newspaper, but after all, American annals are filled with successes whose beginnings were even more dubious."

As a callow newcomer to the paper I was only on the fringe of these great events—one of the cheering mob of fifty-cent subscribers to buy Jim Barrett an engraved watch. But after it was all over I was just as far out on the sidewalk as the fellows who had worked on the *World* for forty years.

The Golden Dome had turned into an Iron Ball.

Oklahoma on the Subway

Each of the 2,867 regular employees of the *Worlds* got two weeks' pay, and Herbert Pulitzer for the trustees promised that the first five hundred thousand dollars received from Howard would be distributed among the ex-Worldlings. I do not know whether this sum was to be in addition to the two weeks' pay or to include it; if distributed equally among the former employees, it would have amounted to $174.43 a head, a slim provision against indefinite unemployment. Since I had been on a drawing account and not a regular salary, I didn't even get the two weeks' pay. This was not a tragedy for me, since I was young and alone, but the plight of the older hands was a lesson in journalism.

I went up to see Stanley Walker at the *Herald Tribune* again, as I had so many times during the preceding autumn, and I made a perfunctory round of other city rooms. The town was like an airfield during a strafing, with hundreds of men trying to get into half a dozen foxholes. I returned to my street-patrolling routine for a couple of weeks and then applied for a job on the *World-Telegram*. I had refrained at first from this obvious démarche, because the pre-merger *Telegram* had seemed to me such a ludicrous rag, written for the most part in an idiom I once described as Oklahoma Byzantine, to the specifications of an owner who had placed on the bulletin board a notice saying: "Remember, New York is Bagdad on the Subway!" I felt a personal resentment against this newsprint Falstaff capering over the dead Hotspur.

The *World-Telegram* was then housed in a crazy old building at Dey and Washington Streets, south of Washington Market.

The atmosphere was as cluttered and confused as the interior; the "new" paper had taken over the *Evening World's* advertising contracts and was consequently swollen to an ungainly size, although the ads, accepted at a rate based on the *Evening World* circulation, were not profitable. More ads necessitated the inclusion of more editorial matter, and the cheapest kind of editorial matter to manufacture is a feature story by a low-salaried writer. So I was in luck. Talcott Powell, an assistant to Lee Wood, the managing editor, was signing on new hands for this hermaphrodite-rigged craft, and he accepted me at once. I was to be paid seventy-five dollars a week.

During the next four years I wrote between seven hundred and fifty and one thousand feature stories for the *World-Telegram,* nearly all under my own byline. The exceptions were second or third stories on days when I had more than one in the paper; we were allowed only one byline a day. Some of them were good. I used a number later in a book called "Back Where I Came From," about New York, and a couple attained a second life in the Whites' "Sub-treasury of American Humor." Here I could write a monograph on feature stories, but I will save it for a course of lectures when the last iron ball hits me and I become a professor in a school of journalism. All I want to say about feature stories here is that they need not be as bad as they usually are.

I might also fill a chapter with jovial reminiscence about the strange people I met while filling space for Mr. Howard, but I have already exploited that material rather thoroughly in the *New Yorker.* Stanley Walker once wrote, in the *Herald-Tribune* Book Review, that I knew more characters than any other reporter in New York. He was probably wrong, but it is nice to have been mentioned for the honor. So all I will say about the creative aspect of my sojourn on the *World-Telegram* is that I learned nothing about writing there.

I did learn a lot about something else. Very early in my *World-Telegram* life I acquired a human responsibility, which through circumstances beyond the control of either of us became at times exceedingly heavy. This took the carefree, juvenile jollity out of journalism for me definitively. It taught me that society is divided, not into newspaper people and non-newspaper people, but into people with money and people without it. I did not belong to a joyous, improvident professional group including me and Roy Howard, but to a section of society including me and any floorwalker at Macy's. Mr. Howard, even though he asked to be called Roy, belonged in a section that included him and the gent who owned Macy's. This clarified my thinking about publishers, their common interests and motivations.

Some thousands of my fellows in city rooms all over the country were going through the same processes of thought at about the same time, which is why the American Newspaper Guild grew so fast. I won't forget the day when Howard came down to the new World-Telegram Building at Barclay and West Streets in his trick limousine to talk us out of forming a real union. This must have been early in 1934. The staff had been cut repeatedly since the paper had lost the edema resulting from the merger. It had been cut without regard to sentiment. Men who had been on the *Telegram* when it was a struggling outsider had been dropped with quite as little ceremony as castaways from the *World* who had swum to the life raft. Selection had been on the single standard of value for the management's money at current quotations. So we who were left had no reason to feel gratitude; we were simply the biggest bargains available in a buyers' market.

Our salaries had been cut twice, in September, 1932, and in March, 1933, by 10 per cent each time, so that mine had dropped first to $67.50 and then to $60.75, or a couple of dollars less than I had been making when I left Providence. My salary was atypical only in that it was so large. Joe Mitchell was getting no more, even though he was a writer unique in America. The paper had recently put on a new Police Headquarters man at twenty-three dollars a week.

I have sometimes been told that I cannot understand the full force of the depression because I was never one of the true unemployed. My interludes of street patrol in 1930 and 1931 weren't long enough to be serious. But living in New York on $60.75 with a wife and a lot of hospital bills is enough to give a fellow a pretty good hint of what economic insecurity is like. Payments on back bills frequently brought our disposable income down to about forty dollars. And of course, as lucky people, we helped newspaper friends who had no jobs at all. This was always a joy, but I sometimes wondered about a system under which the publisher hired a man at a low salary, worked him, and then let him go with nobody to put the bite on but fellow newspapermen. I thought that every laid-off newspaperman ought to be allowed three bites at a publisher—say fifty dollars each time. Not just the publisher who canned him but any publisher who happened to be in the vicinity.

Craftsmanship carried its own satisfaction, but it is a continuing irritation to know that you are an excellent, appreciated craftsman, but that there are so few outlets for your product that you must take what a rube in a purple shirt is willing to pay you. A one-room apartment is not so amusing when you are thirty and married as when you are a cub of twenty-one. There was no housing shortage in 1932–33–34, just a rent-money shortage. And it must be assumed, since I had been pretty steadily employed for eight years by first-rank newspapers, that I was doing better financially than most other newspapermen in the nation.

My Professional Career Ends

A fellow named Dick Joseph, who writes travel pieces for *Esquire*, once told me the story of his first newspaper job, on the Scripps-Howard paper in Columbus, Ohio. Dick, as editor of the student newspaper of Ohio State University, which is in Columbus, got into a row with the university authorities because of a piece he had written about fraternities. They threw him out.

The local Scripps sheet carried an editorial commending Dick for his independence as a journalist. If the university didn't want young men of his type, the Scripps-Howard newspapers did, the editorialist wrote. So Dick, who was afraid to go home to New York City, clipped the editorial and took it to the managing editor. "You said you wanted me," he said. "What do I start doing?"

The editor, who hadn't expected such immediate consequences, stalled for a while, because his bosses had forbidden any increase in the pay roll. Then he said, "All I can offer you is a cub salary—five dollars a week and an expense account. I'll let you knock down twelve dollars a week on the account. You can put down extra taxi and bus rides. That will keep my pay roll from looking too big."

Dick was glad to get the job. This was at the nadir of the depression. He worked for six months, covering good run-of-the-news stories, like executions, he tells me, and then the boss told him he would have a promotion.

"We have never had a night city editor," the Scripps-Howard executive said. It was an evening sheet.

(We used to have a saying on the *World-Telegram*: "A

Scripps-Howard executive is a man who walks fast"—to show he is busy—"smiles a lot"—to show he is a regular fellow—"and moves office chairs"—to show he is never too busy to notice details.)

"You know, someone to come in at midnight, look through the last editions of the big city evening papers and the first editions of the mornings for stories that have a local follow, call reporters if anything big breaks, and generally maintain the continuity of the operation. Unfortunately I am still unable to raise your pay, but it's an opportunity for you."

Joseph felt proud. He was making progress.

Next payday he opened his envelope and began to laugh. This annoyed some of his co-workers. They were sore because the whole staff had had a 10-per-cent cut.

"But I couldn't help laughing," Dick says. "Inside my envelope was a check for four dollars and fifty cents."

I like to think that Joseph was opening his envelope at the precise moment when Roy Howard, sitting on a rewrite man's desk in the *World-Telegram* city room, was chummily telling us that we were not laborers but artists, and that it would be a big mistake for us to affiliate with the A.F. of L. (afterward we quit it and went into the C.I.O.).

I had a colleague on the *World-Telegram* during the depression whose personal and domestic commitments were unusually heavy. Consequently he was more scandalously underpaid than the rest of us. He had a great knack of working up crime mysteries, and could make the unexplained murder of a taxi dancer read like "A Study in Scarlet." He was ingenious and enterprising, and readers lapped up his stuff. But he never could get a raise. In 1934, when Bruno Hauptmann was arrested and charged with kidnaping and murdering the Lindbergh baby, this reporter scooped the entire country by obtaining facsimiles of the signatures on the ransom notes. Lee Wood told the reporter that as a special reward he would be presented with a due bill on a chain clothing store entitling him to a thirty-dollar suit of clothes. The depression was beginning to lift slightly, and when the reporter looked in the glass at the clothing store and saw himself in the new suit, he acquired enough confidence to go out and look for another job. He got one at two-and-a-half times his old salary.

Remembering these scenes of newspaper life, and reinforcing my memories with those of Gene Campbell, which go back to 1906, and of still older-timers encountered, I cannot take seriously the recommendations of the authors of "A Free and Responsible Press" that newspapermen "impose professional standards" on their employers. Elevator boys would have as good a chance.

The Guild has given the newspaperman a modicum of economic security in a great many cities—not as much as a member of Big Six enjoys, but then the Guild is a new union. For example, when the *Herald Tribune* released one of the best-known reporters in the world last winter it had to pay him thirty-six weeks' severance pay—two weeks for each year he had been with the paper. This gives a man a longer tether than he used to have. He can afford to be more independent than in the days when he might be simply chucked out for having the "wrong attitude."

Because of the accumulating severance pay, his independence is even in direct ratio with his length of service. Before the Guild it used to be the other way around. But this is still far from guaranteeing the newsman any "professional" freedom.

When a physician thinks that a patient needs penicillin, he may prescribe penicillin, but when a newspaperman thinks that his city needs a municipal electric plant, he knows better than even to ask his boss for permission to prescribe. I know of few newspapermen who are forced to write things they do not believe, but of many who are prevented from writing what they do. And not a few have had their reports either suppressed or distorted within their own home offices. It is always interesting, for example, to note the divergence between the books written by *Time-Life* foreign correspondents after they leave that organization and the tenor of their despatches as published while in its employ. In Tunisia in 1943 I worked with a pair of earnest and accurate *Time-Life* men, great boosters for the segment of the American Army with which they had lived for months. The cables they sent home were full of approbation, but the reports as they appeared in the air-mail edition of *Time*, which reached the armies with disconcerting speed, were critical in a nasty, patronizing way. They were barred from the headquarters of the best division in the Army even though they produced carbon copies of the dispatches they had sent. These had been twisted at New York, apparently to prove that the Administration's conduct of the war was amateurish. Both men are still working for Mr. Luce and I am sure are still sending accurate dispatches. I am not at all sure that they are that when published.

Newspapermen are quick to get the idea of what the boss wants, but those who get it first have usually had similar ideas right along. The publisher chooses some staff members as his instruments and ignores others (or, if they are obstreperous, gets rid of them). The reporter has as much independent voice as a piano key.

George Seldes, who for years was a foreign correspondent for the Chicago *Tribune*, once told me of a meeting of *Tribune* correspondents in Chicago, shortly after the 1914–18 war, when Colonel McCormick partitioned the known world among the representatives of the World's Greatest Newspaper, like Alexander the Great cutting up the Orient among his generals.

"How many men speak French?" the colonel asked.

A good many raised their hands.

"How many German?"

A good few raised their hands.

"Italian?"

Only a few.

"Russian?"

Perhaps one.

"And how about you, Olaf?" addressing one of his favorites.

"I don't speak any."

"Fine, fine, you'll be unprejudiced. I'll make you a *roving* correspondent."

Olaf, which is not his right name, has been the colonel's pet correspondent ever since. He has, without too much effort, avoided learning anything which might lessen the colonel's esteem for him. But no one can accuse him of becoming ignorant just to please the colonel. The colonel liked him because he was ignorant.

They don't always give a man an ignorance test before hiring him, even on the WGN. A literate occasionally sneaks in—for example, Edmond Taylor, who was the *Tribune's* correspondent in Paris at the beginning of the most recent war. Taylor, who subsequently wrote a remarkable book called "The Strategy of Terror," was sensitive to the purposes and methods of both the Nazis and their collaborators in Allied and neutral countries. He sent a dispatch in the early fall of 1939 about German designs on the Balkans and was rewarded with a cable telling him to take a vacation because he was obviously having a nervous breakdown. He resigned. Olaf arrived to replace him.

So operates the intramural process of selection.

Newspapermen talking about their "profession" always remind me of that grand burlesque entry of Bobby Clark and his partner, the late Paul McCullough, with Clark at once dignified and jaunty, puffing on a cigar butt and swinging a cane, McCullough, dignified and solemn, wearing a high plug hat and the dogskin coat he had bought secondhand in Winnipeg many years before. As they reached the centre of the stage Clark would throw away the cigar. McCullough's dignity would dissolve instantly and he would dive for the discard. Clark, regretting that he had thrown away a butt still worth diving for, would whack at McCullough's fingers with the head of the cane, and dignity would volatilize in a struggle over something worth a quarter of a cent.

Early in the spring of 1935, I quit the *World-Telegram*. I think it was the example of Lou Wedemar, the man in the thirty-dollar suit, that decided me. Or maybe it was all the pugnacious music I heard at the St. Patrick's Day parade, which I attended in company with my wife, who is redheaded. Anyway, on March 22 I told Lee Wood that I had been with the *World-Telegram* for exactly four years and that if he didn't give me my first raise I would quit. "No raise," he said.

So I went up to Mr. Hearst's King Features and got a job that lasted just eight weeks, at eighty-five dollars a week. This was exactly enough time for me to negotiate a steady job on the *New Yorker*. I had done both reporting and rewrite for the Talk of the Town department in the front part of the *New Yorker* while I was still at the *World-Telegram*.

I am glad I worked for Hearst once, because that completes the gamut. The editor of the *Evening Journal* Magazine, to which I was assigned, used to hand me a couple of clippings about a sex murderer in Altoona who had inherited an ancestral estate while awaiting the electric chair. Then he would say, in a cavernous voice: "Dream about it for a while, Liebling. Just dream about it."

A still higher executive told me one day: "The public is interested in just three things: Blood, money, and the female organ of sexual intercourse." He was the last guy who told me about newspapers while I was still a newspaperman.

The Wayward Press

The Wayward Press

I had opportunities to work on better news stories as a member of the *New Yorker* staff than I had ever had on a daily. I am still proud of the job I did getting material for a profile of Father Divine in the spring of 1936. This sable and squatty twentieth-century Joseph Smith had been aided rather than defined by newspaper stories accenting the mystery of his origin and wealth, and repeating, without analysis, his claims of a vast international following. I traced him back to the earliest beginning of his ambition to be God, described the main source of his income, with proofs, and worked out pretty accurately the relatively small number of followers he had, but had absolutely. You can get more out of five thousand people who believe you are God than out of ten million who merely approve of you in a general sort of way. Nothing has happened in the intervening eleven years to change any of the conclusions I set down.

The story of the aged white woman who died early this year leaving Father $350,000 paralleled that of Thomas and Verinda Brown, the colored couple who told me in 1936 how they had made over all their savings to him in the belief he was God. They sued him for the money and got a judgment (on which I don't think they were ever able to collect). Father's surrender of his claim to the legacy when challenged by the old woman's next of kin reflected the legal precedent set in the Brown case. The law assumes that you aren't God, and that if you induce anybody to give you money under the representation that you are God, then you are obtaining the money under false pretenses. Clifton Fadiman wrote in his preface to an anthology of *New Yorker* profiles, "May I remark, in passing, that Father Divine stands out as by far the most powerful personality in the book? Beside him Vincent Astor, for example, becomes merely a boyish millionaire, wealthy enough to be able to substitute a few colorful eccentricities for genuine personality." No reader of innumerable newspaper stories about the Negro hedge-cutter who became a god would have got that impression. Some of the stories were jocular, some patronizing, and all puzzled. Father was a good newspaper subject (or else they wasted all that space) but they muffed him. Any one of a score of good newspapermen in New York could have taken his measure, but no paper would pay a man for a couple of months to do it. The superficiality of newspaper coverage is without excuse; public characters appear as on a child's drawing, two-dimensional and without perspective. All that is lacking is the childish charm. This is not the fault of the reporters but of their employers, who will neither invest in thorough reporting nor even sanction it, because it might disturb their own concept of the world they live in. They like to believe in Astors. I signed the Divine profile with St. Clair McKelway, but I did all the reporting on it. Mac did the writing, after my first version began to look like a million-word book on comparative religion.

When the war began in Europe in 1939, I went to Paris for the *New Yorker,* came home after the fall of France, went to Britain in 1941 and again in 1942, going on to North Africa, came home again in the summer of 1943, and then went to Britain in October to await D Day. I covered the French campaign and came home a couple of days before Christmas, 1944. It was only in 1945, when I was settling down in this country, that I began to read newspapers regularly again.

I read foreign news with constant, involuntary reference to what I had seen in Europe and to my knowledge of the men filing the despatches. I read domestic news in the light of what I had learned between Professor Mecklin's speech and the Hearst executive's dictum about the three things people really cared about. Then I began to read sporting news again, because I like boxing and horse racing a lot, and while I was on the page I looked at other sports stories too. I read editorials because they made me sore, and columnists because they usually made me feel terribly clever. I read book reviews habitually, and quite often dramatic and musical criticism, although my interest in the theatre and music was desultory. Then I read a lot of the other stuff, even though I had already looked at everything that ordinarily had any interest for me, because newspaper reading can become a nervous habit, like wife-beating or small talk.

After a few months at home I began to react to some of the things I read. Some of my reactions resembled severe attacks of mental hives or prickly heat. Occasionally they verged on what psychiatrists call the disturbed and assaultative. So I suggested to Bill Shawn, the managing editor of the *New Yorker*, who relayed to Harold Ross, the head man, that we revive the Wayward Press department.

This had been founded by the late Robert Benchley in 1927, when the *New Yorker* was two years old. Benchley invented the title. He wrote Wayward Press pieces at irregular intervals from then until 1937. In the beginning Benchley reviewed the newspapers in the same spirit as he would have reviewed the vaudeville shows we then still had. I would have taken the same line had I been writing the department at that period, except that I could not have done it one-tenth so gracefully or well. But in the thirties, when the world became more serious, Benchley took some pretty hard socks at injustices and misrepresentations. Benchley wrote purely as a newspaper reader. He had little of what Max Fischel called the newspaper "taint" on him. After Benchley gave up the department—probably because he got interested in so many other activities—it lapsed for eight years, except for a fine isolated piece by Wolcott Gibbs on newspaper handling of the Lonergan murder case in 1944. Gibbs lived in an apartment house two doors from the murder scene. He wrote no more Wayward Presses thereafter, presumably because no more murders occurred on that block.

The situation that inspired my first Wayward Press was the mess over the reporting of the surrender of the Germans at Reims on May 7, 1945, and the ensuing confusion over V-E Day. I was but recently out of the clutches of Army Public Relations myself, and I took up strongly for Ed Kennedy of the Associated Press, who sent out the news of the surrender although he had been forbidden to do so. I did not feel then, nor do I now, that the end of a war should be kept a secret.

The publishing world's handling of Kennedy's feat was typical. The Associated Press capitalized on it by sending it out to all member papers, and they played it to the full. Then, when the State and War Departments made angry noises, the AP repudiated Kennedy, but not the story. He was kept on the pay roll, but without assignment, until he resigned. The War Department reinstated him as a war correspondent late in 1946, when there was no war to go to. This caused me to greet him, next time I saw him, as "my exonerated friend." Ed is now publishing a newspaper somewhere in the wasteland west of the Hudson, in one of those California towns that begin with Santa. I think Monica.

The A. P. Surrender

The great row over Edward Kennedy's Associated Press story of the signing of the German surrender at Reims served to point up the truth that if you are smart enough you can kick yourself in the seat of the pants, grab yourself by the back of the collar, and throw yourself out on the sidewalk. This is an axiom that I hope will be taught to future students of journalism as Liebling's Law. The important aspect of the row, I am sure, is not that Kennedy got his dispatch out of Europe before the SHAEF Public Relations bosses wanted him to but that only three representatives of the American press were admitted to one of the memorable scenes in the history of man, and they only on condition that they promise not to tell about it until the brigadier general in charge of public relations gave them permission. No correspondent of a newspaper published in the United States was invited to the signing; besides Kennedy, Boyd Lewis of the United Press, and James Kilgallen of Hearst's International News Service, the official list included four radio men, an enlisted correspondent for *Stars & Stripes*, and a collection of French, Russian, Australian, and Canadian correspondents. Whether a promise extorted as this one was, in an airplane several thousand feet up, has any moral force is a question for theologians. The only parallel I can think of offhand is the case of Harold the Saxon, who was shipwrecked in the territories of William of Normandy at a time when Edward the Confessor was getting on in years. William, taking Harold into protective custody, made him swear not to claim the English throne after Edward died, but when Harold got home he cocked a snook at William. Anglo-Saxon historians have since expressed a good deal of sympathy for Harold's point of view, but the Church held with William. I suppose that Kennedy should have refused to promise anything and thus made sure of missing an event that no newspaperman in the world would want to miss, but I can't imagine any correspondent's doing it.

I do not think Kennedy imperiled the lives of any Allied soldiers by sending the story, as some of his critics have charged. He probably saved a few, because by withholding the announcement of an armistice you prolong the shooting, and, conversely, by announcing it promptly you make the shooting stop. Moreover, the Germans had broadcast the news of the armistice several hours before Kennedy's story appeared on the streets of New York, and Absie, the O.W.I.'s American Broadcasting Station in Europe, broadcast it in twenty-four languages, including English, within an hour after.[1] The thing that has caused the most hard feeling is that Kennedy broke a "combination," which means that he sent out a story after all the correspondents on the assignment had agreed not to. But the old-fashioned "combination" was an agreement freely reached among reporters and not a pledge imposed upon the whole group by somebody outside it. Incidentally, the *Times* used to make its reporters at

[1] Kennedy told me, shortly after his return to the United States, that immediately after the signing, and before the correspondents had boarded the plane to fly back to Paris, Brigadier General Allen told them that he was sorry, but that when they got there they might find that the correspondents at Headquarters had already been permitted to send a bulletin summarizing the story.

"General Eisenhower is very anxious to have the news sent out as quickly as possible," he said, "because he realizes that getting it spread around quickly will help prevent bloodshed." Allen suggested that they write their stories in the plane, to have them all ready for the censor when they hit Paris. They wrote them, but about a minute after they arrived Allen told them that somebody "higher up" (than Eisenhower, apparently) had ordered the stories held.

Kennedy said that when he heard the Absie broadcast he got watered off and, going to an Army telephone, a direct line to London that he had sometimes been allowed to use, put in a call for an Associated Press colleague in London. The operator, assuming he had permission to make the call, put him through, and Kennedy simply read the story he had written on the plane.

That was Ed's story, and I suspect that part of the other boys' indignation was because they had forgotten about that particular telephone line.

Police Headquarters stay out of combinations. The willingness of the large American news organizations in the European Theatre of Operations to be herded into the new-style combination, in return for favors that independent journalists didn't get, had led directly to the kind of official contempt for the press that the Reims arrangements indicated, with the accompanying view that opportunity to report history was what SHAEF calls a "SHAEF privilege," like a Shubert pass. The Associated Press was a leader in establishing this form of organized subservience, and the jam it now finds itself in is therefore a good illustration of the workings of Liebling's Law.

For many years before this war, the editorial end of the American newspaper business had been turning from newsgathering to shopping for a packaged, mass-produced wordage sold by the press associations and syndicates. A few newspapers, such as the *Times* and *Herald Tribune* here and the *Tribune* and *Daily News* in Chicago, went into wholesaling in a modest way themselves by setting up their own syndicates, principally to peddle European news. The war, coupled with the excess-profits tax (which made many businessmen decide that they might as well pay their extra money to employees as to the tax collector), put an end, in a number of cases, to the newspapers' depending entirely on this sort of ready-made, or store, news, and scores of writers for magazines and newspapers began to arrive in the European Theatre of Operations. The large news organizations then faced the problem of proving that boughten coverage was not only cheaper but better than "original" reporting—say, Ernest Hemingway's. To accomplish this, they either suggested or accepted enthusiastically—it is not quite clear which—the Army's present principle of "limited facilities" for the coverage of news events. This meant that they concurred in the rear-area military maxim that there were never enough accommodations for the number of correspondents who wanted to see anything. The military, in return, conceded that the correspondents of the organizations which had large London bureaus should have first call on whatever accommodations there were. These bureaus established their importance with a SHAEF Public Relations personnel that seldom got out of London. The clearinghouse for the allotment of "facilities," which from then on assumed the character not of rights but of favors, was the Association of American Correspondents, whose headquarters were in London and which was dominated by the representatives of the large press organizations, and any facilities that were left over were distributed among the independent correspondents whom the members found most "reasonable." The key members of the Association further impressed the Public Relations soldiers with statistics about the number of readers each of their organizations served. The Associated Press claims to "fill the news needs of eight hundred million people," I.N.S. two hundred and twenty-five million, United Press (unaccountably modest) fifty-five million "in the United States alone," the Chicago *Tribune* syndicate a hundred and ten million, the *Herald Tribune* syndicate ten million, the *Times* syndicate six million, and Time-Life, Inc., which managed to wedge its way into the Association at an early date, twenty-two million. Together with the major radio chains, which reach a good billion people each, these press associations and syndicates served about twice the population of the world. This total does not even include the readers of the Chicago *Daily News* syndicate, figures for which are not on hand at this writing. Having once accepted the principle of limitation (i.e., to members of the Correspondents' Association) and having made a habit, for thirty months, of shouting publicly, "Headquarters is always right!," the dozen or so ruling members were hardly in a position to object when the Army decided on a further limitation of newspaper facilities—this time to zero.

The story that amused me most during armistice week was the one that appeared in the *Times* of Wednesday, May 9, under the headline "Fiasco by SHAEF at Reims Is Bared: Reporters Barred from Seeing Historic Signing of the German Surrender." It was signed by Raymond Daniell, a sententious little man who, as chief of the *Times'* London bureau, had been the chief promoter of the limitations scheme, back in 1942. "The correspondents never liked the Army's plan, but they accepted it with reservations," Daniell wrote. "What made them especially angry, however, was the fact that when the time came for the surrender, it was the Army's plan for coverage in Berlin that was adopted, instead of an order of precedence drawn up at Dieppe by the newspaper representatives and followed ever since until

last Sunday night by the Army where space was limited."
Daniell, as president of the Correspondents' Association, had
practically imposed the "order of precedence" on the Army
press-relations chief in London after the Dieppe what-was-it. His
reason was that it turned out after the raid that Quentin
Reynolds of *Collier's* had been along without the sanction of
the Association. It was never hinted that Reynolds' presence had
anything to do with the sanguinary unsuccess at Dieppe, but
Daniell and his opposite numbers in the other large news organizations nevertheless felt that magazine men should be discouraged. The bureau chiefs of the syndicates, conspicuously including Robert Bunnelle of the A.P., who is now involved in the
Kennedy trouble, simply transferred to Europe the tendency of
American district reporters to play ball with the police lieutenant on the desk.[2] It is that which makes the rather spluttery
rage of Brigadier General Frank Allen, the Supreme Headquarters Press Relations chief, so comprehensible. The brigadier feels
like a keeper at the zoo who has been butted in the behind by
his favorite gazelle. What made Daniell especially angry, appar-

[2]*This tendency even extended to inciting Army authorities to censor other
correspondents. Harry Butcher, in his book "My Three Years with Eisenhower," p. 59, entry for August 15, 1942, notes: "Considerable talk about
the color problem. A correspondent expressed concern that at least one 'irresponsible and biased' reporter was about to send troublemaking articles
back home about the color question. Someone raised the point that existent
censorship rules bar Negro stories of this type. Ike said, 'Take it off!' Later
he was importuned by a small group of first-rate correspondents to recon-
sider his decision, but he stuck to it. Said in the long run it would be better
for the news, good or bad, to flow freely. Might just as well let the American public know what the problems are and our success or failure in meeting
them."*

*This makes me sad. The picture of first-rate (!) correspondents arguing
for censorship and the West Point lieutenant general against it is priceless—
and as creditable to Eisenhower as it is disgraceful for the alleged newspapermen. I don't know whether I or a talented Negro correspondent for a
colored newspaper named Dunbar was the writer under attack—we were
both writing stories about the colored soldiers in the west of England. Mine
appeared in the New Yorker that fall under the title of "The Rolling
Umpties," a paraphrase of a Negro motor-truck regiment's pet name for
itself—The Rolling Twenty-eighth. My stories, incidentally, went up to
General Eisenhower himself for final censorship. He wasn't too tough on
them, either.*

ently, was that the military found room at the surrender ceremony for twenty women friends of officers but left him standing
outside. He seemed to feel that this was rubbing it in.[3]

The Kennedy explosion has, I imagine, done no harm, except
possibly to Kennedy—one of my favorite reporters, I might add.
The Russians have not declined to end the war because of it.
Maybe, in the absence of opposition, the Russians would have
had to stop anyway, although this does not seem to have occurred to Supreme Headquarters spokesmen. The Russians had
their own surrender show in Berlin, and probably had a better
publicity break on it than they would have had if the two surrenders had been announced simultaneously. (They could do
with a public-relations counsel, anyway.) One unconditional surrender of the Reich a day is about as much as the public can
absorb. Moreover, the row can do a lot of good if it brings into
the clear the whole disturbing question of military censorship
imposed for political, personal, or merely capricious reasons and
reveals the history of the prodigious amount of pure poodle-
faking that has gone on under the name of Army Public Relations. I remember the period in North Africa when, for reasons
of "military security," no correspondent was allowed to say anything against Admiral Darlan even after he was dead, and when
a dispatch of my own was censored because I said that anti-
Fascist Frenchmen thought our indulgence of the Fascists silly
(information which obviously would have been of great interest
to the German General Staff). In France, last summer, another
of my stories was held up a week because I wrote about the
torture and execution of an American parachutist by Vichy
militiamen. It was evidently important to military security that
the American public shouldn't think hard of our enemies. "Horror stuff," by which the censors meant any mention of ugly
wounds or indecorous deaths, was for a long time forbidden, but
recently it has been found compatible with security. Somebody
must have told whoever makes the rules that the Germans know
about it. But the worst form of censorship was the preventive

[3] *One of the friends was Mollie Ford, a very pretty Red Cross girl, now
married to Harry Butcher, who was General Eisenhower's personal aide,
with the rank of captain—in the Navy. The secret was revealed in the press
with the announcement of the Ford-Butcher marriage.*

kind exercised by Public Relations, which, in any echelon higher than an army in the field, acted on the principle that an inactive correspondent was potentially a source of less bother than a correspondent who was going somewhere. While the correspondent was in the United States, the object was to keep him from crossing to England, and once he got to England the game was to stop him from reaching Africa, Italy, France, or any other place he might find subject matter. If he arrived in any of those countries, there was one more line of defense—P.R.O. would try to hold him in Algiers, Naples, or Paris, as the case might be. Actually, he was safe only when he got to a front. He had nothing to worry him there but shells, for the higher echelons of Public Relations left him alone. To give Army Public Relations the only credit due it, some of the younger officers in the field were helpful, hard-working, and at times even intelligent.

The Public Relations situation reached a high point in *opera-buffa* absurdity in London in the spring of a year ago, before the invasion of France. There were at one time nine separate echelons of Public Relations in London at once: P.R.O. SHAEF; P.R.O. Twenty-first Army Group (Montgomery's command); P.R.O. FUSAC (First Army Group, which later became Twelfth Army Group); P.R.O. First Army; P.R.O. ETOUSA (European Theatre of Operations, U.S. Army), which handled the correspondents' mail, gave out ration cards, did publicity for Services of Supply, and tried to horn in on everything else; P.R.O. Eighth Air Force; P.R.O. Ninth Air Force; the P.R.O. for General Spaatz's highest echelon of the Air Forces command; and the Navy P.R.O. The Air Forces publicity people were unpretentious but aggressive; the Navy was helpful; the five other echelons spent most of their time getting in each other's way.

The P.R.O.s, mostly colonels and lieutenant colonels (a major, in this branch of service, was considered a shameful object, to be exiled to an outer office), had for the most part been Hollywood press agents or Chicago rewrite men in civilian life. They looked as authentic in their uniforms as dress extras in a B picture, but they had learned to say "Army" with an unction that Stonewall Jackson could never have achieved. One rewrite lieutenant colonel used to predict casualties as high as 80 per cent in the first assault wave on D Day. He had never heard a shot fired in anger. Others would seriously tell correspondents that they, the correspondents, couldn't go along on D Day because there wouldn't be space enough on the landing craft to hold another man. The P.R.O.s were perhaps under the impression that you load ships for an invasion the way you would ferryboats, without regard to the organization of combat units. There was room for ninety more men on the Coast Guard LCI on which I finally crossed. The one point on which all the London officers were united was their detestation of the field army. One division commander who requested that a certain correspondent be allowed to accompany his outfit into action stirred such resentment in the London army that he was reprimanded by the Chief of Staff of SHAEF. The London P.R.O.s felt that the division commander, being a mere major general rich in battle experience, was guilty of insubordination when he disagreed with non-combatant lieutenant colonels. Daniell, Bunnelle, and the rest of the news-agency men adapted themselves to this squalid milieu and flourished in it. They agreed with everything the dress extras said, especially with the thesis that on fifty miles of Norman coast there would be room for only about twenty correspondents, who would, of course, represent the larger news organizations. The habit of saying yes to people you don't respect is hard to break, which is one reason I think well of Edward Kennedy for breaking it. Also, I think that if any severe punishment is inflicted on the first journalist to disobey an unreasonable order, an era of conformity will set in that will end even the pretense of freedom of the press in any area where there is a brigadier general to agree with.

Having finished with what I consider the deeper implications of the Kennedy case, I would like to say that it has produced some delightful examples of journalism right here in this country. On the afternoon of Tuesday, May 8, after most of the papers had played up Kennedy's story real big and the Army had then denounced it as "unauthorized," Roy W. Howard, president of the Scripps-Howard newspapers and overlord of the United Press, the A.P.'s chief rival, broke into print with a plea for the Associated Press. Howard said that he himself had been pilloried like Kennedy in November, 1918, when he had re-

ported the armistice four days before it had happened. The two
cases were an exact parallel except that Kennedy's report was
right and Howard's was wrong.

The *Times,* on that same Tuesday morning, carried Kennedy's
story in two columns on the right-hand side of the front page,
in twelve-point type, under two cross-lines and two banks drop-
ping from its four-line streamer headline. On Thursday it published an editorial saying Kennedy had done a "grave disservice
to the newspaper profession." A *Times* man I met in a saloon
that afternoon said they had run the story because it looked authentic but they had run the editorial because they didn't like
the way the story had been sent out. On Tuesday they also carried a boxed dispatch from Drew Middleton, one of their own
men in Paris, saying that all the correspondents except Kennedy
had been caught in "the most colossal 'snafu' in the history of
the war."

Wednesday morning brought Daniell's remarkable *Times*
story, cited above (which read exactly the way a *Nebelwerfer*
sounds) and a perfectly deadpan account of the Reims function
by Drew Middleton, who presumably had not been there, since
he wasn't on the list of correspondents invited by SHAEF. Middleton's story appeared twenty-four hours after the *Times* had
carried the Kennedy story and was practically a duplicate of it.
The *Herald Tribune* had an equally deadpan account by John
O'Reilly, who presumably wasn't there either, and an editorial,
better-tempered than the *Times*', chiding Kennedy. It also had
on its front page an excellent eyewitness story about Berlin in
the final days of the Russian attack upon it, written by its own
correspondent Seymour Freidin, who was still under suspension
by SHAEF for having gone to Berlin without Brigadier General
Allen's permission. The story had been held up six days. The
Times had a similar story by the equally excommunicated John
Groth, but it wasn't so good. *PM,* that same P.M., had a long,
involved "Letter from the Editor," by the editor, toward the end
of which it came out that the editor was in favor of the decision
Kennedy had made.

After that the excitement seemed to be dying away, but Friday morning Robert McLean, publisher of the Philadelphia
Bulletin and president of the Associated Press, issued a state-

ment censuring Kennedy. Friday afternoon brought an editorial in *Editor & Publisher*, the trade journal of the newspaper business, a publication that usually reflects high-echelon newspaper sentiment. *Editor & Publisher* made a magnificent grab for the best of both worlds simultaneously, just as if it were a newspaper. It said, "We agree with Kennedy that no military security was involved and that it was political censorship. . . . The Paris correspondents also declare they have no degree of confidence in the Public Relations Division of SHAEF, and we don't blame them. [Actually, when a motion of no confidence was proposed at a correspondents' meeting in Paris after the surrender incident, the correspondents tabled it, preferring to gang up on their colleague Kennedy.] We hope this will serve as a lesson to the military and political leaders of the Allied nations that a story of that magnitude cannot be kept secret." But the editorial also said, "Kennedy apparently violated one of the cardinal principles of good journalism—that of respecting a confidence. No amount of explanation . . . is justification." Of course the Allied leaders would not have learned the lesson if Kennedy had not repudiated the confidence. Neither McLean nor *Editor & Publisher* challenged SHAEF's right to impose such a condition. The top side of the newspaper business obviously believes that freedom of the press goes no farther than the right to complain about corporation taxes.

To wind up, and illustrate, my morality tale, the *Times*, on Saturday morning, carried a story that SHAEF was going to retain control over correspondents in Europe even though fighting has ceased and that censors have been empowered to suppress anything they consider "unauthorized, inaccurate, or false reports, misleading statements and rumors, or reports likely to injure the morale of the Allied forces (or nations)." This means that correspondents may send no news, even though it is verified and vital to American understanding of what is happening, unless it is "authorized" by some Army political adviser like Robert Murphy, who in 1942 gave a sample of his stuff by stopping all stories unfavorable to the State Department filed in North Africa. It also means that the censors—or rather, in the last analysis, the censors' Army superiors—will decide what is true and accurate or false and misleading, and what is calculated to injure the morale of Allied forces. For example, a correspondent might say there was a strong republican movement in Italy, but the censor might decide that such knowledge would diminish the Royal Italian Army's enthusiasm for the Royal House the Allies insist on propping up. So he would stop the correspondent from sending the story to America. And so it might go —and will, if the press continues to truckle to the dress extras.[4]

[4]*Conditions in areas under military government are not too good even now, according to reports received by the American War Correspondents' Association committee on censorship in the field from areas like Korea. The Association is preparing a report which may very well appear before this book.*

Sherman Could Have Been Wrong [1]

The brass in the Civil War had its troubles with correspondents too, it is indicated by a letter from Major General William Tecumseh Sherman to Rear Admiral David N. Porter in reference to a correspondent of the New York *Herald* named Thomas W. Knox, who had sent a dispatch criticizing Sherman's arrangements for a dash into the defenses of Vicksburg on January 1, 1863. The attempt had failed, by a very narrow margin, according to the presumably impartial testimony of Porter, the naval commander of the expedition. That campaign on the Mississippi was amphibious warfare, like the landings of World War II. Porter's version, contained in a letter to his own chief, Gideon Welles, Secretary of the Navy, states:

"General Sherman, having attempted to take the enemy by surprise, lost about 700 wounded, 300 killed, and about 400 prisoners. All this was owing to Colonel DeCourcey (who has since resigned) not following General Blair, who had no difficulty in getting into the works of the enemy. Had our troops been able to hold these works for three minutes, Vicksburg would have been ours; but that chance was lost and will not offer again. . . . The rain forced General Sherman to embark, and we did so without the enemy being aware of it until everything was on board. Not a thing of consequence was left behind. . . . I have always thought the late attempt was premature, but sometimes

---

[1] *I am indebted to Barnes F. Lathrop, of the Department of History of the University of Texas, for the tip on l'affaire Knox. The correspondence about it is contained in Vol. XVII of "War of the Rebellion; a compilation of the official records of the Union and Confederate Armies" (70 volumes in 128, Washington, 1880–1901).*

these dashes succeed, and certain it is that, but for the want of nerve in the leader of a brigade, the army would have succeeded."

This is Sherman's letter thanking Porter for support in the controversy:

DEAR SIR: *I thank you most kindly for your kind and considerate letter, Feb. 3, received this day, and am more obliged than you can understand, as it covers many points that I had neglected to guard against. Before Vicksburg, my mind was more intent on the enemy intrenched behind those hills than on the spies and intriguers in my own camp and "at home."*

The spirit of anarchy seems deep at work at the North, more alarming than the batteries that shell at us from the opposite shore. I am going to have the correspondent of the New York Herald tried by a court-martial as a spy, not that I want the fellow shot, but because I want to establish the principle that such people cannot attend our armies, in violation of orders, and defy us, publishing their garbled statements, and defaming officers who are doing their best. You of the Navy can control all who sail under your flag, whilst we are almost compelled to carry along in our midst a class of men who on Government transports usurp the best staterooms and accommodations of the boats, pick up the dropped conversations of officers, and report their unlimited and tainted observations as the history of events they neither see nor comprehend. This should not be, and must not be. We cannot prosper in military operations if we submit to it, and, as someone must begin the attack, I must assume the ungracious task. I shall always account myself fortunate to be near the officers of the old Navy, and would be most happy if I could think it possible the Navy and the Army of our country could ever again enjoy the high tone of honor and honesty that characterized them in the days of our youth.

With sentiments of profound respect for you and the officers of your fleet, I am, truly, yours,

W. T. SHERMAN, Major-General of Volunteers.

Knox, who had been on the same ship with Blair's men, got their stories, after they had re-embarked, of what must have seemed a monumental snafu. He had sent to his paper a dispatch hinting that Sherman was going mad. I can imagine what the talk of the battered brigade must have been like. The operation had not, as a matter of truth, been carefully mounted; it looks from this distance like one of those improvisations that are remembered as brilliant if they come off. The court-martial convicted Knox of disobedience to orders and excluded him from the military department under the command of General U. S. Grant, which included Sherman's Twentieth Corps. But President Lincoln revoked the sentence and said Knox could go back if Grant agreed to receive him. Grant put it up to Sherman, who of course refused. Knox stayed out.

Sherman was angry because Knox hadn't been sent to jail, and also because Lincoln had interceded for him.

"The insolence of these fellows is insupportable," he wrote to Grant. "I know they are encouraged, but I know human nature well enough, and that they will be the first to turn against their patrons. Mr. Lincoln, of course, fears to incur the enmity of the *Herald*, but he must rule the *Herald* or the *Herald* will rule him; he can take his choice. . . .

"If the press be allowed to run riot, and write up and write down at their pleasure, there is an end to a constitutional government in America, and anarchy must result. Even now the real people of our country begin to fear and tremble at it, and look to our armies as the anchor of safety, of order, submission to authority, bound together by a real Government and not by the clamor of a demoralized press and crowd of demagogues."

"If it be so that the people of the United States demand and must have news, true, if possible, but still news," he wrote to General Blair, Knox's protector, "their condition is likened to that of the drunkard, whose natural tastes have become so vitiated that nought but brandy will satisfy them, and they must pay the penalty. I for one am willing no longer to bear tamely their misrepresentations and infamies, and shall treat Knox and all others of his type as spies and defamers."

Knox had a bit of hard luck in running up against a general as invulnerable as Sherman, a great talent who had the unlimited support of Grant. But the military history of the Civil War, on the Northern side especially, is a long record of bungling expensive in blood by almost every commander, and one can imagine how much all the bunglers wanted to shut up the correspondents. They might have kicked the ball around the infield for another five years without making a put-out if it had not been for the goading of these critics calling attention to their errors. The Grant-Sherman combination itself owed its eventual big chance to the pricking of successive rival reputations by the pressmen. With a good public-relations officer, 1942 style, McClellan might have stayed in command indefinitely.

Sherman's letter to Grant reveals the immemorial confusion of the authoritarian mind, which sees a threat to liberty in the right of criticism, and hope only in "submission to authority."

I am glad that he told the Republicans in 1876, when they wanted to run him for President, that he wouldn't run if nominated and wouldn't serve if elected. The country escaped a dangerous administration.

No Papers[1]

Like most people who once worked on newspapers, I have always been a chain reader of them, when they are to be had. Since I got back to this country from Europe last winter, I have spent from one to three hours a day looking at them. So it surprised me at first, during the newspaper-delivery strike, that, from the minute they began not to be available, I began not to miss them. A friend of mine, another former newspaperman, reported the same subjective phenomenon. Other friends, with and without similar pasts, said that they, too, were getting along beautifully. I heard ten times as much talk about the shortage of cigarettes as about the total absence of newspapers. The only complaints I heard came from commuters who lived at such short distances from the city that it was impractical for them to smoke opium during the trip. Some of these people said that now that they had no newspapers they were compelled to look at the scenery, which revolted them. But it's their own fault that they live out of town. I've tried to tell them that scenery is like that. When, finally, the publishers and the drivers settled the strike, they did well for themselves, because if the strike had continued much longer they might have lost the customers both depend upon. Reading newspapers had turned out to be one of the habits, like gum chewing, that have no really deep hold; people found they could take them or leave them alone. I did not understand why until I began reading the New York newspapers again after the strike.

The face of an acquaintance you have not seen for a while,

[1]Because of a strike of drivers of newspaper-delivery trucks, most New York readers went without papers for the first seventeen days of July, 1945.

even a short while, sometimes surprises you when you meet him again. You had not remembered him quite as he is. It was that way with the papers. I simply hadn't remembered how bad some of them were, and how indifferent the others, and how overstuffed all of them were with blobs of type that you half read only because they happened to be in front of your eyes. The *Herald Tribune*'s front-page story on Wednesday, July 18, about the end of the strike, contained one of the most inexact affirmations that newspaper has carried in any year in which there has been no national election. It's a good illustration of what I mean. "However thankful the drivers and publishers were for the end of the strike," the anonymous author wrote, "the greatest relief was felt by the public." The publishers and drivers were really sweating about the strike; the drivers' livelihoods and the publishers' profits depended on the result. Is it really possible that the *Tribune* writer meant that the public worried more about the strike than the drivers and publishers did? This is a rhetorical question; he meant nothing of the sort. Or else he must have wondered why his paper's half million erstwhile readers (Sundays; weekdays 326,000) weren't picketing, buying radio time to present their case, or burning Louis Waldman in effigy. The statement is a simple example of wishful non-thinking. In a similar way, a sports writer may lead off a story with a statement like "The most popular man in Brooklyn today is Somekus Punkus, of the Dodgers," and go on to explain that Punkus hit a home run that won the ball game. The writer is conscious that actually Punkus is unknown to the million or so Brooklynites who don't give a hoot about the Dodgers and that P. isn't even popular with the few ball-players who know him well. But the writer suffers from the vocational craving to have something to say. The political writer says from force of habit that he detects "a rising tide of Republican sentiment" or talks about a "fast-increasing indignation which may block" an administration bill. He discounts the truth of what he writes before he even sets it down, but he feels that somehow he is performing a function. The reader learns to make the same discount, and after a while, though he continues to buy the paper and look at it, he ceases to pay any attention to what it says. In normal times it requires more of an effort of will to enter the subway in the evening without buying a paper than it does to buy one. When the papers vanished from the stands during the strike, the effect was the same as it would be if restaurants stopped serving the chalky-white cheese-paste they now put on your butter plate. In a word, unnotice-able.

July 18 was, it is true, a bad news day, or at least a day of the kind of news that is unsatisfactory to write about. The *Times* and *Tribune* both carried multicolumn "accounts" of the Big Three conference at Potsdam, which were in fact accounts of how their correspondents hadn't been allowed to find out what was happening there. The *Times*, apparently to make the story more complete, also carried an account of how the Associated Press correspondent had not been allowed to find out what was happening, too. The *Times* and *Tribune* both gave a heavy play to the fact that President Truman and Marshal Stalin had had liver and onions for lunch. The other big story in both papers was about the night shelling of the coast of Japan by the combined British and American fleets. Spot-news accounts of naval actions, however, are simply jumbles of clichés from which any real information is automatically excluded, since correspondents on ships can't see what is being shot at or whether it's being hit, and wouldn't be allowed to tell about it if they could. It is also forbidden to report losses, if any. The result is like an account of an invisible baseball game without the score. There were some interesting minor items of foreign news (all of which could have been got onto less than one page), and the rest of the *Times'* forty-two pages and the *Tribune's* forty-six pages were made up of Arthur Krock and Mark Sullivan and Bonwit Teller. The *Times*, in addition, carried a poem in a headline on page two: "Enemy Firmer in Burma."

There are, of course, days when there is important news and you would give anything to have a paper. There didn't happen to be such a day during the seventeen-day strike,[2] but once I thought there was going to be one. The British general election

---

[2]*Sometimes news disappears for years at a time, as in the period discussed on pp. 64–70, when there was nothing to write about but the Medicine Ball Cabinet and dance marathons. News is like the tilefish, which appears in great schools off the Atlantic Coast some years and then vanishes no one*

was held on July 5, and I innocently thought the news of the results would be available in the morning papers of July 6. I sent an office boy over to the *Times* to get me a paper, and when he brought it back I learned that the results wouldn't be known for three weeks because the servicemen's mail votes had to be counted. This gave me a lot more time in which not to mind the strike. I used some of it in constructive thought about the solution of the whole newspaper problem.

Abolition, I can say immediately, is not the answer. What I'd like to recommend is to get out large newspapers only on days when there is a lot of news, supplementing them on the intervening days with small bulletins containing such essential matter as race charts, market reports, and weather information. This will seem to some a radical solution. I can already hear the first objection editorialists will raise. They will say that to handle big news adequately you must have a big, competent organization in a state of constant readiness, that you can't simply send out a call for newspapermen after the news starts to break, and that then, having this big, competent organization on hand, there's nothing to do but go ahead and put out a newspaper. I think the strike, which taught us that people do not care to read newspapers with no news in them (I do not take into consideration the hundreds of small boys who formed lines at the *Daily News* and bought a couple of hundred papers apiece, in the hope of reselling them to comic-strip fans), has furnished us with the answer to this particular argument. Mrs. Dorothy Schiff Thackrey, publisher of the New York *Post*, improvised, under the pressure of strike conditions, a technique which it seems to me may save New York journalism. During the strike, the *Post*, like all other New York papers, maintained full employment in its editorial, mechanical, and advertising departments. Members of the editorial staff, for instance, reported at their regular hours, received assignments, covered their stories—presumably warning the subjects of their interviews that they were to be quoted—and wrote the stories to meet deadlines. The

---

knows whither, or for how long. Newspapers might employ these periods in a search for the breeding grounds of news, but they prefer to fill up with stories about Kurdled Kurds and Calvin Coolidges, until the banks close or a Hitler marches, when they are as surprised as their readers.

copy was then edited and set up. Up to this point the procedure paralleled that of other struck newspapers. But—and this is the crucial detail, which suggests that Mrs. Thackrey belongs, like T. S. Eliot, among those whom a contemporary critic has termed "culture heroes," the openers of new vistas—*the Post printed no papers!* To carry her innovation one step farther, it is only necessary that, on days when there is no strike, the drivers report with their trucks and make their routes but just don't deliver anything. In this way newspapers could be maintained intact between outbreaks of news, without impairment of employment; the staffs could be kept up to snuff, perpetually rehearsing between incidents.[3] We do not ask of an army under peacetime conditions that it go out and stage a massacre every day to justify its existence. We do not demand that a fire company rush out and break the windows of a store that is not on fire. And the dissemination of news, when there is some, is a matter of public interest, just as much as fighting a war or a fire. If you doubt me, you have only to consult any of the last three thousand and ten public speeches of Dean Carl Ackerman of the Columbia Graduate School of Journalism. Why not, then, a standing establishment of newspapers?

I can anticipate the objections to this plan of a few diehard laissez-faire economists like Dr. Friedrich Hayek and Dr. Ruth B. Alexander, but I am prepared for them too. Let the members of the public kick in with their two or five cents for their favorite daily paper on days when the paper does not appear. If it is worth a nickel to read the *Sun*, it is certainly worth a nickel not to. In fact, it is a bargain. There may be some interesting changes in circulation figures, because it is worth just as much not to read the *News* as it is not to read any of the five-cent papers. The already vast circulation of the *News* would grow vaster. A man who had to pay five cents not to read the newspaper *PM* would be a sucker to give up the money, in fact, when for only two cents he could avoid reading Captain Patterson's little *Ausgabe*. These are details, however, that the circulation departments could work out among themselves. The funnies could be published outright in large, satisfying books,

[3] *Or the reporters could be sent out to dig on long-range stories, the kind that can't be done in a day (see my remarks on Father Divine, p. 115).*

suitable for throwing at Dr. Hayek. There would be, it may be objected, a certain loss in advertising revenue (the newspaper *PM* has, of course, managed to get along without advertising),[4] but I contend that the great saving in newsprint effected by not printing the papers on days when there is no news would more than compensate. This might make it feasible, in time, to refrain from printing a paper at a cost of only four cents a non-existent copy, or, in the case of the two-cent papers, 1.685, which would be even cheaper than the present costs of not refraining from printing them.[5] The newsprint saved could be shipped to southern Tunisia to be made into newspapers for the Arabs, who have been getting off too damn easy so far anyway.

[4]*No longer. Now it is taking advertising but not getting along.*

[5]*Negative economics are a specialty of mine. Thus, on learning that advertising rates had risen, I wrote in Esquire: "This is a break for the publisher of my last book. He will save more by not advertising at the higher rates than he used to save by not advertising before they rose." He also managed to save most of the books.*

Obits

The authors of newspaper obituaries, or obits, are a frustrated and usually anonymous tribe. The biographical notices of public characters which they prepare in advance of their subjects' departures are filed away in the papers' libraries marked, for example, "Hold until wanted—bring up to date 1947," and can be released only by the deaths of the protagonists. This is naturally a source of anxiety to the obit writer who has embalmed a subject with phrases in which he feels he can take some pride. Sometimes the obituarist conceives a deep grudge against an elder notable who, by stubbornly refusing to expire, delays public recognition of a superior rewrite job. The late John D. Rockefeller, Sr., outwore the patience and contributed to the alcoholism of three newspaper generations. Much of the decline in editorial esteem of the late David Lloyd George, and perhaps also of George Bernard Shaw, may be ascribed to irritation of a like origin. Theodore Dreiser, who died on December 28, in his seventy-fifth year, probably suffered somewhat from this professional reaction. By contrast, General George S. Patton, Jr., who predeceased Dreiser by a week, was sixty years old and at the very peak of his obituary value. Patton had been in the news more prominently since 1942 than ever before in his life, and since there was always a possibility during the war that even a very superior officer might decease abruptly, his obits had been kept up to date by highly rated members of the New York newspaper rewrite batteries. It is probable, also, that during the strike last summer of the newspaper-delivery men high-priority obits in all the offices received a good refurbishing. Dreiser's, to judge from internal evidence, had on

most papers been confided to young reporters who had returned
early from dinner assignments where the guest of honor failed
to show up.[1] There was therefore a piquant discrepancy between the newspaper treatments of the two decedents. Only
PM (a day or two late, as usual) gave Dreiser a more considerable send-off than Patton. Max Lerner, of that paper, wrote
a full-page editorial on the novelist, while Ralph Ingersoll pol-
ished the general off in five paragraphs and a line.

A member of the *Daily News* staff named Kermit Jaediker
set the tone for the Patton pieces when he retrospectively chronicled the general's birth as the most prodigious since that of
Pantagruel. "This laconic young man with the pink complexion,
the sandy hair, the steel-blue eyes, and the stuff of legend woven
into his six feet of bone and muscle, was born November 11,
1885, on his father's ranch in San Gabriel, California," Jaediker
wrote. Born six feet high and with all his hair, Patton never
stopped growing in the minds of rewrite men and their editors,
and after his death one or another of the New York papers
gave him credit for every achievement of Allied arms in the
European Theatre of Operations except the battle of Stalingrad.
This is a convention of the Only Free Press in the World, like
a preacher's eulogy at a funeral. When you write a man's obituary, you become his advocate.

It is probably this tradition which explains why the *Sun* said,
"The troops under him, revivified by his leadership, swept up
Gafsa on the long drive to El Guettar, Mateur, Bizerte, and triumph in North Africa." The "long drive" south from Gafsa to
El Guettar is perhaps nine miles, and that is as far as the troops
got under Patton. Mateur and Bizerte are in the opposite direction, about a hundred and fifty miles to the north. The Americans won their great North African victory there—under the
command of General Omar N. Bradley. The *Times* leaned even
farther from the perpendicular when it related that at El Guettar, Patton won "the first major American victory over Nazi

---

[1] *I learned after this piece appeared that John Rogers of the* Herald
Tribune *had written both the Patton and Dreiser obits for his paper. Lest
that seem to detract from my reputation as a connoisseur, however, he admitted that he had written the Dreiser obit in 1938, while he had written
Patton's in 1945, aided by seven more years of experience.*

arms." Major General Terry Allen commanded the First Division when, without assistance from Corps, it won the wholly unpremeditated battle of El Guettar, repulsing a surprise attack by the German Tenth Armored Division. The First was technically under Patton's command, of course, just as he was under the British General Alexander's and Alexander was under General Eisenhower's. But Allen won the battle.

Mr. Jaediker pursued the motif with the not unpicturesque statement "The legend burgeoned in the African campaign when the rasping, swearing tankman, two pearl-handled six-shooters dangling on his hips, led our forces in the conquest of Tunisia." If Patton rasped for Jaediker, he went "swashbuckling his way across the sands of North Africa" for a writer named George Adams, of the rival *Mirror.* "Swashbuckling," I take it, is a sort of third gait, between a walk and a run. The *Herald Tribune* said he had more flair than any other general since Custer, though what poor Custer had a flair for I wouldn't know—certainly not Indians. There are limits, however, even to the convention of the funeral whoop-it-up-and-holler, and I thought that Donald Mackenzie, another *Daily News* writer, transcended them when he wrote of "the brilliant break-through by his [Patton's] Third U. S. Army at St. Lô and Avranches." The Third Army was not activated until after the break-through near St. Lô, which was managed by four infantry and two armored divisions of the First Army, under the command, for the operation, of General J. Lawton Collins, of the Seventh Corps. St. Lô itself had been taken several days earlier, by the Twenty-ninth Division, also of the First Army. Avranches was not reached until after the break-through, and as a consequence of it.

Future Plutarchs, if they use the files, will have the same difficulty in selecting anecdotes to season their narratives as they will in determining General Patton's share in operations. There were plenty of stories, and the obituarists told them differently. The *Herald Tribune,* for example, said that Patton waded across the Sure River on a submerged footbridge, while the *Daily News* said that he swam across it twice (with the corroborative detail that it was flooded "in the depth of winter"). The *Times,* probably referring to the same river, called it the Sauer and said that he had denied swimming in it.

Then there is the matter of narrow escapes. Several of the papers were in accord that he had had three during the European campaign. One was when a large dud shell hit eight feet from his motor vehicle, which is close. Another occurred when a shell hit his headquarters while he wasn't there, which seems to me a rather commonplace type of escape, like that of the people who don't take trains for Miami that get wrecked. On the third escape, however, there was disagreement. The *Herald Tribune* said it happened when flak hit his private plane. The *Times* said it was when a German fighter dived at the plane and Patton's pilot had to touch down quickly. The *Herald Tribune* didn't mention the fighter. The *Times* didn't mention the flak. Could there have been two separate episodes, or did the flak hit the fighter? Mackenzie, the *Daily News* man, added to the standard three/four escapes one that nobody else recorded. He said he had seen a bridge at Chartres blow up "right in Patton's face," covering him with mortar dust but not causing him to turn a hair. Mackenzie could not have been sure of that if the general was wearing a hat.[2] The Plutarchs will learn from practically all the obits that when Patton was a young lieutenant, posted to a new regiment, he asked his commanding officer if there was stabling for his mounts and, when assured that there was, appeared with a whole string of polo ponies. But whereas the *Herald Tribune* said there were a dozen ponies, the *Sun* said twenty-six. And one of the papers even said that only one of his sidearms was a pearl-handled six-shooter. The other, it stated, was a .45 automatic, which he never completely trusted.

The general's temperamental difficulties were conscientiously minimized. The *Mirror's* Mr. Adams said, "Frequently criticized at home, his impetuousness won nothing but admiration from the embattled English and the liberated French." Adams added that Patton got quick results: "When his Third Army slowed at the approaches to the formidable fortress of Metz for lack of gasoline, he acted without hesitation. Officers were sent to the rear with authority to halt all supply vehicles, dump their loads, and send them back for gas. . . . Patton got his fuel."

[2] *He probably was. When he commanded the Second Army Corps in southern Tunisia he made everybody within two hundred miles of the front wear a helmet all the time. If the MPs caught you without one they would impose a fine.*

The fact is that in real life Patton got nothing, and his army was stalled for want of gas—though it was not his fault—for two months. "The thing that we [Third Army correspondents] loved him most for," Mackenzie said, "was that he never took one cent of his pay. He sent it all back to soldiers' charities. Patton was a millionaire and didn't have to fight for money." Even a Third Army correspondent,[3] it seems to me, should have understood that being a millionaire made it easier for Patton to give his pay away. What interested me was the implication that all soldiers not millionaires did fight for money.

The most important thing that any of the obit authors set down about Patton, I think, was buried in the body of a story by Robert Richards of the United Press which I read in the *Mirror*. "Despite his reckless reputation in battle, he seldom wasted lives," Richards wrote. "He took big chances only when the stakes were worth it." As Ingersoll said the next day, "He saved many lives. . . . He won battles with thousands of men that might have taken other generals tens of thousands to win."

Patton labored under continual anxiety. Cautious, hard-working, and terribly ambitious, he was the kind of competitor who, in the old Greek phrase, always smelled of the oil of the gymnasium rubbing room. At West Point he never missed football practice but could never make the team. At polo he developed slowly, by dint of enormous concentration and heavy expenditure for mounts. His highest handicap, 4, was attained in 1932, when he was forty-seven years old. He built up his professional skills in the same way, by internal sweat, but he had them ready by the time of the war. The clownish, swashbuckling façade was as spontaneous as the lobby display at Radio City Music Hall.

I can think of several officers other than Patton who might have commanded the Third Army, but nobody but Theodore Dreiser could have written "Sister Carrie." Only the *Times* and the *Journal-American*, however, thought Dreiser's death worthy of a place on page one. He made page eight in the *Sun*, eleven in the *World-Telegram*, and twelve in the *Herald Tribune*, which in 1944 devoted a two-column spread on the front page

[3]*The First Army had a much better lot. I was with the First Army.*

to the end of William Allen White. The hands that performed the latest revisions of the Dreiser obituaries evidently belonged to men for whom he was already a figure of the past.

Literary historians will have as many conflicts to resolve if they take the Dreiser obits seriously as the military boys will be up against reading the Patton pieces. The *Times* and the *World-Telegram*, for example, said flatly that Dreiser, when he died, was a member of the Communist Party, but the *Sun* said, "He was never accepted as a member of the party," and the *Herald Tribune* said only, "On his sixty-fourth birthday he told interviewers he was through with Communism."

The *Journal-American* obit writer said of "Sister Carrie," "That novel, which, by today's standards, is comparatively harmless, deals simply with the sorrowful life of a village maiden in a big city." The *Herald Tribune* said, more accurately, that the great protest against "Carrie" in 1900, when the book appeared, was based on the circumstances that the heroine was not a maiden and that the story nevertheless had a reasonably happy ending. The *Journal-American* also said that "Dreiser's struggle against the school of Dean [sic] Howells and Louisa May Alcott, his fight against the prettifying of the basic facts of living, opened the door to an era that gave the world such writers as Sinclair Lewis and William Faulkner." These pairings seemed to me a bit mysterious, but at least the sentiment was right.

The *World-Telegram* held Dreiser down to six paragraphs, including the statement about his party affiliation; the *Post* said pontifically that he was "oversentimental from his earliest days in Terre Haute, Ind.," and the *Sun* was sober and factual (except about the party matter). But the *Herald Tribune's* story, I thought, was the daisy of the lot. Nastily patronizing, it began with the premise that Dreiser did not know how to write. "In 1921 the New York *Tribune* wrote of him," the *Herald Tribune* said in 1945,[4] "he is probably the worst writer who ever wrote a good novel in the history of all literature." Since the measure of writing is its total aesthetic effect, this makes as little sense as a reference to a bad cook who produces excellent food. Some good books are better written than others, some bad books are worse written than others. *Herald Tribune*

[4] *In an obit written in 1938.*

'45 contained no hint of who the *Tribune* '21 critic was, or what he has written since, or whom among his contemporaries he considered "good writers."

Having put old Dreiser in his place, the *Tribune* obit man must have reached for another batch of envelopes, which turned out to be full of clippings about the time, in 1931, the deceased had slapped Sinclair Lewis's face. The *Herald Tribune* treated this significant episode at considerably greater length than the story of how Patton slapped the soldier.[5] Mr. Lewis, the obit noted, had (before the slapping, of course) told reporters that if the 1930 Nobel Prize had not gone to him, it should have gone to Dreiser. The obit writer seemed to feel that Dreiser should have been grateful.

The obit went on to quote "one critic" who said of Mr. Dreiser that "he was himself an American Tragedy," and to recite his participation in "various liberal movements that caught his fancy," as a result of which "he raised his voice again and again" as his "liberalism gained momentum." It also talked a lot about a dispute Dreiser had with Paramount Pictures and three times referred to his novel "Jennie Gerhardt" as "Jennie Gebhardt." There was nothing in it to indicate that Dreisers outrank four-star generals.[6]

[5] Two soldiers, in a hospital in Sicily.

[6] The last time I talked with General Patton was in the late Brigadier General Theodore Roosevelt's sickroom in a hospital in London, in March of 1944. Roosevelt had come up from the Mediterranean to join the Fourth Division as Assistant Division Commander, and had promptly gone down with pneumonia. He was convalescing. Patton had recently arrived from the United States. He was still in bad odor because of the slapping episode, but had been promised the command of the Third Army, when activated, if he behaved himself in the interim. He had Major General Troy Middleton with him. Patton had given Terry Allen and Roosevelt a nasty deal in Sicily, and Roosevelt despised him, but now the big man was trying to make friends with everybody. He was carrying a riding crop with a handle loaded with lead; a deadly weapon in a brawl, he told us. He said that once, when starting a hunts race in Virginia, he had become so annoyed at the unfair tactics of one of the riders that he had hit him over the head with the riding crop, knocking him cold.

I had an impulse to say, "Look out, Teddy, you're in a hospital; he'll probably hit you." But I decided that Patton might not see the joke.

The last time I saw Patton was on July 14 at Ste.-Mère-Eglise, in Normandy. It was at Roosevelt's funeral.

Mayor into Columnist

Four pages of increasingly cryptic notes are all that remain to me of a dismal project conceived last summer for an article on New York's newspaper columnists. I suppose I knew exactly what the notes were meant to suggest when I wrote them, but a stream of association has no fixed banks and what I set down then no longer suggests very much. "HI Phillips sun oldfashioned funnyman" and "George Fielding Eliot ht strategist now reconverting to political thought" remain fairly comprehensible entries ("ht" means "*Herald Tribune*"), and "Walter Lippmann ht nowtherefore and whereas and ahem" and "Nick Kenny mirror radio cum sentiment and puffery" still seem to mean something. But "meryle Rukeyser ja tells all, hoohoo" and "Phil Wylie post onceaweek thinks boldly mygod" are less clear. I do have a hazy recollection that I used "hoohoo" as a shorthand term for the lamentatory manner ("ja" is "*Journal-American*") and "mygod" as a marker buoy for prose imbued with cosmicality. This last supposition would help explain "Samuel Grafton post thinks and thinks and thinks and quivers mygod," but is weakened by the entry "Orson Welles post thinkpolit" ("thinkpolit" stands for political thinking). If "mygod" meant to me last summer what I now think it did, why didn't I put a "mygod" after Welles too? And I cannot understand why no "hoohoo" is appended to "mark sullivan ht see David lawrence." As for entries like "Arthur Krock times state of nation funnier than Zero Mostel" and the names of several ladies followed by the single word "glue," I can no longer remember what I was going to say, any more than I can remember what I had in mind when I put down "Ida Simonton Black pm dirty children."

I dropped the enterprise after classifying seventy-two columnists,[1] and I bring it up now only to explain my interest in the
journalistic début of Fiorello H. LaGuardia, who to date does
not seem to be either hoohoo or mygod or, in fact, to belong
under any of my other headings, such as "thinkpolit," "funny-
polit" (George Dixon, of the *Mirror*), "Broadway," or "gastric"
(Dana, of the *World-Telegram*). At this writing, LaGuardia
has produced six columns for *PM*, at the rate of one every
Saturday, and an equal number for Sachs Quality Stores. Sachs
is the installment furniture house that publishes LaGuardia
columns on Thursdays, as part of its advertisements, in several
newspapers in town but not in William Randolph Hearst's
Mirror and *Journal-American*, which have refused the ads. It
is in the mayor's contracts that he can write anything he pleases,
but his Sachs copy has so far been as moderate as the conservative
fan-back chair for $79 that was featured along with his first
column for the furniture firm, to "test his pull," as a gentleman
at Sachs told me. (The Sachs man added that the response was
gratifying.) This first column began, "No Democracy can survive without a free press. As time rolls on, there is more and
more democracy in democratic countries, and more countries
adopting the democratic form of government. Freedom of the
press becomes a mockery unless it is a truthful press." This
seemed to make the Hearst people mad.

Sachs No. 2 was an appeal for clothing for the United Nations

[1]The high total may be explained by the circumstance that there is no
Newspaper Guild minimum wage for columnists. Many of them work for
bubkis (beans), as the boys say, either because they want the publicity for
use in another profession (the stage or radio) or in the hope of catching on
and getting a profitable syndication. The Evening Post in particular reminds
me of a supermarket in which the reader wheels his little wagon among
counters piled high with packaged goods on the sales theory that while
loading up with his staple Wilsons and Graftons he may be tempted to
try a new brand.

Mr. Brown of the Providence Journal Company, which has no local competition, long ago quit buying syndicated columns and began putting the
money saved into improving the Bulletin and Journal's own coverage (they
sent their own man to the Moscow Conference, for example). It is a hopeful precedent, and would, I am sure, pay off in a competitive field if the
paper that cold-shouldered the syndicate salesmen in favor of its own staff
properly publicized its policy.

Clothing Collection, running as an entry with a set of slip covers for $49.95. No. 3 was a protest against cutting the appropriation for the O.P.A., and it ran with a collection of dummy fireplaces (no fire in *them*, either). No. 4 was an appeal not to sell WNYC, the municipal radio station, which Mayor O'Dwyer had already declined to sell. This ran in a reupholstery ad. The next Sachs column was an argument for approaching the housing problem "realistically and intelligently." "Taking first the labor situation," the new columnist said, "I believe it could be easily straightened out. . . . All costly labor disputes should be adjusted without any further delay." He added a plug for the Wagner-Taft-Ellender Bill, which would provide money at two per cent for home construction. The column was sound but not exciting. Only Mr. Sachs can tell whether it sold many modern tables with lucite legs. No. 6 affirmed that even temporary housing ought to be safe, comfortable, and cheerful.

It is in his *PM* pieces that the mayor emeritus is in there swinging. He started off as if he were going to run a Wayward Press department of his own, with two blasts at the *News* and one at the *World-Telegram*. So far, nobody has swung back at him. This probably puzzles LaGuardia, and it also raises an interesting point about the usages of the American press, which we are frequently reminded is the greatest press in the world. When LaGuardia used to remonstrate with some newspaper— as, for example, when he chucked a *PM* reporter out of City Hall and called Ralph Ingersoll, *PM*'s editor, names—every newspaper quoted him and the publication concerned usually replied with an editorial. But now that he is a newspaper writer himself, nothing he says gets any editorial reaction. This may be because of the sincere belief of most publishers that nothing is so insignificant as a man who merely writes, or it may simply reflect the reluctance of businessmen to call attention to a competitor's wares. More probably it is a consequence of the doctrine of journalistic immunity which has accompanied the transition of newspapering from a scrabbling calling to a pompous industry.[2] Newspapers and newspapermen, according to this theory,

[2] *For a masterly exposition and illustration of this point of view, see John Bainbridge's three-part profile of Reuben Maury, editorialist for the New York Daily News and Collier's magazine, in the New Yorkers of May 24*

are advocates without moral or physical accountability for their words, like lawyers in one of Rabelais' courts; there is no reason for them to fight with one another.[3] The *Herald Tribune* may whack away at isolationists and the *News* at interventionists, the *Sun* at labor and the *Post* at the N.A.M., but the *Tribune* must never bang the *News* and the *Sun* must not take notice of the *Post*.

The same code applies to individuals. Heywood Broun once wrote a piece on Westbrook Pegler—I think it was the one in which he said Pegler's trouble was that he had been bitten by an income tax. Pegler's riposte, while hard on Broun, included a plaintive note. "I let him peddle his peanuts," he wrote, as I remember it. "Why didn't he let me peddle my peanuts?" He seemed to consider Broun's direct rebuke unethical. The development of this convention among newspapermen can be traced, I think, to the extreme insecurity of employment on papers before the rise of the American Newspaper Guild. When a man faced the possibility that he might at any time have to ask for a job at the shop across the street, he couldn't afford to be choosy about the shop-across-the-street's editorial attitude. And by the time he had worked for five or six newspapers, as most old-timers had, he could not possibly be expected to believe in the policies of all of them. So squeamishness came to be considered an unpleasant affectation and cynicism was a popular one. A newspaperman left his own ideas, if any, outside the city room with his overcoat when he came to work and resumed them only when he went home, and it was not considered friendly for one newspaperman to remind another newspaperman of what he had

---

and 31 and June 7, 1947. Maury wrote *isolationist* editorials for the *News* and *interventionist* editorials for Collier's concurrently, with the knowledge of both employers. "If anybody wants to know what I think," he said, "let them get enough cabbage on the line for a syndicated column and I'll tell them."

[3]The Hutchins-headed Commission on the Freedom of the Press, in "A Free and Responsible Press," highly recommends mutual criticism among newspapers, but the recommendation is as little likely to be heeded as one for public mutual criticism by allied governments in wartime. There may be personal animosities among publishers, but they are far outweighed by their common interests.

written during working hours. Newspapermen are gregarious and convivial, and the convention made life smoother than it had been in the earlier age, when opposing editorialists horsewhipped one another.[4]

Even LaGuardia made an obeisance to the current convention early in his first *PM* piece. "I find that newspapers very often become rigid in a one-sided viewpoint entertained by their owners," he wrote. "A case in point is the New York *Daily News*. It could be of tremendous influence for good. As it now operates, it expresses the mood, the hates, the hobbies of its main owner, Capt. Joe Patterson. . . . Personally, he is a very nice gentleman." A paper that faithfully expressed the personality of a very nice gentleman, one might think, would be a very nice paper, but LaGuardia indicated, as he warmed to his work, that he thought the *News* was a damned outrage. His text was a Christmas editorial in the *News*, the principal purpose of which, according to LaGuardia, was to stir up bad feeling between the United States and Great Britain. He took exception to the *News* editorialist's device of offering two false premises and then solemnly choosing between them. "As to why we fought in World War II with F. D. Roosevelt, some people feel that Hitler's persecutions of German Jews were what got us into it," the *News* man had written. "We do not believe that theory will hold water." "Then," wrote LaGuardia, "the article shamefully proceeds to say that again in World War II we entered to save the British Empire. . . . Had the U.S.A. not gone to war after Pearl Harbor, the *Daily News* perhaps in its Christmas editorial would gleefully have been singing 'Deutschland Über Alles.' " By this time the

---

[4]*James A. MacDonald, a revered friend who writes a column called "Yea, Verily," for the New York Enquirer under the byline of Colonel John R. Stingo, likes to tell how, when he was a copy boy in New Orleans in about 1885, the publisher of his paper met the publisher of the opposition in an alleyway and stuck an umbrella in the opposition's eye.*

"They were both great thieves," the colonel says, "but they had to fight to maintain an illusion of sincerity." I am not in favor of a protocol of violence, but the participants in the mayhem showed at least a consciousness that they were supposed to be mad at each other. More than once I've heard advertising men and reporters say in barrooms, "We're all whores together." Let the advertising men speak for themselves, and any reporter who really hates himself use the first person singular.

mayor emeritus had apparently forgotten how nice Captain Patterson was.

The *News* made no comment, and the following week LaGuardia, with the angry air of a cairn terrier whose challenge has been spurned by a large sow, resumed the attack with a second essay, which *PM* headlined "LaGuardia Catches 'Daily News' Red-handed." He cited a *News* dispatch of January 3 that began, "The long-concealed pre-Pearl Harbor orders by President Roosevelt for our Navy to escort British troopships in the Atlantic and destroy Axis war vessels on sight were spread into the record of the Congressional inquiry today," and pointed out that the order had not been concealed but had been widely publicized when it was issued, in September, 1941. The *News*, he said, was now trying to help build the legend of a Roosevelt conspiracy to get us into war. He reproduced the *News'* own dispatch of September 11, 1941, announcing the issue of the order. This dispatch carried the name of Doris Fleeson, who, finding it impossible to go along with the paper's policy, has since resigned—an almost solitary example of dissidence on the *News* staff, it may be noted. "Capt. Patterson cannot say that someone slipped up and forgot an old news item," the mayor-turned-columnist said, "because that very news item was the subject of an editorial in the same paper the next day." And he reproduced the 1941 editorial in question, which carried the heading "Roosevelt Eliminates Congress."

I would have liked to see the new columnist go on slugging the *News* for a while, but, terrierlike, he found a new object to bark at in his third piece. In this he called the *World-Telegram* for quoting an anonymous member of Mayor O'Dwyer's city U.N.O. committee. The member had said, according to the *World-Telegram*, "If the U.N.O. is going to be tied up with the Roosevelt name and the Roosevelt traditions, it will amount to the kiss of death—that is the prevailing belief among those who sincerely wish for the success of the U.N.O." LaGuardia wanted to know which member had said it; there were only ten members, all public men of some standing. He implied that this was an example of that nasty journalistic trick, the editorial opinion in the guise of an anonymous quote. (If LaGuardia is looking for another example, he might note that Louis Stark, writing about the steel strike in the *Times'* lead story of January 25, was guilty of as pretty an example of it as anyone would wish not to see.) The *Telegram* man had made the mistake of planting his quote in a field so small that he could be called on it. The *Telegram* city desk, however, insists, to anyone who inquires, that one of the ten *did* say it but still wants to remain anonymous. It has said nothing in print about the LaGuardia column, thus following the precedent of Kid McCoy, who once said to a belligerent customer in his saloon, "I wouldn't dignify you with a punch in the nose."

As for the *News*, it has continued in its own astonishing direction, declaring, in an editorial on January 20, "Evidence is he [Roosevelt] labored with all sincerity to get us into the war, hoping for a One World outcome, and hoping himself to be President of the One World, perhaps with Winston Churchill as his Prime Minister."

Having failed to get a rise out of his new professional colleagues, the former mayor turned to politics in his fourth, and so far most successful, effort. No. 4, under the highly LaGuardian headline "Do You Get that Smell? I Do!," treated of the proposed sale of the city-owned power plants to Consolidated Edison, the announcement of which had caused the threat of a transit strike. "It is not the present power plants that the Edison fears," he wrote, showing one of the best sides of the old LaGuardia, an honest appreciation of corporative motivation. "What they fear is that when these plants are renovated and modernized they will form a yardstick for the true cost of generating electric current. In addition, it would give the Edison a complete monopoly and the City would again be at its mercy." He then scolded Michael Quill of the Transport Workers' Union for having threatened a strike and Mayor O'Dwyer for having promised Quill he would not sell the power plants without a referendum. How the mayor could have refused to do what Quill wanted (which LaGuardia thought was the right thing) without selling the plants (which LaGuardia thought would have been a wrong thing) is one of those intellectual impasses the new columnist used to meet when he was mayor himself by screaming and banging his heels against his desk.

No. 5, a dismal flop, was a plea to the U.N.O. to make its

permanent home in New York City.[5] It was published under the date of February 3, the very day the U.N.O. Site Committee announced its choice of Greenwich-Stamford. This happened, probably, because LaGuardia has to get his copy in by Thursday for the *PM* which is issued Saturday but dated Sunday. His *PM* No. 6 article was an endorsement of the O.P.A., like Sachs No. 3, only with embellishments, prompting a suspicion that the new columnist is already rewriting himself like a veteran. It probably happened, though, because he was on some sort of a good-will mission to Brazil and had left a couple of canned columns behind to be inserted while he was away. This is not a major offense. Ernie Pyle used to write three weeks ahead sometimes.

LaGuardia is not much of a writer. He dictates all his copy and is probably under the impression that you can make a sentence emphatic by saying it louder. He will probably never be a success on big, powerful mygod pieces—he hasn't even done one about the Atom Bomb yet. But as a columnist the little fellow is likeable for his bewildered, old-fashioned idea that a man ought to mean what he says. And there are several subjects on which he should know what he is talking about, a suspicion I've never had about most of his column-writing colleagues. I'd like to read LaGuardia columns on theatrical censorship, horse racing, Bertrand Russell, on the decline of the public library, school, and hospital systems under his own administration, and on Bob Moses and the *Führerprinzip*.[6] That's saying a good deal, because I can't think of even one subject on which I'd like to read a column by a hoohoo.

[5]It has turned out, however, that his confidence in the common sense of the United Nations Organization was not misplaced. It has come to New York City, not, perhaps, entirely because of the LaGuardia plea.

[6]He has lashed out at the multiple-officed Moses often and effectively in his PM columns, but has never explained why he appointed and tolerated the Commissioner of Everything while he was mayor. Moses, whom it would be impossible to elect to any office, has represented the propertied interests against the voters under two successive "people's mayors."

Papers within Papers

This year may go down in journalistic history as the year it became a general practice for newspaper publishers to rent out lodgings to other men's ideas. Editorials that run as paid display advertising have on many days and in many papers taken up four times the space allotted to the kind of editorial the publisher pays to have written. Since they make more typographical splash and get better positions in the papers, they probably reach more than four times as many readers. This, I suppose, might be considered a demonstration of how free speech, dammed in one direction, will find another outlet. It is no longer practical, as it was in the days of Cobbett and Garrison, for a man not extremely rich to found a newspaper to advance a thesis, so nowadays people with a point of view just rent space. In the past couple of months I have noted editorial-content advertising with sponsors as varied as the American troops at the Eastern India Air Depot, in Panagarh, India, who want to come home, and the National Association of Manufacturers, which wants to prevent inflation by eliminating price controls. It is a proof of the freedom of the press that publishers who would hesitate to plump, in a half column on the editorial page, for abolishing price controls are quite willing to sell a full page to the N.A.M. any time.

The publishers were also big-minded enough to sell Maxwell Anderson and the producers of Anderson's "Truckline Café," Elia Kazan and Harold Clurman, space in which to blast the publishers' own critics, the critics having previously put the blast on "Truckline Café." The exchange may have set an interesting precedent, both for the theatrical-advertising departments and for the readers. Playwrights in the future may reserve space—double the amount occupied by the newspaper's critic—for the second day after the opening, and there review the review. In fact, I don't know why they have to wait until their plays open; they could tee off on Burton Rascoe,[1] for example, in advance of the first night. This would put the critic in the position of a man who could be called a poor sport if he pans the play. Under the present system the playwright is called a poor sport if he pans the critic. The practice could be extended to other sections of the papers. Tony Galento could buy space in the *Mirror* in which to express his opinion of Dan Parker; female novelists dripping with book-club money could buy whole pages in which to squelch their scorners.

Following up Kazan's and Clurman's negative contribution to the dramatic pages, Guthrie McClintic, the producer of "Antigone," made an innovation that might be described as positive when he presented a number of newspapers with a review of the play written by John Mason Brown, which had appeared in the *Saturday Review of Literature*. This review, accompanied by Brown's picture, ran at McClintic's expense, and it considerably improved the tone of some of the papers in which it appeared. McClintic evidently felt that in the *Saturday Review* it had not reached enough customers.

Now that advertisers are furnishing newspapers with editorials and dramatic criticism, the next step would seem to be the hiring of reporters to cover news events and write copy to be published as paid advertisements of the Institute of Arab American Affairs, the American Steel and Iron Institute, the International Latex Corporation, or any of the other organizations which are already running their own editorials in the newspapers. It might add to the richness of newspaper reading and also to its confusion. Already, when a man says he has read something in the *Times*, it is not always possible to tell whether he means the *Times*-*Times*, the General Electric-*Times*, the American Dairy Association-*Times*, or the National Committee to Aid Families of General Motors Strikers-*Times*. In the field of foreign affairs there are, among others, a Justice for Greece Committee-*Times*

[1]*Former critic of the* World-Telegram.

and a Committee for a Just Peace with Italy-*Times* that have divergent points of view on reparations.[2]

This conversion of the metropolitan press into a great forum for the expression, at regular line rates, of all shades of opinion causes me only two slight misgivings, each based on a cloud of dust on the horizon no larger than a man's hand the size of a ham. First, the rates are rather high (from fifty cents a line in the *Post* to three-fifty in the Sunday *News*). Second, a newspaper can refuse to publish any ad it doesn't want. The first may account for the fact that, of 25,840 lines of advertising dealing with strikes published by the *Times* (the only paper on which my O.S.S. has as yet checked up) during the first six weeks of the year, 17,255 were on industry's side, whereas only 3,185 were pro-labor. Six hundred lines were classified by my operative as "detached" and four thousand eight hundred as "bewildered." The four thousand eight hundred were signed by Mr. David Silberman, a zipper manufacturer, self-described in the text as a "bewildered small businessman."[3]

[2]*Various factions in the dispute over Palestine have bought a large amount of paid space. Segments of opinion within Jewry have been represented in many of these advertisements, written with wide variations in effectiveness and good taste. But the phenomenon most impressive to me has been the number of pro-Arab ads signed by organizations like the Arab Institute. American Arabs appear to possess an unsuspected per capita wealth.*

All the organizations, prodded by George Seldes' aggressive little weekly In Fact, *have denied that they received funds from sources outside the United States. But the oil corporations with chief interests in the Moslem world have offices within the United States.*

[3]*Arthur Hays Sulzberger, publisher of the* Times, *said at a forum held on May 6, 1946:*

"Mr. A. J. Liebling, in the March 30 issue of the New Yorker, had a brief article analyzing the New York Times advertisements. He raises many interesting problems: pro-capital ads exceeding pro-labor ads in recent time. Was this accidental? Did capital submit more? How many were rejected? . . . The answer to the question is yes, that it was accidental, that management did submit more, and that no ads in that category were rejected. From January 1 to April 21 the score stood: labor unions with 19,000 lines and business firms with 33,000 lines."

Mr. Sulzberger missed the point: it is not accidental that management has more money than labor and will always be able to buy more space. In any contest conducted by means of paid advertising, therefore, labor must always be at a disadvantage.

The only controversial advertisements I know of that any local newspapers have refused to publish so far were the product of a copy writer for Sachs Quality Stores named Fiorello H. La-Guardia. The former mayor writes a weekly column called "Under the Hat," which supplies reader appeal to Sachs offerings of coffee tables and upholstery. In it he has twice attacked the *Daily News* for what he calls its "moronic" opposition to the United Nations Organization. The first time he did it, not only the *News* but the *Herald Tribune* refused the advertisement. The *Tribune* has explained to the curious that it could not permit one retail firm (Sachs Quality) to attack another (the *News*) in its columns, even at display rates. This was the first time in memory that any newspaper had admitted that newspapers were businesses. The official line had always been that they were philanthropies privately operated in the public interest by a dedicated caste. The *Times* accepted this anti-*News* ad, but when LaGuardia tried it again three weeks later, the *Times* joined the *Herald Tribune* in rejecting his contribution and published the explanation that it had omitted the ad "on the advice of . . . legal counsel that the article was libelous." The *Post* and the *Bronx Home News* accepted the ad and have not been sued.

The LaGuardia incident raises the question whether newspapers, since they have the power to refuse an editorial in the shape of an advertisement, can escape responsibility for the contents of the editorials they do accept. The newspaper-within-a-newspaper is a field almost uncovered by postal law, which has been designed to deal with advertising that tries to sell merchandise. A dentrifice manufacturer who advertises a cream that will grow teeth can be prosecuted for using the mails to defraud, and so can the publication containing his ad. A racing tipster is not allowed to advertise "confidential information" or "stable connections" when he hasn't any. Most reputable newspapers have codes of their own that go beyond the government minimums. The *Times*, for example, will not publish any medical advertising that contains testimonials, or any "advertisements that make false, unwarranted, or exaggerated claims." It maintains an Acceptability of Advertising Department that appraises the amount of exaggeration in every commercial ad presented.

This winter, however, it published a quarter-page advertisement with the simulated news headline, "7,750,000 OWNERS OF AMERICAN SMALL BUSINESSES HIT BACK AGAINST THE UN-AMERICAN OWNERS OF 'BIG LABOR.'" This ad was sponsored by an organization known as the Conference of American Small Business Organizations, with an address in the Board of Trade Building, Chicago. The implication of the headline was that 7,750,000 small businessmen belong to the Conference, or at least agree with it, which remains to be proved in, I should roughly guess, 7,749,000 cases (if there are that many small businessmen). Also, the headline stated that labor is "owned," which is neither demonstrable nor true. The story in the body of the advertisement began, "Months ago, one of America's top labor leaders said to one of us: 'You haven't seen anything yet. We are going to pull a general strike. First, the automotive industry. Then steel. Then the electrical workers. *We are out to get exactly what we want, and we are prepared to go just as far as we have to to get it.*'" The rest of the screed ran, "Can you doubt that they and the theorists are out to debase all American business—so that they can build out of the ruins a planned economy of their very own?" and is based on the conversation with the labor leader who is not named. He is in a class with the source of the tout's "confidential information." The chance that a "top labor leader" would predict a general strike is infinitesimal. Events since February 7, when the ad was published, make it appear unlikely that a progressive strike was ever contemplated; in fact, the steel and the automotive workers are already back at their jobs.[4] But since the purpose of the advertisement was not to make money but to influence public opinion, the standards of the Acceptability of Advertising Department apparently did not apply.

That sort of text would be acceptable neither as a commercial ad nor, naturally, as ordinary editorial matter in the *Times*. Nevertheless, it is not libelous, because it mentions nobody and you can't libel a class. But it seems reasonable that newspapers

---

[4]This type of ad, published in formidable numbers, over innumerable signatures, some as nebulous as this one and others as forthright as Edward F. Hutton's, helped create the atmosphere that American employers needed to obtain the passage of the Taft-Hartley Act.

will soon have to impose some standards of accuracy and even, perhaps, of style on their paying guests. Restrictions on style might deprive us of some rare joys. Never, in the days when *Times* editorials were written by old gentlemen in velvet jackets, did the paper boast a *prosateur* like H. N. Light, president of the Light Company, of 223 South Main Street, South Bend, Indiana, who contributed 360 lines (by advertising measure) and $504 to the News of the Week in Review section one calm Sunday last month. The Light Company operates an electrical-appliance store. Mr. Light:

If I ran for President of the World, following would be my platform, Nationally and Internationally:

STRIKES MUST BE OUTLAWED

No. 1. Why should man pay his hard-earned money to give a big, fat man a big, fat salary of $75,000.00 a year plus an unlimited expense account, which could easily double his annual salary. Think!!! Don't just listen to some flowery orator. THINK!!! That is why God gave man his brain—to work out his own Salvation.

No. 2. What man helps produce, man must be privileged to share in the profit in proportion to his contribution to make a profit possible.

No. 3. If there be an annual deficit, man must pay his just share in proportion to his inefficiency which caused the deficit.

No. 4. Man needs man's whole-hearted co-operation always.

No. 5. To live, No. 1, 2 and 3 will bring about No. 4 and No. 4 is what every humanitarian honestly desires.

No. 6. Before we were physically born here on this planet, regardless of how long we have been here, time has been so much longer before we came. History proves that, and I think our intelligence tells us after our physical carcass is ebbed out, it is going to be a long, long time after that. So now while we are privileged these few years of physical life here on earth, there are so many more things to this idea called living, or life than the DOLLAR. We are all put here on this earth to help mankind, to make possible a more abundant life for all. Man is privileged today with an opportunity, the like of which he has never before been privileged in the history of time. Let us all take advantage of it *today while we still have this glorious opportunity. Man's extremity is God's opportunity.*

My South Bend correspondent informs me that when Mr. Light gets an idea for an ad, he goes into a corner, thinks it out by himself, writes it down, and then shows it to his wife for comment. Mrs. Light is the talkative member of the family, and Mr. Light is the thinker.

The most notable flower of paid-advertisement editorial writing, to my taste, was a full-page editorial that appeared in the *Times* on February 27, sponsored by the Military Order of the Purple Heart. For the occasion, the Order had apparently switched to the Purple Prose. The advertisement was signed by Russell Birdwell, identified as "one of America's most distinguished public relations counselors." It was a protest against the atomic-bomb test off the Marshall Islands. The title, in bigger type than the *Times* has ever used in a headline, was "WHERE ARE WE GOING?"

The piece began, "The time has come again when America must use its voice, use it in one mighty crescendo—as it was used after Pearl Harbor." Birdwell's rhetoric continued in one mighty crescendo from that point on: "Let us have no sentiment as we consign these victorious veterans of World War I and II to graves that will vomit with revulsion as man dares to talk of Heaven and prepares for Hell. . . . Let us forget, if we can, that scientists cannot yet guarantee to mankind that additional explosions of the diabolical instrument may not start a never-ending chain of atomic disturbances that will wipe out large areas of the globe, perhaps turn it back to its flaming guts. How quaint to believe this good old world of ours will really come to an end. Ignore the Book of Revelations, laugh off the Biblical prophecy, 'I am Alpha and Omega, the beginning and the ending.' The Four Horsemen of the Apocalypse are merely out for a joyride. . . . Save those precious American ships—they may be needed—sooner than you think!"

Mr. Birdwell galloped up to his conclusion, still topping himself in every sentence, although a lesser man would have missed out long before: "Ask President Truman to advise peoples everywhere that there will be no choking, belching clouds of death over the Bikini Atoll in May and July. . . ." And then, pulling out the vox humana, he ended, "But instead there will be a rainbow in the sky."

After the *Times* had collected the $2,640 for the ad and climbed out from under the debris of the Birdwell explosion, it tried to straighten its hair and look as if nothing had happened, but it has never been quite the same spinsterish newspaper since. It seems to have lipstick all over its face.

A couple of weeks after the publication of the foregoing Wayward Press I received a pleasant note from Arthur Hays Sulzberger of the *Times* reminding me that it was easier to criticize than to operate, and asking me to offer suggestions for the improvement of the papers-within-papers situation on the *Times*. I waited until I could formulate a few remedial ideas and then get time to set them down. Early in May I sent him the following letter:

May 8, 1946

Mr. Arthur Hays Sulzberger
Publisher
The New York *Times*
Times Square
New York, N.Y.

DEAR MR. SULZBERGER:

I was flattered to learn you had read my *New Yorker* piece on Papers within Papers. I have been in Washington for the past ten days, trying to get material for a Profile, and hadn't a chance to write anything more on the subject for your consideration. Your note proves that there are subjects on which it is more important to be amusing than sympathetic. By being amusing you get read by the people you want to reach. By being sympathetic you get to be a lovable old city-room character and eventually a teacher in a school of journalism.

I don't want anything done about the merely silly ads, like the one I said got lipstick all over the *Times*'s face. They probably brighten the paper, if you will concede that the *Times* occasionally needs brightening.

But I do think there should be a check against misrepresentation, just as there is in the case of commercial advertising and of news writing.

The advertisement to which I particularly objected recounted that a "top labor leader" had come to the advertiser and outlined the strategy of a general strike which, the t.l.l. threatened, would take place if labor didn't get all its demands immediately. The identity of the advertiser was questionable.

The inherent improbability of a top labor leader tipping such an intention was enough to mark the story as almost surely a fraud. If one of your reporters had brought in such a story, an editor would have asked him who the labor leader was. If the editor were convinced that such an interview had taken place, but that to preserve a news source the man's anonymity had to be protected, he *might* run the story (although in my opinion 98 per cent of the effectiveness of a story is lost when the source cannot be named). But before running it even then he would seek all sorts of corroborative evidence. And he would have, as a starting point, his faith in the credibility of his own man.

There are criteria of intent as well as probability, or rather of intent in its relation to probability, which every decent reporter uses. The ad was signed by "a small businessman's committee," equipped with an advertising fund of large business proportions and quartered in the Board of Trade Building, Chicago, which houses more large than small businesses. It also housed the America First Committee in 1941. There were no individual names attached to the ad; there was no indication of the number of small businessmen represented. Not a reassuring setup for a reporter concerned with authenticity.

In order to forestall the mythical strike, readers of the ad were invited to purchase quantities of pamphlets at 5½ cents each and distribute them among their friends. (I am not sure that this does not constitute a simple swindle; telling a lie to sell something.) As a matter of fact, we now know that labor didn't get all its demands as of last February, and that a number of the strikes from then on have since been settled, without any indication of a general strike developing.

Would the *Times* run an ad beginning: "A prominent Jew came to us and predicted that if the Zionists didn't get everything they wanted the Jews would poison the water supply"?

Or, "A leading figure in American industry told us confidentially that if labor didn't consent to go back to a fourteen-hour-day, manufacturers had agreed to close down all their plants simultaneously and starve the so-and-sos"?

Would it take a toothpaste ad saying "A leading American doctor came to us and said, 'Average life expectancy in the United States will increase by ten years if people use our silly paste'"? We know the answer on the last one, of course. The *Times* wouldn't print it, because it is patently the kind of thing the Federal Trade Commission and the Post Office would raise hell about.

A newspaper is held accountable for the accuracy of commercial advertisements; a good newspaper feels responsibility for the accuracy of its news columns. The *Times* tries to be a good newspaper. Why should this new kind of ad escape all controls?

Now for the practical side of the deal. (I can hear some lovable old city-room character saying, "There is nothing *constructive* about this criticism.")

It is not impossible to apply the above-mentioned criteria of intent and probability to advertisements that are essentially paid editorials. It would involve some expense, but after all, the ads bring in a good deal of money, from a source hitherto unexploited, and it needn't be *all* clear profit. Better a large profit and a clear conscience than a very large profit and an untenable ethical position. That, I believe, has always been the *Times's* *Weltanschauung* anyway.

Advertising men are not trained to evaluate truth outside of the face-cream and garden-shrubbery field (for which they have printed manuals).

Why don't you set up a staff of experienced newsmen to screen these new ads? Let a good hardheaded desk man give them a quick once-over for obvious flapdoodle (like the top-labor-leader thing). Have a good investigator or two to determine the real provenance of each ad. Then insist that the real sponsor of the ad sign it. Example: if your men find that the small businessmen's association consists of three employees of the Quaker Oats Co. released for temporary duty, with funds contributed by Midland Steel and Montgomery Ward (this is all imaginary, of course), or that a Pan-Arabian Institute consists of one (1) Arab tablecloth peddler and $50,000 contributed by the Sinclair Oil Co., I think you would owe such information to potential readers of the ad (if you still were willing to run the ad).

A very great number of these ads, all dogmatically citing "promises" and treaties difficult for the casual reader to check on, deal with international subjects. I should suggest that one good copyreader with experience on the *Times* cable desk, or even a redundant foreign correspondent (of whom you probably have a few now that war has ended), be assigned to edit this stuff for factual basis.

I expect you are being subjected to a good deal of argument for *laissez-faire:* that a newspaper should sell space to anybody, in which to say anything, for any purpose.

When Walcott complained to the referee that Carter was biting him the referee replied, "Bite him back." So labor should buy space to lie about capital, capital to lie about labor, Jews about Arabs, Arabs about Jews, and the newspaper publisher sit in the middle and take the money, like Tom Sawyer taking apple cores to let the other boys paint his fence. That is an NAM conception of freedom of the press, and some of your associates may consider that it is a profitable, ethical one as long as the newspaper does not engage its own responsibility. I can even imagine a new paper in New York to be called the *Daily Pontius P.*, with a basin and ewer at the masthead, and *no* content for which it is responsible—just syndicated columnists and controversial ads. It is a humiliating conception, for the publisher, who becomes merely the proprietor of a *maison de passe*, rents the rooms and doesn't care what happens in them. I have never heard that you are a particularly humble man.

The *laissez-faire* argument, besides being humiliating for the publisher, is of course disingenuous. Walcott and Carter embody only the romantic aspect of *laissez-faire* (the rugged man's doctrine, advanced by customers of Pirie MacDonald).[1] Economically applied, it is " 'Every man for hisself,' said the elephant as he jumped up and down among the chickens." If both parties to a controversy are *allowed* to buy space, the one with the more money will buy more space. The figures on lines of strike-controversy material in my article point this truth: employers

[1] *Walcott and Carter were the same weight.*

had outbought unions about 6 to 1 during the period checked. The NAM has bought miles of space attacking OPA, and people of moderate means who are protected by OPA have bought damnall. I should not be surprised to find that the corporations which chip in for these NAM ads are allowed to count them as business expenses and deduct them on their tax returns. It is just another means of beating people over the head with money. But the application of the system of scrutiny I have suggested would at least prevent advertisers from hitting people below the belt with it.

Faithfully yours,
A. J. LIEBLING

I received a gracious note of thanks on May 16.

"The problem that you raise is indeed a difficult one and we're keeping at it constantly," Mr. Sulzberger wrote.

Then the *Times* (and other papers) proceeded to run a long series of violently anti-labor ads sponsored by the "Tool-owners' Union," an organization which the New York State Labor Department in 1947 forbade to operate in New York State, because it was simply a corporation owned by three people in Lexington, Massachusetts. The Tool-owners' "Union," according to the Department's Bureau of Standards and Appeals, was a "fascistic organization, with all potentiality for undemocratic action and danger to our way of life."

Somehow I don't think Mr. Sulzberger set up that investigating staff.

Mamie and Mr. O'Donnell Carry On

The editorial column of the *Daily News* for Monday, May 27, had both an explicit and an implicit importance for the connoisseur of newspapers, a hobby at least as defensible as railroads or majolica.

"Joseph Medill Patterson, publisher of this newspaper and the man who directed this page from the day the *News* began, June 26, 1919, is no longer with us," a notice midway down the page said, which was the column's explicitly important part. "The story of his death will be found in the news columns." Patterson had died the previous day at Doctors Hospital of a diseased liver.

"Those who are left behind will do their best to keep this page and the paper what we believe he would want them to be," the notice continued and ended. The rest of the editorial column was blank. That was the part of the column that had implicit significance. There was nobody left to tell the highly paid editorial writer what to think.

It will be particularly hard to interpret the wishes of the late publisher because there is no way to be sure that Patterson in 1948, or in 1947, or even late 1946, would favor the same policies he did on the day of his death.[1] He had made an abrupt shift, in the early thirties, from sexy buffoonery to earnest plugging for the New Deal, and another, in 1941, from supporting Roosevelt to opposing him, a switch based primarily on foreign policy.

[1] *The News, however, has proceeded on the theory that he would have remained steadfast to reaction. I must admit that his age makes this seem probable. Many a leftist becomes a tory with advancing years, but few reverse the process after decay has set in.*

Economically, Patterson had moved from the N.R.A.'s position to the N.A.M.'s, and he was still in motion when he died. Since he had carefully discouraged independence of expression among his subordinates, nobody outside the News Building can even suspect what *their* ideas may be. So the paper with the largest circulation in America (over two and a quarter million weekdays and twice that Sundays) was left like a steam roller with full way on whose operator has gone off for a beer and forgotten to come back.

Even the *Times*, printing a properly respectful, although non-committal, editorial on the departure of so prosperous a competitor for advertising, evinced a certain timid curiosity about the *News's* future. It said, "The *Daily News* was so peculiarly Captain Patterson's individual creation from day to day that it will be interesting to watch what changes, if any, his death will bring."

A convention has grown up among newspaper publishers that public discussion of a newspaper's mundane affairs is slightly sacrilegious. So, although what happens to the *News* will affect the lives of New Yorkers more than, for example, the freedom of Rumanian elections, most of the papers said little or nothing about the oversized orphan's future. Only *PM* was sufficiently impolite to speculate in detail about it. On Wednesday, May 29, *PM* listed a number of possibilities: that Mrs. Eleanor (Cissy) Patterson, the dead man's sister, who publishes the Washington *Times-Herald*, or Robert R. McCormick, his first cousin, who publishes the Chicago *Tribune*, might come to New York to take charge of the *News*; that the publisher's widow, his daughter Alicia, and the Washington Mrs. Patterson might administer it jointly; or that a board of *News* executives might be set up to run the property as a sort of crown colony. "One thing, however, seems certain," *PM* announced. "With control both of the parent Chicago Tribune Co. and the News Syndicate Co. [which handles the *News* cartoon strips] in the hands of the Patterson-McCormick clan, the New York *Daily News* will remain a family affair." The majority of the stock in the Chicago Tribune Co. is inalienably vested in the Medill Trust, which is shared by the Washington Mrs. Patterson; the estate of the late

Mrs. Ruth McCormick Simms,[2] the *Tribune* McCormick, generally known as the Colonel; and Joseph M. Patterson's heirs. They enjoy the income from the trust but have no right to sell their shares in it.

The catch is that none of the survivors even remotely resemble the strange and fearsome man who built the *News* from scratch during a period in which the total number of major New York dailies dropped from thirteen to nine. He did it without throwing in any great amount of money, either, although he potentially had the backing of his family's great newspaper fortune. During the same stretch, William Randolph Hearst had to fold his morning newspaper, the *American*, and Roy Howard succeeded in converting three papers (one of them excellent), with a combined circulation of eight hundred thousand, into a single, mediocre survivor with three hundred and eighty thousand. Mr. Hearst and Mr. Howard have sometimes been mentioned as dragon rivals of the late Mr. Patterson, but in the New York field he made them look like the boxed salamanders children buy at the circus.

The *News*, not unnaturally, took a sentimental view of Mr. Patterson's demise. Ed Sullivan, one of the paper's two Broadway columnists, wrote, "Walt Whitman's 'Captain, My Captain' sums up this reporter's feelings at the death of Capt. J. M. Patterson, who engaged me for this post 14 years ago, with a handshake as the only contract." (Mr. Patterson was frequently called Captain from the time of the first World War, in which he commanded a battery in the 149th Field Artillery. He never gave writers contracts, because he believed it made them feel too

[2]*In my original draft I pulled a terrific boner on this one. Unaware that Mrs. Simms was dead, I wrote that she herself shared in the Medill Trust. Geoffrey Hellman, the New Yorker's shark on necro- and genea- logy spotted it reading the story in a "rough copy" of the magazine, but it had already gone out in 100,000 copies of the out-of-town edition. It was all right in the New York copies. I felt particularly vulnerable since I had so often picked on the errors of others. But I didn't get one call on the bull. I did get a whole flock of letters from News readers—the circulations of the News and New Yorker evidently overlap—denouncing me for misinterpreting the plot development of Little Orphan Annie and for saying that an old character in Terry and the Pirates was a new one. (He was new to me.) Characters in the funny pictures are evidently far more important to News readers than members of the McCormick family are.*

important.) Carl Warren, a byliner chosen to write the *News's* obituary, turned out a tuberose of a story, using the device of an obit within an obit, a kind of play-within-a-play idea, as in "Pagliacci" or "Hamlet."

"Joseph Medill Patterson once wrote the obituary of his best friend," Warren began. "It was a three-line memo to Max Annenberg [*News* circulation manager, who died in 1941] which said in part: 'Good-by. I am going to miss you a lot. . . . Hope to be seeing you some day. J. M. Patterson.' Perhaps he would have liked some such unpretentious farewell written to him now. It was typical of the man who, to himself, was an humble person. To others he was a genius who possessed and used the magic gift of human understanding." If Mr. Patterson would have liked a three-line obit, he didn't get it. Warren's piece ran five columns.

Writers on other New York papers, while feeling perhaps as bad as Mr. Warren, exercised a commendable restraint. The *Times* and *Herald Tribune* detailed the 1906–1910 phase of the late publisher's career, when, turning his back on the family wealth and retaining only a modest allowance of ten thousand dollars a year, he went in for Socialism and fiction writing. Warren mentioned the fiction but not the Socialism. The *Times* indicated that the *News's* switch to America First isolationism before Pearl Harbor, although it brought Mr. Patterson into line with his sister and cousin, had not reflected the unanimous sentiment of his countrymen. The *World-Telegram*, the *Sun*, and the *Journal-American* were, if not brusque, perfunctory in their treatment of what the *News* called a "newsprint-and-ink saga." *PM* moralized and oversimplified a bit. A young woman named Eleanor Morehead, the author of its Patterson obit, wrote, "The *News's* phenomenal growth is easily explained: it played up the gaudiness of the post-war period, purveying the forbidden thrills of sex and homicide, squeezing the last drop of scandal from every divorce, murder, kidnaping, and movie case." The *Graphic*, which purveyed and squeezed just as gaudily as the *News*, never got anywhere, and expired, and the *Mirror*, as uninhibited as Mr. Patterson's relict ever was, has never been able to give it a rub.

But Mr. Patterson did not have to depend entirely on the

pages of his own newspaper for a good press. The Washington *Times-Herald* received the Warren story by wire and printed it in full, without changes, inside black borders. The Chicago *Tribune* made a few interesting changes in it and also added to it. One of the *Tribune* additions was: "Patterson was the eldest of a family trio of publishers whose exploits, leadership, and genius for success made history in 20th century journalism. . . . Surviving members of the famous trio are his sister, Eleanor M. Patterson, publisher of the Washington *Times-Herald*, and Col. Robert R. McCormick." McCormick was also in the field artillery during the first World War. The *Tribune* relegated the discreditable fiction-writing interlude to the tail of the story, saying in its chronology of Patterson's life that he "worked on the *Tribune* intermittently during this period [1906–11]." It also buried far down in its text an anecdote that Warren had played pretty near his opening—about Patterson's affection for the common people, which caused him to have chiseled across the front of the *News's* skyscraper the last six words of a quotation attributed to Abraham Lincoln: "God must have loved the common people, because He made so many of them." The *Tribune* inserted a long new anecdote, though, about how Patterson insisted on being boss. "The fact that I decide against you is no proof that I'm right and you're wrong," it quoted Patterson as telling an editor. "It's purely because of an accident of birth that I happen to be in a position where I get my way. But, I do get my way and don't ever forget that." And, added the *Tribune*, he banged his fist on the desk to help the man understand.

The *Tribune* naturally omitted a bit that Warren had slipped into Captain Patterson's military saga, as distinguished from his newsprint-and-ink saga. "After the [first] War," Warren wrote in the *News*, "Gen. Douglas MacArthur, his former division commander, referred to Patterson as 'the most brilliant, natural-born soldier that ever served under me.'" Everybody on the *Tribune* knows that Colonel McCormick is the most brilliant, natural-born soldier that ever served under anyone. To appease Patterson's sprite for the omission, the *Tribune* ran a subhead, "WAR HEROES PLAN FUTURE," over a paragraph describing a business conference the cousins had held in France in 1918. The *Tribune* also devoted nearly a column to anecdotes about Pat-

terson's part in originating cartoon strips—such as "The
Gumps," "Gasoline Alley," "Orphan Annie," "Smilin' Jack,"
"Dick Tracy," and "Smitty"—that the Tribune-News Syndicate
peddles. These strips, besides being immensely profitable merchandise, are formidable assets of the *Tribune* and *News* in their
respective competitive fields.

On the editorial page, the same day, the *Tribune* mused, "You
can't wholly explain genius. A very few men—and Capt. Patterson was one of them—have it and the great majority don't.
Somebody, some day, may find out why this is so. The best we
can do now is to say that he was born of the right parents, in the
right place [Chicago], and at the right time. He inherited the
blood of the founder of this newspaper, the grandfather for
whom he was named [who was Mr. McCormick's grandfather,
too], and he inherited also an interest in the ownership of the
Tribune. . . . These circumstances, surely, are not the whole
explanation of the man and his career, but they are a most important part of it."

The *Tribune* editorial acknowledged what the *News* had not
dared to mention—the defunct genius's early sins—and gave him
a cousinly absolution for them. "In early manhood he was a
Socialist," it stated, "because, as he once said, he couldn't find
answers to the arguments of his Socialist friends. When he did
find the answers he quit the movement. He had joined because
he saw Socialism as the hope of the common man. Years later, in
much the same spirit, he supported Mr. Roosevelt thru two
terms. He broke with him dramatically over foreign policy. Capt.
Patterson, who knew war and history better than Mr. Roosevelt
did, couldn't believe that the common man's lot in America was
going to be improved on European battlefields."

There is a tone in the *Tribune* treatment of the obit that
presages ill for the *News* if Chicago takes over its editorial operation. Patterson would never have told the common man, from
whom the *News* makes something like five million dollars a year,
that an "accident of birth" had happened to bestow on him,
Patterson, the right to bang his fist and have his way. Under his
direction, *News* editorials were sweetly reasonable even when
they didn't make sense, and superficially simple even when their
motivation was complex. His Harun-al-Rashid sojourns in Bow-

ery flophouses and two-bit movie theatres were not eccentrici-
ties; he studied people as closely as the Plains Indians studied
the buffalo herds—and for much the same reason. The *Tribune*
editorialist, trying to account for the *News's* success, probably
hit nearer the truth than Miss Morehead of *PM*, although the
truth he hit near is enough to drive you crazy. "Patterson had no
formula," he wrote. "What he had was something infinitely
more precious, and that was a sense of what the masses of the
people, rich and poor, smart and dumb, were interested in and
how to tell it to them. The *Tribune-News* comic strips display
this understanding . . ."

As I write this piece, the stricken tabloid seems to have recovered its aplomb, if not its sense of direction. The paper looks
pretty normal, anyway. In the number in front of me, Mr. Sullivan reports that New York restaurant waiters are using their war
earnings to fly to Europe to see parents and relatives. He does
not say how they get visas. Doris Blake, the lovelorn-column editor, heads her piece, "WHEN HE WALKS OUT, GIRLS, GET ANOTHER,
DON'T PINE." Elinor Ames, the "Correct Thing" editor, says,
"Try to keep conversation general. It's tactless to ignore completely the man present while you chat about styles, shopping,
and such feminine subjects." This is accompanied by a photograph of a bored young man being ignored by two young women
looking at each other with their mouths open. Jimmy Jemail, the
Inquiring Fotographer (why not "Fotografer," or "Photogra-
fer"?), has asked six people whether the state should award
$140,000 to Bertram M. Campbell, who was unjustly imprisoned
for four years (four said he should get it). The headlines run
about as usual: "HIS REFLAMING YOUTH BURNS HER, SAYS WIFE"
(middle-aged husband acting up); "TOWN'S AILING GOLDEN GIRL,
4, DIES IN SLEEP;" "2 HELD IN RAPE MURDER, PAL SAYS CONVICT DID
IT;" "BLUM FLIES HOME WITH U.S. CREDIT;" "WHO KILLED BUMMY?
HEARING SLATED;" "MP SOCKS TWO RED OFFICIALS." Bill the
Bumblebee, the nom de plume of a correspondent of the "Voice
of the People" department, says, "It's about time the proper-
tarians and libertarians woke up and put these shirkers in their
proper place. You don't find any strikes in Russia, the worker's
paradise. Uncle Joe won't stand for any of that nonsense. . . ."
C. D. Batchelor, the editorial-page cartoonist, has done a con-

ventionalized but sexy figure of Columbia kneeling at a soldier's grave, which is decorated with a cross marked "Unknown." It is Memorial Day. Columbia is saying, "Your best memorial and most durable is a country made free from enemies without and within." The same figure, with a skull for a face, used to be labeled "World War II" by the cartoonist. There is a Memorial Day editorial, which says, "The only ending we can think of for this editorial is: God save us all from any more 'idealistic' Presidents." Only John O'Donnell, the Washington columnist, seems a little off his feed. He writes about Roosevelt in a vein that is almost nostalgic: "Since the by-gone days of Roosevelt press agentry, the old magic of bemusing the people of the Republic has lost its touch." A practiced *News* reader can tell what he means. O'Donnell then goes on to explain how useful Roosevelt's sense of timing would be to Mr. Truman.

As for the cartoon strips, a character named Rex, in "Smilin' Jack," is drifting downstream toward the falls while a girl named Cindy is trying to rescue him. Baron De Plexus, a rather new character in "Terry," is plotting against the Dragon Lady. A little girl named Honey, who has befriended Orphan Annie, is about to be dispossessed from her homestead. Nilon, the latest in the long series of murderous females apprehended by Dick Tracy, shrieks, "It's no use. *I'll tell everything.*" Andy Gump is being hoodwinked by a French countess. Skeezix, in "Gasoline Alley," is attempting to get a garage job for a legless war veteran. A short man in "Harold Teen" is trying to impress a tall girl whom he calls Dream Dust from Dixie. A horrible talking infant in "Smitty" is lisping about giving his dog to a blind boy. And Mamie is making Uncle Willie stand with his face to the wall, so he won't see Moon Mullins' new girl friend, Dodo Van Dazzle.

And the Sun Stood Still

I am always curious about the state of our nation, so when I learned from an advertisement in a morning newspaper some weeks ago that Mr. Ward Morehouse, dramatic critic of the *Sun* (an evening newspaper), was going to make a cross-country motor trip and describe it in a series of articles to be called, simply but inclusively, "Report on America," I determined to follow his peregrinations with fidelity. My plan, I foresaw, would entail giving some attention, even if involuntary, to other ingredients of the *Sun*, and I looked forward to this with sentimental disquiet. All my recollections of the *Sun* are associated with my maternal grandfather, whose favorite evening paper it was. I have seldom had occasion to look at it since his death, twenty years ago. I feared, in renewing the acquaintance, the sort of shock experienced by the city man who returns to the site of his boyhood toboggan slide and finds it occupied by part of a Robert Moses *Autobahn*.

As soon as I bought a copy of the *Sun* containing the first installment of Mr. Morehouse's Report, I could see that I need have had no apprehension. Nothing essential had changed since 1926. It seemed as perfectly preserved as the corpse of Lenin, a first impression I subsequently confirmed by examining a couple of July, 1926, examples in the Newspaper Division of the Public Library. Morehouse, who has been on the staff of the *Sun* since 1926 and is well preserved himself, contributed to my reversed-time-machine illusion by beginning his Report with a dispatch date-lined June 3—no year specified—from Baltimore, entirely devoted to an interview with H. L. Mencken. Mencken, who is sixty-five, complained that soft-shell crabs, for which his mother had paid twenty-five cents a dozen, were retailing for twenty-five cents apiece. This he cited as a sign of the decay of the times, adding, as another, that he never saw any beautiful women any more, an observation that may have had a subjective basis. Mencken's income as a writer—seven dollars a week in 1899— has, Morehouse failed to note, risen rather more than twelve times. The philosopher's value has therefore been inflated, rather than diminished (as he seems, without statistical basis, to believe), in terms of soft-shell crabs. The *Sun* is a Republican paper, and this summer, as in 1926, the Republicans are thinking about presidential candidates two years in advance. Mencken told Mr. Morehouse that Senator Vandenberg was the best man the Party had but that the nomination would probably go to "some fraud like Bricker or Stassen." (I noticed in the course of my Public Library research that twenty years ago George Van Slyke, who is still one of the *Sun's* political experts, was telling his concerned public that President Coolidge would not run again. The choice for the nomination lay between Longworth, Lowden, Dawes, Hoover, and Watson—news which, viewed in retrospect, renewed my faith in the designers of the Constitution. Had they provided for a plural presidency, 1928–1932 might have been five times as bad.) "People are in a state of imbecility," the Baltimore bonze told Morehouse in valediction. "The country is a wreck. Don't ask me the remedy."

Morehouse, having established suspense by this beginning ("Will he find the remedy?" I asked myself. "Will he save us?"), pressed on to Washington. There, under the date line of June 5, he interviewed, by coincidence, Senator Vandenberg. He described Vandenberg as the "bland and incisive . . . tall, articulate . . . suave, vital, cigar-smoking, Grand Rapids-born Senator, who, in the opinion of many observers here, is the outstanding man in the Republican Party." The most cheerful words America's Reporter could wring from the incisive and articulate statesman were: "President Truman is a dear personal friend of mine. He has my very great sympathy in the tragic responsibilities which he bears." So, Morehouse, leaving behind him what he called the "Potomac city of the incommunicable beauty," pushed on South, the remedy still undiscovered.

Vandenberg, who is sixty-two, is a callow interviewee by Morehouse standards, but the *Sun* man built up his average at Raleigh, North Carolina, by seeking counsel of Josephus Daniels, a very elder statesman of eighty-four. Mr. Daniels said, "I've seen the days when capital said, 'The people be damned,' but I never expected to see labor say the same thing."

Banging along indomitably in his car, "the doughty little coupe, WM 125," which he has implacably personalized throughout his journey, Morehouse Reported two days later, "It's wet, as wet as only north Georgia can be during a cloudburst." (How wet was that? I wasn't sure.) But he kept right on going, apparently hitting his typewriter as the doughty coupe ran itself. "I've slowed down to a crawl," he reported. "Something's in the road ahead—— Yes, a mule cart driven by a colored man." ("Stop typing, Ward!" I caught myself crying. "Grab that wheel! Don't hit that colored man!") Apparently he didn't hit the colored man, for a few days later he was calmly filing from Laurel, Mississippi. "Some day I shall write a book about going across America with two typewriters, three extra tires, a camera, a shotgun, half a case of shells, and a case of neuritis," he said in beginning his Laurel dispatch, and one found oneself suspecting that perhaps he was already doing so. "Mississippi—here's a State with all the languor of the deep, deep South. . . . Soothing on the ear are the sounds of the South—the Sunday morning tolling of church-bells in an Alabama hamlet and the low, faraway whistle of a locomotive in the middle of the night." Up here in New York, we-all Yankees put whistles on the churches and automatic electric guitars on the locomotives.

On June 25, still in quest of the remedy for the nation's ills, Morehouse arrived in Tishomingo, Oklahoma. There he sought the wisdom of former governor Alfalfa Bill Murray, seventy-six. This brought the average years of his major political consultants to seventy-two. "If you want me to tell you about the country right now, I can only tell you it's crazy," Mr. Murray said. "I'm telling you that the groundwork for a panic is already laid; it will reach its zenith in about 1953. The Republicans will have a chance in 1948, a good chance, and they probably will be blamed, but Roosevelt really started it." Turning to foreign affairs, he said, "You can't harmonize a pagan mind with a Christian mind, an Asiatic mind with a Caucasian mind. When a person talks of stopping war, he's going against all the lessons of history." Evidently the Murray interview was discouraging, for Morehouse quickly got away from politics and has since confined his Report to observations of a more superficial nature. Soda clerks and filling-station attendants are civil or uncivil or tolerably civil, he has Reported, and traffic on the road is sometimes heavy and sometimes light, depending. Hotel rooms are hard to find, many veterans are back in civilian life, and the legitimate theatre outside New York is not what it was when it was in a more flourishing condition than it is now. Morehouse arrived on the Pacific Coast early in July, tying the transcontinental record for oxcarts with gentlemen outriders, and not long afterward interviewed Jim Jeffries, seventy-one, on the state of the prize ring. Mr. Jeffries took a dim view of it. He lost his most recent fight to the late Jack Johnson, in 1910.

Mr. Morehouse chronicled an interlude of gaiety under the date line of July 10, from Beverly Hills, Reporting that he had on that day seen Howard Benedict, Howard Reinheimer, Howard Clothes, Natalie Schafer, Hicks Coney, Tom Cobley, Sammy Colt, Colt 45, Grace George, Radie Harris, Tommy Guinan, Lana Turner, Jimmy Stewart, Beulah Bondi, Lucille Hille, Arthur de Liagre II, Vinton Freedley, Bob Taplinger, Alvin de Liagre III, Ray Massey, Marjorie Rambeau, Reginald Denham, Mary Orr, Peter Davey, José Iturbi, Hugh G. Flood, Alexander de Liagre IV, Man Ray, Arch Selwyn, Selig Archwyn, Mary Anderson, Ethel Barrymore, Billy Selwyn, Belwyn, Jessie Royce Landis, Battling Norfolk, Louis Hayward, Joseph Cotten, Monty Woolley, Jimmy Gleason, Humphrey Bogart, Jack Goodman, Angelo Rizzo, H. B. Warner, H. B. Twentieth Century, I. J. Fox, Charles Trowbridge, Armand de Liagre, Alaric de Liagre, Hume Cronyn, Pat O'Brien, Walter Slezak, Lionel Barrymore, Ray Arcel, George Brown, Eddie Bitzell, James A. MacDonald, the Original Dixie Kid, Frank Morgan, Leon Ames, Bob Montgomery, Oscar Karlweis, Isobel Elsom, Ollie Thomas, Delmore Schwartz, Corporal Izzy Schwartz, Cyril Connolly, One-Eyed Connolly, Jr., Jimmy Cagney, Angus de Liagre, William Harrigan, Jackie Kid Berg, Van Heflin, Barbara Stanwyck, Katherine Emery, Burgess Meredith, Peggy Wood, Edmund Gwenn, Will Rogers, Jr., William S. Hart, Jr., and Alfred de Liagre, Jr.

As I write, Mr. Morehouse has arrived in the state of Washington, where he may either jump in the Pacific Ocean (since there is so little hope for us) or decide to come home in time for next season's first nights.

While pursuing Mr. Morehouse, I have been, as I had anticipated, bemused by other of the *Sun's* archaic charms, which, like the taste of Proust's *madeleine* steeped in tea, brought back the sensations of an earlier, happier time. I have discovered, for example, with a curious atavistic excitement, that H. I. Phillips, the *Sun's* artisan of light verse, still conducts the column called "The Sun Dial." Mr. Phillips, in the summer of 1926, wrote like this:

> *Here lies Mary Jane McNeil,*
> *Shot down by Henry Wumps*
> *For asking after ev'ry deal—*
> *"Now lemme see—what's trumps?"*

I am happy to report that he has lost none of his skill, and that he has adapted his themes to the times. One of his recent poems, slyly entitled "Readjustment," goes like this:

> *Hunter College bids farewell*
> *To the U.N.'s cosmic spell.*
> *Now the Bronx from fog is cleared—*
> *Double talk has disappeared.*

And another, entitled "Epitaph for Any Statesman," like this:

> *Here lies "X"*
> *Flat on his musha;*
> *He tried to get*
> *Accord with Russia!*

This one could as well have run in the *Sun* on the July day in 1926 it carried the headlines:

100 M.P.'S MEET
IN ANTI-SOVIET
MOVE IN LONDON
MOSCOW SENDING AIRPLANES
TO AFGHANS

You all remember the destruction of London by the Afghan Air Force, or *Afghawaffe.*

Fontaine Fox's Toonerville Trolley still clangs through the *Sun* comics, as it did two decades ago. What I took at first glance to be a new comic strip called "George Sokolsky" (I was perhaps misled by the illustration) turned out instead to be an anti-labor column written by a man named George Sokolsky, who once broadcast for the National Association of Manufacturers and made speeches for the American Iron and Steel Institute. Dr. Sokolsky (he received an honorary degree from Notre Dame recently) uses much of his space to denounce propagandists for the Political Action Committee. The column points up the one perceptible difference in the *Sun* since Grandpa died. Its political and economic position is the same, but whereas in 1926 the tone was always complacent, it is now occasionally querulous.

The *Sun* still tries to be decent to those it opposes, however. For example, David Lawrence, a *Sun* writer, called upon Truman in a first-page editorial on June 10 to sign the Case Bill, in order that the President might gain the support of more voters at the next election. But when, one day later, the President, ignoring this solicitous advice, vetoed the bill, the *Sun* ran another first-page editorial, under the heading "MR. TRUMAN'S SHOES DON'T FIT." " 'Get the votes' was the Pendergast creed on which Mr. Truman was reared, and 'Get the Votes' is his motto now," the editorial said. The *Sun*, of course, was not being consistent. Also, it made the President look like a pretty altruistic man. The editorial was illustrated with a cartoon showing Mr. Truman wearing shoes far too big for him, which in some papers might have seemed a belated tribute to Mr. Roosevelt. In order to make sure that its readers, evidently an unsubtle lot, got the point, the *Sun* had labeled the shoes "PRESIDENTIAL SHOES," and the editorial ended, "In brief, Mr. Truman's presidential shoes don't fit."

Most of the sports writers are the same ones I used to read when I was a boy, after Grandpa finished with the paper, and in the case of the changes made necessary by the deaths of the incumbents, the new men, like Grantland Rice, who is sixty-five, employ the idiom of their predecessors. The dazed Dodgers still reel in defeat in the *Sun's* baseball stories, and it is a safe bet that, according to the *Sun*, any Southern football team scheduled to play Princeton will come North from a campus with a tradition of swords and roses to twist the Tiger's tail while the shades of Big Bill Edwards and other Nassau greats look on in dismay.

I do not remember having seen before "The Word Game," a form of self-torture which invites the *Sun's* readers to find as many words as possible concealed in one big word and write them down in a given time limit. This time is based, I suspect, on the trajectory between Grand Central Terminal and a median point like Cos Cob or Darien. Specialized departments are the *Sun's* long suit. It has one called "First Aid for the Ailing House," which tells how to make a studio skylight by sticking broken glass ashtrays together with scotch tape, and another called "Let's Make Pictures," about photography. It runs "Culbertson on Contract," "The Garden Guide," "The Choir Loft," "The Quester" (antique collecting), and departments on philately, astronomy, cats, tropical fish, and the diseases of dogs.

The paper still carries, as it did in 1926, a higher percentage of Associated Press stories than any other daily in town. It has few special correspondents. For local coverage, the *Sun* used to depend heavily on the defunct City News Association. I don't know what it does now about things that happen on Manhattan. Its local staff has always been small. Some years ago, when I was working for another evening newspaper, I soon got to know the *Tribune, Times, Post,* and *Hearst* men who covered the same type of assignment, but it was rare that I met a *Sun* reporter. Very early one morning, in 1932 or 1933, I covered a stabbing in the *Sun* city room itself. One of the night Associated Press machine operators had carved up a colleague. The only *Sun* men present at the crime, a couple of old lobster-shift rewrite men, wearing green eyeshades, had not even looked up to see if the victim was dead. They were busy sorting clippings from the morning papers for rewrite. An ancient compositor who met me as I came down the stairs from the city room with my notes asked me if I was Frank Ward O'Malley. He explained that nobody in the *Sun* building had hurried since O'Malley left, in 1919.

In the first weeks of Mr. Morehouse's anabasis, while I was wallowing nostalgically in the *Sun*, I occasionally felt that my pleasure might prove of short duration. Grandpa, had he survived, would now be ninety-six, and other readers of this delightful anachronism, I feared, must be dying off rapidly. Would all the *Sun's* readers soon be officially dead? Its circulation problem, I figured, was something like that of the foreign-language press since the severe limitation of immigration. It never occurred to me that there would be *new* readers. I was reassured on consulting a newspaper directory, however, to find that the *Sun's* circulation had not only held up but had risen—from 257,000 in 1926 to 293,000 now. The gain of 14 per cent during a period in which the city's population has increased 24 per cent is not sensational, but it is heartening (and confusing) nevertheless. I can account for it only by one or more of three suppositions:

a. The tide of the elderly, which for so long flowed from the Eastern seaboard toward the milder climate of California, has turned, and Dr. Townsend is promoting a mass infiltration of New York.

b. The people who like the show at the East Fifty-fourth Street night club called the Gay Nineties (strong father and mother fixations) read the *Sun*.

c. A certain number of Republicans seep into the city every year, probably following returning vacationists who have been kind to them during the summer.

[My first intention had been to title my Sun piece "Joshua, X, 13" and then leave the readers to look it up and find "And the sun stood still." I was deterred from doing this by Shawn, who pointed out very reasonably that not all our readers lived in hotel rooms, where there were Gideon Bibles readily available, so that many might miss the allusion. It provoked a formidable riposte, as you will see from reading the following correspondence.]

For the Defense

A few days ago the editors of the *New Yorker* received a genial letter of correction from Mr. Charles A. Wyer. They turned it over to me to think about, and I have thought about it. Mr. Wyer's letter follows, along with a few querulous footnotes of my own:

DEAR SIRS:

As one of the old fuddy-duddies employed on the New York *Sun,* I would like to offer my belated condolences to A. J. Liebling upon the death of his maternal grandfather twenty years ago.

If I remember correctly, I joined the *Sun* staff only a few weeks before Grandfather's passing and I doubt not but that the youthful enthusiasm which even the copy desk could not wholly erase from my stories of that day hastened his death. I was only twenty-five then and knew not what I was doing.

As Mr. Liebling says in his recent article in your Wayward Press department, the *Sun* has not changed since 1926, and it is indeed regrettable. And neither have the *Times,* the *Herald Tribune,* and the *Journal-American*[1] changed. Nor even the *New Yorker.*[2] What a world!

I would not for anything pick a quarrel with Mr. Liebling concerning his appraisal of Mr. Morehouse and "other of the *Sun's* archaic charms," but I would urge that he do a little research before he attempts to put down on paper things about which he seems to know so little that is true.

[1]There was no *Journal-American in 1926. Just the* American (morning) and the Journal (evening).

[2]*It has, too.*

For example, he worries about the size of the *Sun's* staff and wonders how it gets along now that the City News Association is no more. The City News, by that name, is no more, but it was promptly replaced by a special local Associated Press service which, like City News, protects all the city's newspapers on stories they do not desire to cover themselves. Had Mr. Liebling delved into this subject a little, he would have discovered that for many years the *Sun* did not subscribe to the City News or any other local news service but preferred to use its own coverage exclusively.[3]

As for the size of the *Sun's* staff, the records show that it is the largest of any evening New York newspaper and that it has been for many years.[4] There has never been an important story or an important district that the *Sun* did not cover with its own men, and the writer recalls vividly that in the days when Mr. Liebling was one of his personal competitors it was Mr. Liebling's habit to arrive at the scene of a story late and rely on this reporter and others to supply him with the bulk of his story.[5]

As for the stabbing of an Associated Press machine operator by one of his colleagues in the city room of the *Sun* some fourteen years ago, the stabbing actually involved two Postal Telegraph men[6] and occurred in the wire room, many feet away from the city room. Mr. Liebling said that the only *Sun* men present at the crime were "a couple of old lobster-shift rewrite men, wearing green eyeshades—busy sorting clippings." There has been but one green eyeshade in the *Sun* city room in the last forty years and that was worn by an elderly copyreader long since dead.[7] The *Sun's* lobster-shift men are far from venerable, and, in fact, comprise the youngest men on the staff.

[3]*He has me there. No wonder it ran so few local stories.*

[4]*The management of the Sun declines to give out any figures on the size of its staff.*

[5]*This has the ring of authenticity, but I do not remember Mr. Wyer. I always thought that the reporter who filled me in was the representative of Collyer's Eye or the Pesti Hirlap. Anyway, the names I cribbed from his notes were usually misspelled.*

[6]*Postal Telegraph blood ran just as red as Associated Press men's.*

[7]*How does Mr. Wyer know what happened on the Sun between 1906 and 1926? He has been there only since 1926, according to his own statement. If eyeshades have not become popular there, it is doubtless because they*

Since the afore-mentioned stabbing occurred two hours before the lobster shift assembled at 3 A.M., and since the first edition did not come out until 10:45 A.M., it is little wonder that the *Sun* staff was able to treat this minor knife battle with considerable calmness. The men in charge doubtless reasoned that a paper capable of getting out an extra edition, such as on V-J Day, in twelve minutes, could handle an unimportant stabbing in seven and one-half hours.[8] One might question Mr. Liebling's judgment in rushing around like the late Frank Ward O'Malley on such a story. Was he afraid the *Sun* would not help him on that one, as it had on many others?

Mr. Liebling notes that in the last twenty years the *Sun's* circulation has risen from 257,000 to only 293,000, or 14 per cent. The latest Audit Bureau of Circulation figures available disclose that the current *Sun* circulation is above 306,000, representing a 20-per-cent increase.[9]

Mr. Liebling might also like to know that the *Sun's* staff is not only the largest on any evening New York paper but in all probability the most youthful. It has the largest Washington bureau, the largest sports department, and the largest European staff[10] of any evening New York paper. It prints more news than any

---

are too much of an innovation. (Since writing footnote 7 I have been informed by Mr. Edmund (Bunny) Wilson, who worked on the Sun in the early twenties, that a green eyeshade was de rigueur in the city room in his time. Once he came to work without one and was docked a day's pay.)

[8]*How could they reason on the basis of something that didn't happen until thirteen years afterward?*

[9]*Average daily circulation, A.B.C., for six months of 1926 ending September 30, weekdays, 259,817. Average circulation for six months ending March 31, 1946 (latest available half year), Monday to Friday, 306,819; Saturday, 210,397. Average of Monday to Friday and Saturday figures: 290,748. Percentage of increase, 11.9. When I wrote 14 per cent, I must have been thinking of the rise in the cost of living since last Tuesday.*

[10]*See footnote 4. The World-Telegram also declines to give out information on the subject, but it is a matter of record that it has no correspondents abroad, since it relies for foreign news upon Scripps-Howard agencies, and that it has one Washington man. Probably the Sun beats it in both respects. Both of these papers seem to have lots of sports writers. The Journal-American has four correspondents in Washington, nobody overseas, since it relies on Hearst agencies, and a hell of a lot of sports writers. The Post has seven men in its Washington bureau, and it has ten overseas,*

other evening paper in the entire world and more than any morning paper, with possibly three exceptions.[11]

It prints more local news than any other New York paper and more sports news than any other paper extant. To paraphrase the title of a book I read several years ago:[12] Why, Mr. Liebling, don't you go back where you came from?[12b]

Sincerely yours,

CHARLES A. WYER

Just as sincerely,

—A. J. LIEBLING

My struggle with Mr. Wyer was not yet ended. Months later he wrote informing the editors of the New Yorker that the Silurians, a club of men who had worked on newspapers at least thirty years ago, had voted Morehouse a prize for his series of articles. They would have been all right thirty years ago, when all the men he interviewed, with the exception of Jeffries, were in their prime. Jeffries was passé even then.

---

which I will bet Mr. Wyer a green eyeshade tops the Sun. The only Sun correspondents in Europe, so far as I know, are Gault and Wendy Mac-Gowan and Judy Barden. PM, which says it wants to be considered not an afternoon but an "all-day" paper, has five people in Washington. It also has one overseas, which gives it an edge of one over the Telly and Journal but leaves it two down to the Sun. (I learned later that the Sun did not have the largest Washington bureau.)

[11]It prints more lines, exclusive of advertising, than any other evening newspaper in New York—7,482,355 to the Journal-American's 7,010,288, for the first seven months of this year, according to Media Records—but this figure includes, as I was at some pains to point out in my previous Wayward Press article, notes on rare stamps, antique crockery, and Chappaqua social events, easy recipes for one-egg banana rum cakes, David Lawrence, George Sokolsky, rippling rhymes by H. I. Phillips, long pieces on who was the best running back developed at Lafayette before 1895, interviews with H. L. Mencken, lists of people who speak to Ward Morehouse, editorials on Mr. Truman's shoes, and selections for a couple of race tracks. How much of all this miscellany is news, and to whom, I leave to the judgment of The Quester, who runs the Sun's antiques column and is presumably an authority on crazy quilts.

[12]"Back Where I Came From," by A. J. Liebling, Sheridan House, 1938, out of print.

[12b]I came from Lexington Avenue, but I can't find an apartment there.[12c]

[12c]Or anywhere else.

[With the following piece I began to get down near the bone. The misuse of words should be punished as severely as the misappropriation of funds, and can have far more serious consequences.]

Antepenultimatum

Journalists, and particularly the fellows who write for the press associations, have a habit of using the strongest word they can think of in the lead of a story, even when the word really means something else. Headline writers often base their eye-smackers on the strongest word in the lead. That's the only excuse I can find for the use of the word "ultimatum" by every New York newspaper on Thursday, August 22, to describe the note sent by the United States to the government of Yugoslavia the day before. It was a conspicuously civilized note, telling the Yugoslavs that if they didn't turn loose the surviving occupants of two American planes shot down by them, the United States would complain to the Security Council of the United Nations. This message, to me, marked a great advance in relations between governments—an advance in a class with that of an individual who, instead of threatening to break an irritating neighbor's neck, tells him he will swear out a summons and hale him into court. An ultimatum, I had always understood, is a threat to break the neck, and no country, or man, can submit to one without loss of self-respect. Serbia received an ultimatum from Austria in 1914.

So when I saw the lead on Jay Reid's *Herald Tribune* story, "The United States Government today served an ultimatum on Yugoslavia," and the *News* headline, "ULTIMATUM GIVES TITO 48 HOURS TO FREE FLYERS" (based on an Associated Press story beginning, "In an angry ultimatum . . ."), and the *Mirror's* "YUGOS GET U.S. ULTIMATUM" (built on an International News Service story beginning, "The United States served a forty-eight-hour ultimatum . . ."), I felt that we had left the diving board and would hit the surface of the third World War any second. As soon as I read the text of the note itself, I felt a whole lot better. There must have been millions of people, however, who didn't read the note, newspaper reading being as perfunctory as it is, and these millions must have spent the next day or so in a Pearl Harborish gloom.

Even the *Times* story by Anthony Leviero, who is ordinarily a conscientious chap, had "ultimatum" in the second paragraph. The three-line, eight-column banner across the front page of the *Times* said, "U.S. GIVES BELGRADE 48 HOURS TO FREE FLYERS OR FACE ACTION BEFORE U.N. SECURITY COUNCIL; REJECTS RUSSIAN SHARE IN STRAITS DEFENSE." That seemed to me tying in the note to Yugoslavia rather closely with one to Russia about the Dardanelles, as if the two were facets, and comparable facets, of the same dispute. Whatever I thought of Russia's ancient pretension to Constantinople, I didn't think it was an outrage—whereas I thought the killing of our fliers was—or that, considered separately, it would have rated more than a one-column head on a dull day.

The *Sun*, that afternoon, carried an eight-column head, "U.S. SET FOR SHOWDOWN ON YUGOSLAV ULTIMATUM," which made it look, at first glance, as if Marshal Tito had sent an ultimatum to us. The *World-Telegram*, often one step ahead of the rest of the world in looking for trouble, had a first-page streamer announcing, "TITO REPORTED SET TO DEFY U.S. ULTIMATUM ON AIRMEN." It wasn't ahead of the *Post* this time, however, for that paper proclaimed, "SPOKESMAN SAYS TITO TO SNUB ULTIMATUM." The heads were based on United Press stories, date-lined London and Belgrade, that quoted "an informed Yugoslav spokesman." In both cases he turned out to be ill-informed. *PM* also used the word "ultimatum" in the lead of its story, supplied by the Chicago *Sun* syndicate.

The *Daily Worker* used a United Press story about an ultimatum. (It is strange to think of Roy Howard accepting Moscow gold, but the United Press is a profit-making service.) It also carried a covey of headlines, among them "UNITED STATES SWINGS 'BIG STICK' IN EUROPE" and "U.S. THREATENS YUGOSLAVIA IN NEW NOTE," with leads such as "Secretary of State James F. Byrnes took a hand in the 'crisis' manufactured over the American vio-

lation of Yugoslav sovereignty yesterday." (Next day, Friday, the
Worker performed the remarkable squiggle of filling three pages
with squawks about the "ultimatum" with only one obscure reference to the fact that some Americans had been killed before
the note was dispatched.)

A fairly late edition of the Thursday *Journal-American* managed to change its headline to "TITO RELEASES YANKS, ACTS AFTER
U.S. ULTIMATUM" and to insert a bulletin to that effect, but it
had not had time to change its lead on the story, which remained
"London, Aug. 22 (I.N.S.)—Yugoslav sources in London predicted today Marshal Tito will reject the U.S. forty-eight-hour
ultimatum on Yugoslavian armed action against American aircraft." (The I.N.S. seemed to have discovered the same Yugoslav source as the United Press—perhaps a member of the anti-
Tito ex-government in exile.)

After reading newspapers about the "ultimatum" all day, I
began to wonder whether I *did* know what the word meant. It
was as if I were in one of those dreams in which familiar words
become dissociated from their usual meanings, or as if I were
listening to Whitey Bimstein talk double-talk. So I got down a
ninety-five-cent dictionary which I bought one time in a cigar
store and which gives only one meaning for each word, and that
the commonest one; it is an excellent guide to everyday usage. It
says, "Final conditions offered as the basis of an agreement, prior
to the declaration of hostilities"—which is how I have always
used "ultimatum." Only in part reassured, I carried my research
to Webster's unabridged, which says, "A final proposition or
condition; esp., the final propositions, or terms, offered by either
of the parties in a diplomatic negotiation; the best terms that a
negotiator will offer, the rejection of which usually ends negotiations." It was evident in the note to Yugoslavia, though, that
the United States contemplated further negotiations, via the
United Nations, in the event of a rejection. To make surer than
sure, I went to the thirteen-volume Oxford Dictionary. It de-
fines "ultimatum" as "In diplomacy, the final terms presented by
one power (or group of powers) to another, the rejection of
which may lead to the severing of diplomatic relations, and
eventually to a declaration of war." The rejection of the note to
Tito could have led immediately only to a complaint to an in-

ternational diplomatic tribunal, and while that might have eventually led to a break, and that to war, the note could at worst have been described as no more than a kind of antepen-ultimatum.

The appearance of the word "ultimatum" in all the stories makes it look, I freely grant, as if the papers had some common excuse for its use—perhaps permission from a State Department public-relations official who, asked at a press conference "if it is all right to call this thing an ultimatum," may have answered, "Sure, boys, go ahead." But public-relations men do not origi-nate meanings for words; nor, fortunately, do they compose the diplomatic communications that pass between the United States and other governments.[1]

I fear that I detected, in their taking the gloomiest possible view of the situation, a certain eagerness on the part of most of the newspapers. The *Times*, for example, in attempting to chart for its readers the probable course of events, interviewed the Premiers of Italy and Greece—two countries on the outs with Yugoslavia. It also carried a long dope story by Herbert Mat-thews, who said that "the violent incident with the Yugoslavs is considered in these [diplomatic] circles as merely the beginning of a long series of incidents calculated to maintain the tension." The "circles," the "well-informed spokesmen," and all the other anonymously ominous sources had a clambake. The *Mirror*, on Friday, went as far as to express editorial regret that the Ameri-can note had mentioned the United Nations and implied an even more profound sorrow that the Yugoslavs had complied with its terms.

Marshal Tito, whose unfortunate photographic resemblance to the pre-Nuremberg Göring was impressed that week on news-paper readers as never before, did nothing throughout the inci-dent to win international esteem. His complaint, reported in the papers of August 26, after he had yielded up his prisoners, that "a hundred and ten American aircraft, ninety-one of them war-planes," had flown over Yugoslavia between August 9, when his

[1]*Six months later, when the* New Yorker *applied to send Miss Janet Flan-ner (Gênet) to the Moscow Conference, it was royally snubbed by a Mr. McDermott, public-relations chief for the State Department. I wonder if he could have been the guy who said "go ahead"?*

men shot down the first unarmed transport, and August 19, when they dropped the second, set one musing about the fiery, unbridled temperament, as the Yugoslav apologists called it, of an air force that passed up ninety-one potential opponents to await one safe target.

The complaint also set me, personally, to remembering a fellow I knew who was killed quite a while back, during the war, while riding in an American transport plane over the territory of a country with which we were not at war. I have always considered him, like the five boys in the second American plane shot down over Yugoslavia, the victim of a cowardly and malicious act. The transport, a lumbering C-47, like the jobs shot down by the South Slavs, could not possibly have been mistaken for a bomber or a light, fast photo-reconnaissance plane. The pilot had lost his way while flying across some mountains and thought he was over an American field, so he started to land. When he was a hundred and fifty feet from the ground, the fiery, unbridled heroes who were jealously protecting *their* sovereignty cut loose with a machine gun. One of the bullets went through the head of this man I knew, a radio correspondent—he was a French-Canadian and an obliging sort—whom I last had seen in Algiers, acting as spokesman for a group of correspondents in a long squabble with General Giraud. The shooting took place on January 25, 1943, over Spanish territory in North Africa, and the plane was on its way from Algiers to the Casablanca Conference, carrying a full load of war correspondents. The pilot managed to get away from the field, though his plane was full of holes, and to make French Morocco. I didn't see any American newspapers, since I was in Africa myself then, but I had always assumed that the shooting must have caused great indignation in the United States. The other day I looked into the files of the *Times* to see how the newspapers in 1943 had handled this incident, and this is the full, and the only, story I found (with a one-line head of minimal size):

CANADIAN BROADCASTER KILLED

Mrs. Edouard Baudry has been advised of the death of her husband, thirty-three-year-old Canadian Broadcasting Corporation correspondent, in North Africa. It was learned here today that Mr. Baudry was killed by anti-aircraft fire when the plane in which he was a passenger flew off its course and appeared over Spanish Morocco.

News values seem to depend very largely upon who does the shooting.

The antepenultimatum story was well received, but I decided on a change of pace for my next effort, since I was afraid the hoohoo's union would send me a membership application to fill out as a professional deep thinker, and I didn't want to break Walter Lippmann's rice bowl. So I thought I would write a jesting piece about sports writers. The effect was a smouldering resentment that has impaired the pleasure of all my subsequent visits to the office of Harry Markson, the press agent of the Twentieth Century Sporting Club. All my ex-friends sit around Harry's desk and look at me with pain in their eyes. "Here is Liebling, who knocks your brains out for money," Jim Dawson said, with only sorrow in his voice, the first time I showed up there after the appearance of the piece.

The Scribes of Destiny

Newspaper people speak of a police reporter, a City Hall man, and a Washington correspondent, but always of a sports *writer*. The sports writer is not expected merely to tell what happened. Upon small, coiled springs of fact, he builds up a great padded mattress of words. His readers flop themselves down on this Beautyrest and escape into a dream world where most of the characters are titanic heroes, devouring monsters, or gargantuan buffoons, and the rest are clean, high-type, aristocratic sportsmen who own yachts, racing stables, or baseball clubs and are occasionally depicted as setting up schnapps for the scribes (a sports-page word for sports writers).

The scribe is expected to be entertaining even when there's nothing to be entertaining about, and whereas the City Hall man or the police reporter doesn't have to write anything unless something is happening, the sports writer has to burn the old adverbs across every day. A baseball player may have his name in print for as many as ten or fifteen seasons, but the really enduring names in sport appear at the heads of syndicated columns, and these are trademarks of great value. All the as yet unsyndicated scribes are trying to establish trademarks too. The competition gives rise to a considerable divergence between exactitude and narration. If I knew a man who had read sports pages since his youth without ever attending a sporting event, I should congratulate him and advise him never to attend one, because he would be disillusioned. If, again, I knew a man who had attended sporting events since boyhood without ever having read a sports page, I should counsel him never to read one, because he would be confused. Most of us who occasionally watch sporting

events and afterward read about them gradually are led to believe
that we saw something like what the sports writers tell us happened.

A while back, as an example of what I mean, I saw a fighter
named Rocky Graziano knock out a fellow named Davis, and
Graziano looked to me like just a strong little fellow who threw
too many right hands to have any brains.[1] Recently, however, I
have seen him described by W. C. Heinz, a sports writer for the
Sun, as "the young fury-fighter they are . . . calling the new
'Golden Boy' of the ring . . . the guy with the rock for a right
fist, the new killer inside the ropes." And now it seems to me, as
I think back to the Davis fight, that the ring was littered with
greening corpses, like the road through St. André de l'Epine in
1944. A wisp of cordite smoke was curling around Graziano's
nostrils (a detail Mr. Heinz omitted), and he had a big, square-
cut rock, like a mounting block or a five-hundred-dollar tomb-
stone, at the end of his golden right arm, and strong men all
around me were whimpering in dismay, half fearing to look, yet
held riveted to their seats by the horror of the spectacle.[2] One
fellow the Golden Rock might well be matched with is Willie
Joyce, who, according to Jim Jennings, in the *Mirror,* uses his
left hand as a "most potent rapier." The clash of steel against
granite, and the chink of gold!

Even a rock or a rapier would be overmatched against Pete
Reiser, a Brooklyn ballplayer. "Pistol Pete Reiser is what they
call him in Flatbush with undisguised affection," wrote James
Parnell Dawson, of the *Times,* in reporting a ball game not long

[1]*Events made my estimate of Mr. Graziano look very good a few days
after this piece appeared. He fought Tony Zale, the middleweight champion, at the Yankee Stadium, and although Zale was thirty-two years old
and supposed to be past his prime, he knocked Graziano out in the sixth
round. Zale even in his prime had never been hailed by the scribes as an
"immortal," which with them is a term of very mild praise.*

[2]*I have had a letter from Heinz which illustrates the pathos of the sports
writer's plight. "Dear Joe," he wrote, "I saw a lot of roads from France
through Belgium and Holland and into the middle of Germany and the
end of the war, and I still feel that I saw more fury and animalism and
hate in Rocky Graziano the night he knocked out Marty Servo than I saw
in the kids, say, of the First Division with whom I clung to the top of a
tank moving in over the Ardennes snow. Sincerely, Bill Heinz." This proves
that after a while they begin to believe it themselves.*

ago, "but yesterday at the Polo Grounds he developed all the power of a siege gun as he clubbed the Dodgers to a ten-inning 3-1 victory." Obviously, a man with a Stone Age rock or a baroque rapier would have slight chance against a siege gun, a weapon only lately become obsolescent and especially lethal when used as a club. The scribes inevitably have an atomic weapon too. "A new mighty atom of the tennis courts put on the mantle of Bitsy Grant today," wrote Allison Danzig, of the *Times*, in an account of this summer's Southampton tournament. The newcomer is a Filipino tennis player named Felicisimo Ampon, who is not very big (that's where the atom comes in, see?). Jeane Hoffman, of the *Journal-American*, writing about him on the same day, presumably without looking over Mr. Danzig's shoulder, described him as "a mighty up-'n'-atom," whose "chain-reaction shots" beat some other tennis player he was playing tennis with.

Foibles are dealt with by the scribes as forthrightly as epic achievements. Take what Roscoe McGowen, of the *Times*, said in his opening sentence about the Brooklyn ball club on the occasion of its losing a game three or four weeks ago. "Proving apt disciples of the cult of fumble and futility," McGowen wrote, "the erstwhile league-leading Dodgers closed their western invasion by helping the Cubs to their seventh straight triumph, 3-2, before a crowd of 38,499 at Wrigley Field today." McGowen meant they made two errors. The sentence, by the way, is a good example of the all-purpose—or *multum in multo* —sports lead in the *Times*. When I worked, briefly, on the *Times* sports-department copy desk in 1925, whimsy had not yet been allowed to work its way uptown from the *Herald Tribune*, and the stars of the staff used to try to get all the essential facts of a story into the first sentence. In those days an acceptable lead read about as follows: "Billy Petrolle, 139½ pounds, of Fargo, N.D., defeated on points by a decision of two judges [here names of judges] and the referee [here name of referee], Phil McGraw, 137, of Detroit, Michigan, before a crowd of 16,487 persons of both sexes, who paid $74,215.63, including Federal and State taxes, at the new Madison Square Garden last night." (This is just a hypothetical example; I don't remember whether Petrolle even fought McGraw, or, if he did, who won.) In 1925,

I would have sent McGowen's lead back for clarification. How much money did the crowd of 38,499 at Wrigley Field pay, and how many sexes was it composed of? And what did the Dodgers weigh? What you get now in a *Times* sports lead is a welded job, as if "The Wind in the Willows" and the *World Almanac* were bound together in one volume.

A game, contest, clash, or head-on collision that one sports writer sees as a ghastly fiasco for the losers may seem to a colleague a romantic accomplishment by the winners. Bob Cooke, of the *Herald Tribune*, summarizing in his lead sentence the same game Mr. McGowen sneered at, wrote, "Inspired by the faint flicker of a pennant dream . . . the Chicago Cubs turned Brooklyn's sunshine into gloom this afternoon as they swept a two-game series with a 3–2 victory that left Brooklyn two and a half games behind the St. Louis Cardinals." Cooke's lead does not tell how many people were there, but he got in a nice touch about sunshine and gloom which not everybody would have thought of. On the other hand, the word "inspired," when used by scribes, is an adjective usually preceding the word "effort," so to many of Mr. Cooke's colleagues his use of one without the other must have seemed a solecism.

Among sports writers, an inspired effort, if continued longer than five minutes, becomes a surge. What a surge is was explained one day a few weeks ago by Garry Schumacher in the *Journal-American*: "It is only in there in the tough going that team members learn to rely on each other, where confidence and morale is forged, and where the will to win becomes a surge." Schumacher was expressing reservations about the Boston Red Sox, who were apparently winning the American League pennant without recognizing the necessity for even an inspired effort, an intermediary link in the chain of combustion which he bypassed in his explanation.[3] To be technically precise, the will to win becomes an inspired effort, and this in turn produces the surge.

The team that has been surging to victory recently (or seemed

---

[3]*Schumacher may have been right. In the World Series the St. Louis Cardinals, National League champions, who had had more experience in surging, defeated the Red Sox. The Cardinals had won their pennant only in a postseason play-off, while the Red Sox won theirs easily.*

to be up to last week, at any rate) is St. Louis in the National League. "The St. Louis Cardinals once more are breathing on the necks of the National League-leading Dodgers," a roundup story in the *Post* reported during the mid-August stage of the surge. On the same day Arch Murray, of the *Post*, put it this way: "Disaster and those relentless Cardinals pounded hard on the spikeprints of the Dodgers today in the wake of yesterday's lethal double dose of defeat by the Phillies, their old-time whipping boys. . . . The worm turned with a vengeance." As a rewrite man on *PM* interpreted it, here's what happened: "The Dodgers' jinx over the Phillies exploded yesterday at Shibe Park with a bang that blew all the Flatbush athletes off the bench." The warm neck, the loaded jinx, and the double dose that left a wake did not, however, prove immediately lethal to the Dodgers. "Showing no after effects from Sunday's double dose of defeat prescribed by the Phillies, the Brooklyn Dodgers tasted of the cup of victory yesterday at Ebbets Field," the *Herald Tribune* reported a day later. That was when the Dodgers still "teetered precariously on the edge of first place," according to the *Mirror*, but looked as if they might yet show that Herbert Goren of the *Sun*, had been on the right track, nine days earlier, when he wrote, "They called the Dodgers the 'team of destiny' in 1941, and perhaps the same tag-line applies this year. It must have been destiny which carried them over all the rough spots in last night's 3–2 victory." (The Giants haven't done so well this year, but they have not fallen so low that any sports writer has reported that they merely won or lost a ball game. The day after they played their hundredth and hundred-and-first games of the season, James Dawson wrote in the *Times*, "The Giants roared past the century mark in the 1946 playing schedule yesterday at the Polo Grounds, beating the daylights out of Frank Frisch's docile Pirates in a doubleheader that attracted 27,709 fans.")

Destiny, extensively used in press releases about Napoleon, established itself in the sports pages in the fall of 1922, when a successful Princeton football team became known as the Team of Destiny. Since then the word has acquired Bronx and Brooklyn applications. The *Enquirer* referred to Tami Mauriello, before he got knocked out by Joe Louis last week, as The Bronx Boy of Destiny. Since the end of August, when the Cardinals surged past the Dodgers, or to the fore, to employ the more usual expression, the destiny of Brooklyn has appeared kind of dubious.

Another destiny kid this year is Jack Kramer, a tennis player even mightier than the Mighty Atom. Mr. Danzig, describing in the *Times* how Kramer won the national championship, wrote, "John Kramer had his rendezvous with manifest destiny yesterday." Kramer needed all the destiny he could scare up to help him, because in Tom Brown, the runner-up, he was meeting no commonplace tennis player. In reporting Brown's quarter-final match with Frank Parker, Danzig had already written, "Not since Ellsworth Vines . . . has a tennis gallery seen such electrifying maceration of a fuzz-covered ball as was wrought by the 23-year-old Californian from San Francisco in defeating Parker. The crowd of 8,000 spectators at Forest Hills yesterday did everything but tear down the stadium in its uproarious enthusiasm over the scorching all-court attack that was almost beyond credibility in its deadly targetry." Kramer was lucky to have a stadium left to play Brown in at all. By the time of the final, Brown must have lost some of his speed, for Danzig found his shots no longer macerating but just lacerating. According to the *Times* sports writer, Kramer kept on "such grinding pressure with his lethal service, return of service and volleys that the lacerating drives of Brown were reduced to impotency."

There is a human aspect to these struggles of the roaring, spike-print-pounding, vengeful-worm-turning Children of Destiny, and some of the scribes occasionally touch on it, like Sophocles recording the conversation of the smitten Ajax in his tent. "In a blind rage, Mel Ott kicked the ball bag across the locker room and cursed all umpires in general and Umpire Art Passarella in particular," Al Buck, of the *Post*, wrote as he began one recent vignette of the intimate genre. (Ott was lucky that, in his blindness, he did not kick a bat bag full of bats.) Mr. Buck's fellow-*Post* writer, Mr. Murray, topped him, I think, with an understanding essay on Bill Dickey, who until just the other day was manager of the Yankees. "Outwardly, Bill remains the serene and gracious fellow he was when he was riding high as baseball's greatest catcher," wrote Mr. Murray, during Dickey's last days in office. "But inwardly, he is a brooding, lonely man, striving desperately to find the solution that isn't there—the means by which he can get his Bombers back in a lost flag fight." It is good for the public to know the secret sorrows of the great. It is the sort of thing that helps prevent revolutions.

I have been either out of the country or just preoccupied during most of the past seven years, and in consequence my reading of sports pages between 1939 and the start of this season was meagre. Upon returning to them, I found them so enjoyable that I decided to catch up on some of the things that had happened during the years I had other interests, and with this in mind I picked up a volume called "Best Sport Stories of 1945," which includes three prize-winners, or *best* best sport stories of 1945, which tied for the first award of excellence. These were selected by F.P.A., John Chamberlain, and Quentin Reynolds. It seems that the sports writers kept on writing just as well as ever while most of the able-bodied athletes were away, which may indicate that the mere presence of a man in a baseball or football player's uniform is all the scribe needs, and then only as a preliminary stimulus to composition. The presence may someday be replaced by a picture, a recorded sound (as, for instance, that of a wet boxing glove's impact on a fighter's elbow), or by the ringing of a bell (as in Pavlov's experiments in inducing salivation in dogs). The scribe needs the athlete about as much, before setting to work, as Keats needed a Grecian urn.

Jimmy Powers, author of the first of the prize-winning stories in order of appearance (from the *News* of October 11, 1945), provided a nice study in the transplanting of terms from one sport to another, a device that always pleases experienced sports-page readers, who react like old burlesque customers, judging the conventional bits by the skill with which they are performed. Mr. Powers, telling about the final game of last year's World Series, between Detroit and Chicago, wrote, "The deciding contest, a comparatively sane affair, was won for Detroit by Hal Newhouser, a left-handed bowler. [Your skilled sports writer, in describing a cricket match, would call the bowler a pitcher.] Hank Borowy . . . lasted exactly four and a half [minutes] . . . and was practically slugged silly before he rose from his stool after the first bell rang. [If Mr. Powers had been writing of a knockout in a boxing match, he probably would have said

that one contestant banked a four-bagger against his opponent's
chin.] The Tigers socked Borowy and his relief, Paul Derringer,
for five runs on four hits and two bases on balls in the opening
chukker. [If Mr. Powers had been writing about polo, he could
have said "inning."] They kept hammering away . . . until they
had, as the dugout patois goes, the old ball game in the old
burlap." This last phrase is considered by the trade to be more
adroit than really using dugout patois and saying "in the bag,"
and it is also simple enough not to confuse *News* readers, as
Mr. Powers well might have done if he had referred to the *ludus*
being in the reticule, or the *giuoco alla palla* being in the *sac
à main*.

The third prize-winning story is by a writer named Jerry
Nason, of the Boston *Globe*, about last year's Army-Notre
Dame football game, and is an example of the grand, uninhibited sports-page manner. (The other prize-winner was taken
from a magazine, and is therefore, as a scribe might put it, a
few feet outside this department's foul line.) Mr. Nason began,
"With a crash that no doubt dislodged the plaster in every
subway where self-appointed South Bend alumni are reputed to
gather, Army's strong-arm boys slammed the gates of mercy on
Notre Dame's stricken football team today." Mr. Nason's assumption was not, I believe, justified; at any rate, I have heard
of no series of cave-ins in the city's rapid-transit system during
the afternoon of that particular Army-Notre Dame game, and
Notre Dame's subway alumni were, as Mr. Nason went on to
demonstrate, attending this football game, aboveground, when
the gates slammed.

"The nation's No. 1 gridiron colossus, namely, Army," the
Boston scribe let his thin trickle of understatement continue,
"raced enthusiastically to and fro upon a carpet of Kelly-green
jerseys for a 48-0 result which was fraught with nightmarish
events for the keelhauled Irish in Yankee Stadium." Upon
reading this, I made a rapid calculation. The Notre Dame team,
even if each member were three feet wide and six feet long, a
generous estimate, would, recumbent, cover an area of only a
hundred and ninety-eight square feet. How far to and how far
fro could Army have run upon this limited surface? Laid end
to end, the Kelly-green jerseys would have extended sixty-six

feet in a straight line, which is more than enough for a first down, of course, but suppose the keelhauled Irish had cunningly laid themselves end to end *at right angles to the sidelines?* No play could have gone further than one yard. I concluded that Mr. Nason was kidding.

"Army sparred around tentatively for the first period," Mr. Nason continued, making use of Powers' gambit No. 1 by writing about one sport in the terms of another. "The Cadets started waving confidently to friends at the ringside and toe-danced and jabbed, so to speak. . . . Then, in the most cold-blooded manner imaginable, it suddenly fell upon this game but doomed Notre Dame aggregation and proceeded to mop up the front porch with it." (What was that house doing by the side of the ring?)

"Before dusk fell mercifully upon the scene," Mr. Nason added, "Glenn Davis had drummed over the stadium sod for three touchdowns . . . on inimitable escapades of 26, 31 and 21 yards. . . . The two Army horror twins had the Cadets in a 35-0 lead going into the final 18 minutes of play. . . . Thus the Army scored five times by infantry tactics. . . . Army's set of linemen have chained atomic power to the degree where it includes immediate and alarming inertness on the part of the opposition but which still enables the swashbuckling Cadets to escape manslaughter charges."

At this point the book fell with a crash from my nerveless fingers, and I went out to the pantry and poured myself a stiff bracer, so that my hand wouldn't tremble as I signed my name on a check for my 1946 Dartmouth football tickets. I certainly missed a lot of excitement by staying in Europe so long.

[A deceptively encouraging American phenomenon is the universal readiness to laugh at any mention of Colonel Robert McCormick or his Chicago Tribune. Bertie is always good for a laugh, like the word Brooklyn in a radio script. I have little need to read the Tribune regularly; readers in its area keep me bountifully supplied with clipped and mounted specimens of the colonel's thinking. I say that it is deceptively encouraging because the Tribune circulation remains more than a million weekdays, a million and a half Sundays, and people who read it acquire a habit, not of agreeing with Colonel McCormick, which would be almost impossible, but of thinking of anybody slightly less reactionary than the colonel as a liberal. No Wayward Press I wrote got a sunnier reception than the following piece, but I sometimes wonder if ragging the Tribune isn't like punching the heavy bag. The colonel is in the direct line of Dickens' Colonel Diver of the Rowdy Journal and of Elijah Pogram, who "Defied the world, sir—defied the world in general to com-pete with our country upon any hook; and devellop'd our resources for making war upon the universal airth." He is in an old tradition.]

Two Pounds for a Dime

It is always salutary to find out how we look to an acute observer from outside our own cultural area—a de Tocqueville, an H. G. Wells, or even a Lin Yutang. I was therefore delighted at the opportunity to read a series of three articles by Charles Gotthart, a Chicago *Tribune* foreign correspondent assigned to New York, which recently ran on the front page of the Sunday edition of the World's Greatest Newspaper. I had been going along in my effete, Eastern way, feeling fairly well pleased with my environment, and then, bang!—the Gotthart trilogy arrived in a lump, each installment embedded in a heavy Chicago Sunday *Tribune*, all three issues bound together with baling wire by a scout I had sent out into the Sears, Roebuck country to trap specimens for this department. Mr. Gotthart, an accompanying note from my scout explained, had been dispatched to New York by his employer, Colonel Robert McCormick, to do a series on the newspapers and magazines of the East. The headlines on the first piece read:

THE ALIEN EAST:
A THING APART
FROM AMERICA
ITS MILLIONS LOYAL TO
LANDS THEY FLED

Gazing at this simple message, I could see Mr. Gotthart (whom I pictured wearing a coonskin cap) feeling as out of place in Times Square as Ilya Ehrenburg or Konstantin Simonov, and trying to attune his ear to the harsh-sounding speech of the natives as he sized up the merchandise on the newsstands.

This article was mostly background stuff, designed to acquaint the reader back in America with the ecology of Eastern journalism. Mr. Gotthart delimited what he meant by the East at the very beginning. "Geografically speaking," he ruled, employing the Chicago *Tribune's* simpliphied orthografy, "the east is east of the Hudson." Having thus annexed Sneden's Landing, Woodstock, Newburgh, and Kingston to the Chicago *Tribune's* American intellectual empire, though leaving Riverdale, Beacon, and historically blighted Hyde Park to the East, he got busy punching.

"The midwesterner who accepts the east as something apart knows from his history books that all of the seaboard states had their foundations from England," he wrote, making no shrift at all of any Dutch pretensions to a hand in settling the area. "The Tory influence was always strong in them, and in New York in particular. When the Declaration of Independence was approved by the Continental Congress in Philadelphia, the last to sign was New York—after considerable hesitation. Historians have attributed this reluctance to the fact that New York was the most strongly pro-British of the thirteen colonies. Many of the Tories exiled from the seaboard states for treasonable attempts to hamper the Revolution returned afterward. In New York City they have remained dominant. Those who pushed across the mountains became purely American, but those who remained on the seacoast never did. . . . In the entire country, three out of every ten persons are foreign born or the children of foreign born. In New York the proportion is six out of ten." Consulting United States census figures, I discover that in Chicago it is also six out of ten.

In his second article Mr. Gotthart introduced the theory that British influence still fouls the alien Eastern press. The headlines on this one were:

ONCE GREAT N.Y.
PAPERS HIT NEW
LOW IN ESTEEM
REPLACE PATRIOTISM
WITH ANGLOMANIA

At the outset Mr. Gotthart made one rather grudging concession to our papers. "With all its shortcomings, the eastern press
is still superior to that of England, where journalism is not acknowledged of equal rank with other professions," he admitted,
and somewhat later he added, "In New York there is a barrier
between newspaper owners and workers not found in the west,
but even so, the city's reporters are vastly better off than their
British brothers, who call themselves 'journalists,' and who have
to use the back entrances and servants' stairs because they are
not accorded equal rank with other professions." By coming out
into the open with all this, Mr. Gotthart called attention to a
lamentable state of affairs which I became aware of while living
in London in 1941 but which I was not allowed to mention because of wartime censorship. In those days, whenever American
correspondents went into London pubs with English "journalists" they had befriended, they were compelled, by social
law, to leave these ragged, low-caste acquaintances in the three-
ales bar, where there were shavings on the floor, while they
themselves went into the saloon lounge, where there was a carpet. One of my own English-press protégés, a man on the *News
Chronicle*, had to rise before dawn every morning to soap his
publisher's hunting boots. Another had to serve his publisher
tiffin when the old man clapped his hands three times. To clinch
his argument that the press is discriminated against in Britain,
Mr. Gotthart pointed out that English publishers, when they
are made peers, seldom get anything higher than a viscountcy.
"Viscount," he added acridly, "is the title given unsuccessful
soldiers like Generals French, Montgomery, and Alexander."

All this had the tone of a man who intended to make no
other concessions, but Colonel McCormick's nuncio, surpris-
ingly, reported that he found the Eastern daily press in pretty
good shape: "The *Sun* and the *World-Telegram* now reflect
all of the best in the eastern rich, a characteristic also of the
Times, which presents the best of the eastern point of view
and extends its influence well beyond New York City. . . . The
New York masses are reached by the Hearst papers—*Journal-
American* and *Mirror*—and by the Sunday and Daily *News*,
the phenomenally successful tabloid, all of which reflect the
midwestern and western origin of their publishers." This, I took

it, meant that the Chicago *Tribune* had given its imprimatur to six of the nine major New York · dailies, with a total of 4,994,238 circulation out of the city's 5,763,444 circulation. I had always feared that most New York newspapers were editorially out of bounds, from a Chicago *Tribune* point of view, and I was pleased to discover that so many of them were acceptable.

Mr. Sulzberger, the publisher of the *Times*, may have been less pleased, because, shortly after the Gotthart series appeared, the *Times* sent Felix Belair, Jr., out to Chicago to write a comical interview with Colonel McCormick. It looked like an attempt to get him to withdraw his endorsement. But perhaps Mr. Sulzberger never even saw the Gotthart series and I am just reading meanings into the Belair interview.

It was then revealed that the New York papers of which Gotthart disapproved were the *Herald Tribune*, *PM*, and the *Post* (plus the *Daily Worker*, which he included just for laughs). The *Tribune* (the alien-Eastern one), he said, was an "anglomaniac supporter of all 'causes' intended to promote the British empire," and he had an unanswerable explanation of how it got that way. It is the product of a merger of the old *Herald* and the old *Tribune*. James Gordon Bennett, Jr., who inherited the *Herald* from his father, was "horsewhipped by his fiancée's brother after his engagement was broken off in 1877. Thereafter he lived abroad. . . . The *Herald* became completely a British newspaper (it was violently pro-war in 1914) and has remained pro-British ever since." As for the pre-merger *Tribune*, it belonged to the Reid family, as it still does, and "in promoting internationalism under the influence of worship for everything pertaining to the British nobility, whom they fawn upon, the Reids have aligned themselves with domestic crackpots who have become expert in the art of smearing American citizens." You put two papers like that together and what have you got?

PM, Mr. Gotthart decided, is another example of the insidious British infiltration. It is not really, he says, "the New York version of *Pravda*." That is just a blind. Marshall Field, its proprietor, "has posed all these years as something between a pink and a red, but there are many who say he is not pink at all but is so devoted to the British empire, associating entirely with anglomaniacs of the Park Avenue and Long Island social set, that his red stand is designed to weaken America and so strengthen the empire."

Mr. Gotthart has little to say of the *Post's* motivation, but he does call it "a vicious paper, reflecting mental turpitude."

The headlines over his third story read:

REAL AMERICA
A MYSTERY TO
PAPERS IN EAST

BRITISH-RED BIFOCAL

VIEW NO HELP

This, one might assume, referred only to the three excommunicated papers, but most of the space beneath it was devoted to magazines. Mr. Gotthart bore down harder on the Eastern weeklies than on the newspapers, possibly because the weeklies have a larger circulation in the Chicago *Tribune's* territory.

"The pattern of Anti-Americanism is found again in such magazines," he writes, "as the Luce trio: *Time, Life,* and *Fortune;* in *Look, New Republic,* the *Nation,* and *New Masses;* and considerable pink has colored the political complexion of *Collier's,* the *Saturday Evening Post,* and *Harper's. . . .* [I should have thought, incidentally, that these last three magazines would have got a passing grade from Mr. Gotthart, but they appear dangerously subversive to him.] *Life,* most successful of the Henry Robinson Luce periodicals, heads the procession of 'cheesecake' magazines. . . . *Life* frequently publishes lengthy textual matter to justify its sex appeal photografs and drawings." I noticed that the *Tribune* uses the spelling "photograf," though the *News* has an inquiring "Fotographer," and wondered whether it was a difference over how to spell this word that for ten years had come between the *Tribune* publisher and his cousin, the late Captain Patterson. But I was glad, in any event, that someone had offered an explanation for the text in *Life.*

When Mr. Gotthart got on to the *Saturday Evening Post* and *Collier's,* he made what I was quick to recognize as a major contribution to the apparatus of criticism. "Pink has colored the formerly great weeklies of large circulation—the *Saturday Evening Post* and *Collier's,*" the Man from America wrote, restating his thesis. "Lacking in qualities inspired by the midwest brand of Americanism, these weeklies fail to offer their readers anything remotely approaching the physical content of a good Sunday newspaper. The CHICAGO SUNDAY TRIBUNE, for example, weighs 32 ounces; *these magazines, five.*" The italics are mine; I use them because I immediately realized that Gotthart had discovered a tangible basis for the appraisal of journalistic values, and, what was equally important, a procedure for its application. Under Gotthart's Law, it was no longer necessary to read a publication in order to evaluate its contents. It was enough to weigh it. There had been no comparable boon to humanity since the discovery of anesthesia. I raced to the laboratory and, picking up the first magazine to come to hand, the then current issue of the *New Yorker*, I threw it on the scales. I was slightly chagrined to find that it weighed but ten ounces, which put it in the same relation to the Sunday *Tribune* as a pan fish is to a two-pound sucker. It was scant consolation that, as I directly ascertained, the *Morning Telegraph* weighed only five and a a half ounces, *Marvel Comics* three, and *Laff* three and a half. A *Daily Worker* I borrowed from the polo editor weighed but two ounces, a figure that should reassure Colonel McCormick. But when I placed the latest Sunday *Times* on the scales, I began to wonder whether the *Tribune* proprietor would stand by *la méthode Gotthart*. The *Times* weighed two pounds and fifteen ounces, exceeding the *Tribune* cited by Gotthart by just one ounce less than a pound.

I then weighed a Chicago Telephone Directory for June, 1943, the latest available in the laboratory. It came to four pounds, fourteen ounces. A Manhattan Telephone Directory weighed three pounds, eight ounces; a Brooklyn one two pounds, five ounces; a Queens one a pound, twelve and a half ounces; a Bronx one a pound, five and a half ounces. Aggregate for the city, exclusive of Richmond, whose directory I couldn't find in the laboratory: eight pounds, fifteen ounces, or as much as the Chicago Telephone Directory and *two complete Sunday Tribunes combined!* I didn't know what to make of these findings until I decided that Mr. Gotthart might have had in mind the division of publications into weight classes, like boxers or game chickens. The *New Yorker* may be O.K., after all, for a welterweight periodical. I hope so.

Post Scriptum: Pursuing the subject of weights, I have just learned from the Museum of Natural History that Mr. Gotthart's brain, if of normal size, weighs approximately forty-nine ounces, or as much as one complete Sunday *Tribune* and the news, sports, theatre, and first advertising sections of a second.

Little Landslide

[A golden glow of myth already (June 23, 1947) surrounds the elections of 1946, which are now represented as a certain sign that Mr. Dewey will be the next President of the United States. This Wayward Press piece, written immediately after the election, helps keep matters in perspective.]

Some time ago, when there was what looked like a synthetic war scare on, I had occasion to write about how most of the newspapers of the nation used the word "ultimatum" when what they were talking about was just a fairly brusque note that we had sent to Yugoslavia. The *Times*, which had erred as much as the rest in abusing the word, indirectly acknowledged its error, after all the excitement was over, in a story from Washington by James Reston headed:

WAR TALK IN U.S. IS BELIED
BY PLAIN FACTS IN CAPITAL
NEW LANGUAGE OF DIPLOMACY APPEARS
TO HAVE CREATED ARTIFICIAL TENSIONS

"It is felt here that the new language is being overplayed by press and radio in this country and is creating a war psychology that is not justified by facts," Mr. Reston explained, rather self-righteously for a representative of a journal that had overplayed it.

I have continued to note instances of that addiction to the strong word, even when it is not justified, which is destroying the values of language in the newspapers. If, for example, you use the word "famine" in a headline to indicate that lamb chops are hard to find in markets that are gorged with poultry, fish, and eggs, what are you going to use when you mean the kind of famine they have perennially in India? "Delicatessens Closing Tonight in Meat Famine," the *Herald Tribune* reported a few weeks ago, and the *Times* of the same day announced:

COUNTRY IS NEAR 'FAMINE' IN MEAT, CENTRES REPORT

Repetition of a word like "famine," however qualified, has a cumulative effect that can scarcely be achieved with words like "Meat Hard to Find," and a few years from now there may be people going around saying that they survived the Famine of '46, and eventually believing it. "If we could stand it, they can," they will say when funds are being raised to relieve an old-fashioned, starving-to-death famine in, say, Greece or Korea.[1]

A word that was applied as loosely during the past week as "ultimatum" or "famine" had been was "landslide." The *Daily News* announced on the morning before Election Day that its straw poll showed that Governor Dewey would be re-elected "in an Election Day landslide unparalleled since the post-World War I sweep of Warren G. Harding." Mr. Dewey, the *News* went on, would be elected by 1,610,000 votes—no more, no less —if five million people voted (which they did). On the same day the *World-Telegram* and the *Journal-American* said in their headlines that the election was going to be a landslide. Now, "landslide," as a political term, has a fairly generally accepted meaning. It signifies that the losing candidate is buried under a great mass of votes, like a man the side of a mountain falls on. The Harding election of 1920, to which the *News* referred, was

[1] *"Crisis," as used in the discussion of the Truman proposal to lend money to Greece and Turkey, furnished another example of the devalorization of a word. No evidence was offered that any new emergency had arisen in the affairs of either country; there was no reason why the British couldn't have announced their withdrawal from Greece months before it became imminent, or why they couldn't stay on a bit longer, as they have. It was implied that something sudden and unforeseeable had happened, and that our only choice was between shelling out money to a vicious regime and seeing the Russians waltz in. If Russian might is so negligible that it can be stayed by a small handout to a slippery kinglet, there is nothing at all critical about European affairs. I can imagine a panhandler approaching a prospect in the street, if such usage spreads, and saying, "Hey, buddy, can you spare the price of a beer? It's a crisis."*

a landslide. In New York State the Republican presidential candidate got 1,871,000 votes against Cox's 731,000, a plurality of more than a million in an election with less than three million voters. Roosevelt's victory over Landon, in 1936, was another classic instance of the landslide, at least in electoral votes—523 to 8. A candidate who wins by a landslide naturally acquires prestige and is attractive to future nominating conventions, so it is to the advantage of a candidate's supporters to magnify his triumphs. But Governor Dewey actually got less than 57 per cent of the popular vote (instead of the 66.1 per cent the *News* had predicted for him)—that is, a shade less than four votes out of seven, instead of two votes out of three. (Roosevelt, running against Willkie in 1940, got 55 per cent of the national popular and 85 per cent of the electoral vote, and nobody ever called that contest a landslide.) In comparison with Harding's plurality, or the plurality of 870,000 that Calvin Coolidge got over John W. Davis in New York in 1924, when 3,250,000 voted, Mr. Dewey's margin of 675,000, with five million voting, seems of the same moderate stature as the governor himself.

Sticking to their stories, on the day after the election practically all the papers referred to a Dewey "landslide." Among them was *PM*, which had fought Dewey dutifully but hopelessly throughout the campaign. "Dewey Landslide," said the top line on the front page, perhaps because *PM* is too young a newspaper to remember what a real landslide looks like. Robert G. Spivack, in the *Post*, the only other paper that opposed the governor, spoke of the victory in the same terms. The *World-Telegram* called it "a great personal victory," the *Journal-American* "a tremendous victory," and the *News*, although acknowledging that its poll had made a slight error, still said "landslide." The slight error was that it had overestimated his plurality by 138 per cent. Incidentally, everyone conceded that Dewey would win; the margin of victory was the only subject of speculation. The *News* poll had predicted that he would carry New York City as a whole (he lost it by 190,000), and also that he would carry Manhattan (he lost it by 60,000) and Brooklyn (he lost it by 167,000). The *News*, it would appear, was functioning about as accurately as a gypsy tea-leaf reader working with tea bags.

Before I leave off discussing large, over-all statistics, I should like to point out that Mead, who is not my idea of a dynamic candidate, had the support of only two city newspapers out of nine—two that have less than 10 per cent of the city's total daily circulation—but that he received more than 50 per cent of the city's vote. This, I'm afraid, is probably an index to the New York citizenry's evaluation of the gentlemen who write the editorials. Several local Republican candidates, both for Congress and the City Council, managed to win despite the handicap of being supported by seven newspapers. I am inclined to attribute the defeat of former Colonel Frederick van Pelt Bryan by Vito Marcantonio, in the Eighteenth Congressional District, to the circumstance that the *Post* also came to his support. No candidate can survive the endorsement of *eight* newspapers. About 5,763,000 newspapers are sold in New York City every day, and 2,549,000 votes were cast here on Election Day, which indicates that every voter buys 2.3 papers a day and disregards them.[2]

The *News* poll, bulletins on which ran every day from October 17 through November 4, was an aesthetic, if not a mathematical, success, and provided my favorite reading matter during the campaign. Seven crews, each commanded by a manager whose name was also published every day, traveled fourteen thousand miles throughout the state, according to Jack Turcott, the *News* byliner who furnished the continuity. I got to know the names of the managers by heart—G. Hussennetter, of West Upstate; John Campbell, of Center Upstate; Art Noble, of East Upstate; Raymond Dowd, Suburban; Clyde Brady, Brooklyn; Edward Dillon, Bronx-Queens; and John Hughes, Manhattan-Richmond. I frequently tried to visualize them as I read the results of their investigations. I would picture Dowd collecting twenty-four Dewey straw ballots one day in Riverhead-Aque-bogue-Jamesport and three for Mead in Mattituck-Cutchogue-Peconic; Hussennetter feeling the pulse of Bloomingburg, Wurtsboro, and Monticello; Brady pushing doorbells between Brighton Beach and Brooklyn College; and all of them shipping

---

[2]*This should cure me of getting jocular about statistics. I received half a dozen letters gravely pointing out that my figures were wrong because a lot of people who bought newspapers didn't vote, and besides, not all the voters had disregarded their papers, because a large minority had voted for Dewey after all.*

their specimens in, day by day, to Turcott, whom I imagined crouching between two comptometers, each as imposing as the globe on the ground floor of the Daily News Building, tabulating the returns that showed Dewey winning everywhere by percentages unequaled since the plebiscite in the Saarland in 1935.

Each installment of the poll was accompanied by a map divided into tiny sections, like a diagram of how to buy beef. The sections were shaded to show where Dillon had been, where Noble had sounded sentiment, where Hussennetter, staggered by an avalanche of Dewey ballots, had fallen to one knee, only to rise again and stumble bravely forward in the direction of Big Flats. Some of the installments were also accompanied by small rectangles—gray for Mead, black for Dewey—showing how big 61.1 per cent was in relation to 38.9, or 80 per cent to 20. Then came little drawings of Dewey wearing a high, 74.1 *straw* farmer's hat (get it?) and Mead in a flat, 25.9 *straw* boater; Dewey sitting on top of a high, 70.3 haystack (hay, straw—see?) and Mead with hardly enough hay to keep the seat of his pants off the ground; Dewey riding an elephant far in advance of Mead on a donkey; and other designs of the same nature. All in all, it was quite artistic.

There was a slight contretemps—which the *News* did nothing to bring to its readers' attention—during the last week before the election, when a *PM* reader named Kaplan, in the Bronx, telephoned to his favorite newspaper that a *Daily News* straw crew (presumably Dillon's) was in the neighborhood taking the sometimes jumpy Bronx pulse, and that one of its members was throwing ballots marked for Mead down a sewer. Mr. Kaplan had given a small boy a Roosevelt dime to scramble down to the sewer trap after them, and the boy had retrieved a dozen, photographs of which *PM* duly published. The managing editor of the *News*, apprised of *PM's* coup, told a *PM* man that the guilty straw-vote taker should be "decapitated." But the executive editor, who apparently ranks his colleague by a half stripe, characterized the whole charge as "hogwash." I do not think that the *PM* man quoted him in full. I am sure he must have said, "Trumped-up, New Deal, Red hogwash."

When the campaign came to an end, I was sorry to say good-by

to beautiful Big Flats and nice Mr. Hussennetter and Mr. Turcott and their friends, and I can hardly wait until they start
building up that unparalleled statewide Republican majority in
1948. With a bigger registration to work on, they ought to miss
that one by two million.

As a sustained effort in entertainment, the *News* poll had no
rival in campaign journalism, though a few stories, or parts of
stories, in other papers stand out in my memory. There was,
for instance, the lead on a *Sun* story: "For the record, it may as
well be stated now that Gov. Dewey is not a baby-kissing cam-
paigner." Then, as if reflecting that so blunt a statement might
alienate the doting-parents vote, the writer added, "That he has
a genuine fondness for children, however, is quite apparent from
his treatment of scores of those whom he has met while visiting
veterans' housing projects in upstate New York. . . . In some
cases the young mothers were quite awed and correspondingly
speechless, but the Deweys usually set them at ease quickly and
loosened their tongues." Mrs. Dewey was, of course, accompanying the governor, and I am sorry I was not present to see her
drawing a stoup of custard or a handful of calf's-foot jelly from
her reticule to bestow on the beaming tenants as the young
mother brought the governor a bowl of milk still warm from the
as yet unwired refrigerator.

The most stimulating news item provoked by the election was
probably the Washington dispatch reporting a suggestion by
United States Senator J. William Fulbright, of Arkansas, that
Mr. Truman first appoint a Republican Secretary of State and
then resign, leaving the responsibilities of government with the
Republicans, who now had the legislative power. The beautiful
simplicity of this notion, which, if acted upon, would also serve
as an edifying example to the Russians—Mr. Truman would be
voluntarily abandoning his veto power—impressed me instantly.
So I was not surprised, the next morning, to see that it had been
taken up by another serious political thinker, Mr. Marshall Field,
proprietor of *PM* and the *Chicago Sun*. Mr. Field had appropri-
ated the top quarter of the inside front page of his New York
property for a letter urging Mr. Truman to ask the Republican
members of the House and Senate to suggest a man to be named
Secretary of State, in whose favor he could resign. On the same

day Max Lerner, one of Mr. Field's employees, filled three times as much of *PM's* space—salable for advertising purposes since November 5—to refute his boss, successfully and solemnly, in the Lerner way, like an elephant treading the dead body of a mouse into the floor of its cage. Under this system, the Republican heir apparent would be selected not by Republicans in Congress but "by the Republican party bosses," Lerner wrote, "by Joe Pew of Pennsylvania, by Col. McCormick of Illinois, by Carroll Reece of the Southern Republican carpetbaggers."

I couldn't help thinking it would be fun to have Colonel McCormick in the White House, even though he might expel from the Union that part of the United States lying geografically east of the Hudson River, just sending a gunboat around now and then to protect American property like the News Building. It would be nicer still, I thought, if Mr. Truman and the Republicans just got together and named somebody they both liked—perhaps Ralph Bellamy. I had never before thought of the Presidency as something you could give away once you got it. The concept opens up a lot of new vistas. It may, in fact, become a convention for the starting candidates of both parties to act only as hors-d'œuvre, like the third-stringers with whom Knute Rockne used to open his games. If so, the better Presidents will be kept on the bench, to be sent in when the going gets tough, with maybe a couple of specialists, presidential drop-kickers, being held in reserve for rare contingencies, like having to shoot a deer for the newsreels. The incumbent of the moment could resign in favor of the shooting President for ten minutes, while the newsreel boys got their stuff, and then the specialist could resign in favor of a President with a good radio voice for a scheduled broadcast. This would make it even harder for the ordinary citizen to call the next play than it is now.

It is quite an idea that Senator Fulbright and Mr. Field have got—that when you elect a man President or Vice-President for four years, you don't necessarily want him to stay in office that long. It seems that it's really more like giving him tickets to an inferior concert you don't want to go to yourself, and your feelings won't be hurt if he gives the Presidency away to his janitor or some fellow in the other party.

[A steak I helped eat at my sister's home in Norwalk, Conn., crystallized my conviction that the meat "shortage" blamed on price regulation in the first two weeks of October, 1946, had been a hoax. My sister served the steak only ten days after the price ceiling had been lifted by a bamboozled Administration, and it was one of the best I have ever bitten into in my life. Take it from a gouty carnivore, my praise is not given to steaks lightly. But at about the third bite I realized that a steak to be that good must have been in an icehouse for a couple of months, months during which the newspapers had been assuring us that there wasn't any meat in the packers' refrigerators, and that the steer from which the steak had been cut must have been lovingly grain-finished for weeks in somebody's corn lot, while the papers had been saying that there were just a few old cows on the range but no fat cattle. I knew that the Norwalk butcher hadn't fed any steers, and I was pretty sure he wasn't a big enough operator to hold carcasses for months. When I got back to New York, I consulted an eminent beefsteak expert named William Wertheim and confirmed my estimate of the time necessary to produce a perfect steak. I haven't had quite such a good steak since, probably because packers now have no inducement to season meat so long having no price ceilings to outwait.

The meat hoax may yet prove an important episode in the history of our country. More than anything else it was responsible for the election of the present reactionary Congress (see my quotation from John O'Donnell, no leftist). While the price of meat has since risen to unprecedented heights—$1.25 a pound for steak in New York as I write—the Congress has interpreted the stimulated meat hunger of 1946 as a mandate to legislate against labor unions.]

The Great Gouamba

It is too early, as I write, to present a detailed critique of the way our press has handled the news about the coal miners' latest abstention from work. I sometimes fancy, however, that I detect a shift in the papers' economic line since October, when the meat producers were abstaining from the sale of any meat at ceiling prices. Jack Werkley, a *Herald Tribune* reporter who flits about the country in what his paper reminds its readers, every time it runs one of his stories, is a twin-engine Lockheed Lodestar flying newsroom, did, it is true, call the October episode a farmers' strike, and Will Lissner, in the *Times*, wrote accurately, if inconspicuously (page seventeen), that "the main reason why feeders are buying and growers are holding cattle is that it appears to be profitable." But there was a note of understanding approval—even, I might say, of affection—in most of the stories about the cattlemen, who were represented as rugged, wholesome, humorous individual enterprisers standing with their gum boots solidly planted in hog slop while they told the rest of the country to meet their terms. Maybe it is just my imagination, but the papers seem to me to be taking a bleaker view of the coal miners, who are using exactly the same tactics. The cattlemen held on to their beasts until they got their price (whereupon meat appeared in quantity), the miners are withholding their labor; but the press seems to have missed the parallel. The *Herald Tribune*, which on October 14 published a long piece about how decontrolled grain prices would affect the cost of raising hogs (it consisted entirely of quotes from a handout from the Republican Congressional Food Study Committee), has so far printed no companion piece on how decontrolled meat and other prices affect the cost of raising miners.

The *Herald Tribune* has me in its debt. It was a *Herald Tribune* editorial of November 26, warning labor against starting an inflation, that sent me scurrying back among my souvenirs to disinter some notes I had made on the journalistic episode I call the Great Gouamba ("gouamba" is an African word meaning "meat hunger") to verify my impression that the newspaper line had changed. I first encountered "gouamba" in "Stories of the Gorilla Country," by Paul Du Chaillu, an African explorer, lecturer, and author of boys' books who lived toward the end of the last century and whom in my youth I read with the rapt attention I now reserve for the daily press. Dormant for thirty years in some stratum of my unconscious, the word popped to the surface on October 9 while I was reading a piece by John O'Donnell, the political columnist of the *Daily News*. "Come what may," O'Donnell predicted, "this battle for the control of Congress will go down in our political history as the meat campaign." "Gouamba," I suddenly heard myself saying. Later in the day I checked, in the Public Library, on my recollection of the word's meaning. "On our return to Obinji," Du Chaillu wrote, in a prose I admire even more than O'Donnell's, "we were overtaken by my good friend Querlaouen, who had shot a wild pig, of which the good fellow gave me half. The Negroes feasted on the *koo loo* meat [Du Chaillu described a *koo loo* as a "new type chimpanzee"], which I could not touch. So the pig was welcome to me, as indeed it was to Quengueza, whom we found almost crying with an affection which is common in this part of Africa, and is called gouamba, but for which we happily have no name. Gouamba is the inordinate longing and craving of exhausted nature for meat. For days, and sometimes for weeks, a man does not get any meat at all; and whenever any other food is brought before him you will hear him say, looking at the food with disgust, 'Gouamba,' which means literally, 'I am sick of food; I have a craving for meat; I care for nothing else.'" Ever since that day I have thought of the period from October 7 to October 14, 1946 (President Truman decontrolled meat on the night of the fourteenth), as Gouamba Week, or the Newspaper Mardi Gras.

Gouamba Week began, for me, with a picture layout and story on the first page of the *Sun* of Monday afternoon. The *News* was caught more or less flat-footed at the beginning of the week, and it looked as if the other publishers had not told Colonel McCormick, way out in Chicago, what was going to happen. The *News* devoted its front page on Monday to a wedding picture of a bride who had dropped dead a minute after being photographed, and it didn't really seem to grasp the horror of the meat situation until Wednesday. The feature of the *Sun's* Monday layout was an Associated Press wirephoto of William Saier, of Detroit, a man who clearly lacked two lower molars, sitting in a restaurant in Windsor, Canada, and shoving a large piece of steak into his widely opened face. Mr. Saier appeared to be in little need of nourishment, since he rather resembled the late William Howard Taft (minus the mustache), but the *Sun's* headline on the Associated Press story it ran alongside brought out the pathos of the situation. "AMERICANS DINE WELL —IN CANADA," it said. The caption under the picture read, "'Yum-mm—Detroit is NOT like this,' William Saier seemed to be saying as he feasted on a large, juicy T-bone steak in a nearby roadhouse inn yesterday." How Mr. Saier could seem to be saying all that with a large piece of steak stuffed in his mouth, the caption writer did not explain. "A thick, juicy steak, luscious pork chops, tender roast beef, remember?" the A.P. story began. There was a second photograph in the layout, showing American automobiles from Detroit lined up at the customs station in Windsor and filled with people who wanted to get into Canada to satisfy their gouamba.

On the following day the papers published the report (which recommended decontrol) of the Beef Advisory Committee of the O.P.A., which was composed of representatives of the industry, and on Wednesday the *Sun's* headline on its leading gouamba story read, "POLITICAL STORM SWEEPS NATION IN MEAT SCARCITY." On Thursday a piece on the front page of the *Sun*, headed "ILLEGAL DEER BAG LAID TO MEAT LACK," told how gouamba-maddened poachers pursuing deer in the Adirondacks had accidentally shot to death a seventy-three-year-old farmer, a clear case of homicide traceable to the mistakes of the Administration. It should be noted that the headline writer did not get the farmer into the headline, presumably because he was not edible.

The *Times*, which had got off to an early start with a rush of stories that seemed a bit heavy, hit its stride, I thought, on the same day with a piece headed "QUEENS RESTAURATEUR, WORRIED OVER MEAT, DIVES OFF BROOKLYN BRIDGE AND SURVIVES." The restaurateur's wife, interviewed by a *Times* reporter, did not say what paper her husband had been reading. Some of the other *Times* entries for Miss Gouamba of 1946 (which prove that the *Times*, as I have often contended, is not nearly so unimaginative as people think) were "MEAT HUNTERS BEAT PATH TO JERSEY HAMLET," "BURGLAR IN BUTCHER SHOP FINDS CUPBOARD ALL BARE," and "CHINESE VISITORS EAT BEEF AT CITY LODGING." This last was the headline writer's way of saying that some Chinese police chiefs had tasted the stew at the Municipal Lodging House on East Twenty-fifth Street.

The *Herald Tribune*'s most ambitious contribution to gouamba was the aerial voyage Mr. Werkley made through the West in quest of meat, but I thought that a brief and simple improvisation by the paper's ship-news man, headed "STELLA POLARIS IN, 106 BID MEAT GLUM FAREWELL," had a much more gouambaceous effect than its air-borne reporter's expensive set pieces. The ship-news man described the terror in the faces of the passengers disembarking after a nineteen-day Caribbean cruise and confronted by life in a meatless New York. The cruise rates ranged from $425 to $1,475 a passenger, and I felt sorry for people with only that kind of money to spend faced with the sort of hell they were coming back to. The best Mr. Werkley could do was tell about a ranch owner who fed him meat off a roast of beef as big as a medicine ball, but since I had never wanted to swallow a medicine ball, my gouamba was not stimulated very much.

The *Journal-American* made a double enveloping advance on the subject of the week. It ran one series of articles from Canada by a reporter named John C. Manning, designed to prove that there was meat in that country (where rationing had been in force almost continuously since 1943—a cogent argument for the abandonment of control here), and another series, by a reporter named Kent Hunter, that was meant to indicate that our meat had gone, via U.N.R.R.A., "into the larders of the Russians and their satellites." Mr. Hunter, who not very long ago was General George Patton's uniformed press agent with the Third Army in France, announced on October 9 that 375,490,719 pounds of "the meat, sugar, bacon, butter, and concentrated foods that American housewives cried for" had been shipped to Austria, Czechoslovakia, Hungary, Finland, Poland, the U.S.S.R., Yugoslavia, and Albania. That works out, if you are good at figures, to one and one-third pounds of food, mostly cereals, per inhabitant of those countries, and could have provided every American citizen with a good buffet lunch. But it is much more impressive if you put it in pounds instead of tons. In tons, it is, to be specific, 187,500, or about three substantial shiploads per country. Incidentally, Hunter might have said that it was more than six billion ounces (6,007,851,504), or 170,322,590,138.40 grams, figures that obviously would have been more important to the stimulation of metropolitan gouamba than any stories about the number of beef cattle in the hands of the ranchers.[1] The head on the story was "SENATOR CHARGES FOOD DIVERSION FROM U.N.R.R.A. TO RED ARMY USE." This piece of Hunter's was surpassed, however, by one he wrote a couple of days later. It was headed "SENATOR BRIDGES CHARGES U.N.R.R.A. STEAKS SOLD IN EUROPE BY BLACK MART." The Journal editors must have had as high an opinion of it as I did, for they moved Hunter up from page two to the front page. "Civilians on the ship [the aircraft carrier Franklin D. Roosevelt] brought back a detailed report," Hunter wrote, "of two-inch-thick steaks served in black-market-supplied restaurants in Naples, in Athens, and along the Morocco-Algiers coast, at a time when American housewives cannot buy hamburger." Naturally the implication was that the steaks must have come from U.N.R.R.A. Mr. Manning's Canadian jaunt pro-

---

[1]Precisely the same chestnut has reappeared this year. Wholesale butchers in New York, chided because meat has risen far above the 1946 black-market prices, blamed the "shortage" on the export of meats to Europe. The Sun followed up with a "revelation" from its Washington bureau that 300,000,000 pounds of meat had been shipped out of the country during the last six months. This would be about two pounds per inhabitant of the United States, or less than an ounce of meat a week diverted from each individual American. It would be less than a tenth of an ounce subtracted from each meat meal. You could hide that much meat behind a green pea.

duced mostly photographs of hunks of meat, the idea being
that there were no hunks of meat on this side of the border to
photograph and that we knew whom we could blame for that.

The *Mirror*, ever a younger sister in Hearst journalism, produced little notable gouamba stimulus during the festival. Its
best offering was a story by a reporter named Henry Hillman,
headed "MEAT FAMINE HAS STATE ON GUARD FOR RUSTLERS" and
explaining, "The arrest Wednesday of a Manhattanite for a
butcher-and-run assault on a docile, three-year-old Holstein cow
near New Paltz seemed to justify the jitters, and many farmers
have reached a state of sirloin tremens where they're about to
move their cattle into the front parlor for safety. A high State
Police official at Albany, however, informed the *Mirror* that the
scare is without foundation." This sort of marched-up-the-hill-
and-then-marched-down-again journalism would never have
started the Spanish-American War.

The *World-Telegram* proved disappointingly uninventive. Its
Frederick Woltman, the fellow-traveler-collector, was apparently
miffed because Hunter had beaten him to the Red angle, and
he sulked behind his file of the *Daily Worker* all through Gouamba Week, not even bothering to go out and see if he could
discover a soup bone concealed beneath the plinth of the Independent Citizens' Committee of the Arts, Sciences, and Professions. The *Post* whimpered a few quiet suggestions about measures Mr. Truman could take against the meat men if he felt
like it, and then subsided when it became evident that he didn't.

The white-horse team in the chariot race, which overtook the
whole field, after being left standing at the start, and passed
them all in a cloud of flying gouamba, was, as any connoisseur
of the kiosks might have anticipated, the *Daily News*. The issue
of Wednesday, October 9, which I keep pressed between rose
leaves, served notice on all lesser newspapers that since Colonel
McCormick and Mrs. Patterson had now taken cognizance of
the emergency, it damn well *was* an emergency. The front page
carried a picture of a band of steers tottering out of a freight car
in Flushing, where, according to the publicity man of a company out there that manufactures steel lockers, they were to be
knocked on the head and distributed in bits to the firm's employees. Mr. O'Donnell, in his column about this being the meat

campaign, had apparently blown the whistle for all hands to turn to, and they did, with the alacrity of so many koo loos. That day the lead Washington story opened with "A ray of hope for the meat-famished East appeared today." The lead editorial, headed "LET 'EM EAT HORSE MEAT," began, "The above should be the slogan of the Truman Administration, according to Representative Charles A. Halleck (R.-Ind.), chairman of the Republican Congressional Campaign Committee." The editorial cartoon showed a flabby, dissipated-looking pugilist, labeled "New Deal Crackpot Economy," supine on the floor of a ring and shouting "Conspiracy! Conspiracy! Conspiracy!" while a handsome young boxer, ticketed "Facts of Life," stood victoriously over him.

On the following day, "DEMS, FEARFUL OF VOTERS, ACT IN MEAT CRISIS" shared page three, the *News* equivalent of the right-hand side of the first page in a standard paper, with "SLAIN PAIR FOUND IN DEBRIS," a story about a double murder in Florida. Mr. O'Donnell played a reprise on the viol de gouamba, and there were two divertissements, called "COOKIE PLANT MAY CLOSE [FOR LACK OF LARD]" and "MEAT STOPS MINE WALKOUT." The second was about how fifteen hundred miners quitting their jobs in Logan County, West Virginia, had been lured back by a promise of free pork chops—a trick that has not yet been tried in the new emergency. On Saturday a photograph of the Duke and Duchess of Windsor had to share the front page with a picture of a meat queue in the Bronx, captioned "Grand Illusion." Saturday's biggest gouamba feature was, however, a mighty funny photograph of a straw-hatted butcher in Johnson City, New York, who happened to be named Harry Truman and who was quoted as saying, while he held a cleaver over a carcass of lamb, "Get rid of those price ceilings and we'll have meat." He evidently considered lamb a vegetable.

With all the newspapers except the gently sniffling *Post* and an imminently apoplectic *PM* joining in the crashing chorus of "Gouamba! There is no meat!," like a refrain by Vachel Lindsay, the week rolled on to its predestined end. The *Sun* cried, in one frantic subhead, "SCARCITY SWELLS HOURLY!" In another hour, it would have been a matter of minutes. Mr. Werkley's climactic *Herald Tribune* story was headed "CORN BELT FATTENS FLOOD

OF BEEF, WAITS FOR O.P.A. DAM TO BREAK." On the second Monday evening of the Great Gouamba, the dam went out.

PM, very ungenerously, I thought, used the front-page headline "TRUMAN SURRENDERS" to record the event. What the President had done was simply yield to a spontaneous demonstration of public opinion. Personally, I much preferred the *Journal-American's* triumphant paean: "HOG PRICES SOAR TO ALL-TIME HIGH."[2]

[2]But they are higher as I write (June, 1947).

[*This piece contains "The Philadelphia Story" in one sentence, a quotation from a Philadelphian journalist: "Apparently there is something about getting drunk in New York that has it all over getting drunk in Philadelphia."*

My affection for that city is, to me at least, apparent between every two lines, but it was taken in ill part. A German refugee professor in particular wrote to me from Rutgers that if citizens of two cities in the same country were mean to each other there was precious little hope for the international harmony.]

Who Killed the Monkey?

The alacrity with which the delegates of the United Nations accepted John D. Rockefeller, Jr.'s, offer of a site in Manhattan caused only slight manifestations of emotion here. Perhaps that was because New Yorkers are used to people arriving from out of town and saying they wouldn't live here if you gave them the place and then, if they can find an apartment, settling in for life. This complacency, plus a rooted New York habit of not reading Philadelphia papers, prevented us from grasping the tragic import of what happened when, on December 12, the General Assembly Headquarters Committee voted to recommend housing the United Nations headquarters in a group of skyscrapers to be erected on the East Side. A couple of days later the Assembly voted to accept the committee's recommendation, 46-7; only Australia, El Salvador, and the *shish kebab* states—Egypt, Iraq, Syria, Lebanon, and Saudi Arabia—held out against the New York charm. The Saudi Arabian delegate furnished a light touch by demanding a guarantee against smoke and odors in the proposed area. The humor was especially pungent to anyone who had ever smelled an Arab city.

Most of the New York press treated the news with polite and restrained enthusiasm, directed principally toward Mr. Rockefeller's generosity. The *Daily News*, however, ran a couple of editorials putting the blast on the whole business. "If you ask us, Mr. Rockefeller has now done something completely cockeyed, at the urging of his eldest son, Nelson," the *News* said. "The voters of New York City have not been asked whether they want the U.N. to be located here forever or until the next war. . . .

We are surprised, though, at the way the city authorities are at
this writing falling all over themselves to snap up this alleged
bargain. . . . All in all, this is one gift horse which should be
looked carefully in the mouth; and it is the city authorities' duty
to do that looking." It complained again, a few days later: "The
world capital is simply being crammed down their [New Yorkers'] throats—and incidentally, the city loses a potential $3,000,-
000 a year in real-estate taxes. . . . All in all [evidently this
editorial writer's favorite windup before he throws his fast one],
it looks to us as if New York has been better off with the meat-
packing houses now on the world capital site." It would be rude,
and probably useless, to inquire whether the editorials reflected
the News ownership's nostalgic Chicagoan predilection for abat-
toirs or its pique because the United Nations had not located
in the Chicago Board of Trade Building, which was the old
headquarters of the America First Committee.

While Colonel McCormick's and Mrs. Patterson's paper was
being mad because the United Nations had decided to live in
New York, all the newspapers in Philadelphia were being still
madder because that body had decided not to live there. For
months, I have learned from a retrospective perusal of the Philadelphia press, that city had had its cap set for the United Nations
with the single-mindedness of a homely woman who sees a
chance of making a creditable marriage at last. While West-
chester thumbed its nose at the delegates and New York tolerated their tenancy—first of a girls'-college gymnasium and then
of a skating rink—Philadelphia's hopes had risen. The city fathers
had offered to the United Nations, as her dower, twelve hundred
and eighty suburban acres, which, according to la presse indigène,
are a cross between the Vale of Kashmir and an American-born
Irishman's dream of Killarney. She was determined to prove to
the handsome stranger from overseas that understanding and
home cooking are better than a dashing manner.

"CITY FIRST IN LINE FOR HOME OF U.N.," a headline in the
Philadelphia Daily News, a placid tabloid not to be confused
with the New York one, announced on December 7. The story
below it said, "Philadelphia, by the process of elimination,
seemed today to be the logical site for the capital of the world."
But even then there was a certain foreboding, which was implicit

in a sentence on the editorial page of the same issue of the paper: "There is no real reason why the U.N. should not decide to locate in the City of Brotherly Love." This is the sort of reassuring thing a woman says to herself when she has been too often a bridesmaid. On December 9 the *News* ran a New York dispatch under the disquieting headline "FICKLE N.Y. IS BACK IN U.N. HOME SITE FIGHT." On the same day the panicky editorialist headed his contribution "Skulduggery at U.N. Crossroads." I was reminded of the emotional reaction of the wholesome Marjorie Jones in "Penrod" when she saw advancing across the floor at Penrod's birthday party the slim little girl from the East who always got all the boys. "What Goes On?" the heading over the editorial demanded on the next day, and the editorialist cried, "What is going on behind the scenes? . . . Let there be no more manipulation! . . . The man on the street [which street? Chestnut? Walnut? Filbert?] is aroused!" Three days later a United Nations story, by a correspondent named Harry Glover, began with the grim sentence "New York got it and Philadelphia didn't." New York had got it.

The villain of the story, in the opinion of the *News* and all the other Philadelphia papers, was Warren R. Austin, the chief United States delegate to the United Nations. The *News* ran two pictures of Mr. Austin the day before the United Nations finally decided for New York. The caption under the first said, "Appears Unfriendly to Philadelphia," and the second said, "Warren Austin Shies U.N. from Philadelphia." Ivan H. Peterman, of the *Inquirer* staff, called the chief delegate "that magic mandarin of Turtle Bay, the Right Honorable ex-Senator from Vermont, Warren R. (for Railroading) Austin, who can claim distinction for the session's slickest legerdemain. As chairman of the U.S. delegation, Austin got fifty-three visiting nations to accept eight and one-half million Rockefeller dollars as better than Philadelphia's twenty millions, seventeen and one-half dead-end acres rather than the twelve hundred and eighty prescribed in the Permanent Headquarters Committee orders." Peterman is a man given to vigorous expression of his moods. (While he was a correspondent in North Africa he jumped into a ditch so hard that he broke his arm, and that is the way he denounces.) "It is time we learned," he wrote, winding up his account of the

United Nations session at which the decision was ratified, "and got rid of the Austin-type windbags now speaking for the U.S.A."

The angriest writer in the City of Brotherly Love, as far as I could see, was a man named John M. Cummings, who writes a column on the editorial page of the same *Inquirer*, a paper which, I discovered, had absorbed the old *Public Ledger*, which was supposed to have some connection with Benjamin Franklin. Mr. Cummings headed an explosion of his "Hot Spots or Country?—U.N. Should Think Twice." "Austin was up until the unseemly (for a Vermonter) hour, scheming with others (the old smoke-filled-room business) to keep the committee on the site from selecting Philadelphia as the world capital," he wrote. "These delegates were sent to the area of the 'dead-end kids' because the State Department was playing its last card. It was the rolling countryside of Philadelphia, a few miles removed from the center of the city, against the night spots of New York. If the State Department could have its way, the gilded saloons of the metropolis would win over the quiet of Philadelphia's suburban countryside because the spats and the striped pants just doted, don'tcha know, on the glamorous drunks, the hot gossip, the latest stuff from the bedrooms and the men's rooms. . . . Apparently there is something about getting drunk in New York that has it all over getting drunk in Philadelphia. . . . From the start, the lads of the State Department, with head delegate Austin as their spearhead and spokesman, have been fighting the case of New York against the country."

That day's editorial cartoon in the *Inquirer*, by a man named Hutton, showed a forlorn female wearing a slip and sandals and labeled "World Peace" sitting on the stringpiece of a pier, dangling her legs over the water. A coal pile, a gasworks, and the Chrysler Building in the background indicated where the pier was, in case you couldn't read the legend on the stringpiece, which said, "New York's East Side." The female held a brief case marked "U.N." in one hand and was apparently trying to decide whether to throw it into the water or jump in herself. The editorial alongside it said, "Compare . . . the cultural background, the historic traditions, the true American spirit, the quiet friendliness that Philadelphia has to offer the visitors from abroad with the blatant commercialism that pervades New York.

. . . Aside from Philadelphia's wishes in the matter, it should be evident that the United Nations would be making a colossal mistake to submerge itself and its hopes of success in the welter and bedlam of New York's masses."

Melvin K. Whiteleather, another returned war correspondent, wrote, in the *Evening Bulletin:* "Under the whiplash of the United States Government, the U.N. has made its choice of a headquarters. . . . When he [Austin] manipulated the offer of a sewer exit site along New York's East River, he worked like a demon to put it over before anyone could stop to ponder. . . . Gone are the dreams of a sylvan world capital. . . . For sylvan beauty there is to be a hothouse geranium on a thirty-story window sill bravely trying to hold up its head." (Dr. Zuleta Angel, of Colombia, the chairman of the committee that decided on the site, said, "The skyscrapers and chimneys of Manhattan will not hinder our work. . . . On the contrary, they will constantly recall us to reality and life.") The *Bulletin* found consolation in the possibility that New York would have a nasty traffic problem. "Philadelphia would have had a problem in congestion handed it if U.N. had located here," it observed, not without pleasure, "but it would not have been comparable to the one New York has been given."

The *Record*, whose staff has been on strike for two months, was at a disadvantage in the controversy; apparently its first-string denouncers, as well as Jerry Doyle, its editorial cartoonist, were on the picket line with the rest of the boys. It seemingly had no correspondent of its own covering the United Nations meetings in New York, for it was running the New York *Times* stories written by George Barrett, who of course favored the acceptance. It was like the *Daily Princetonian's* having to run the Harvard *Crimson* account of a Princeton-Harvard game. J. David Stern, the *Record's* publisher, did write a first-page editorial in the guise of a telegram to President Truman, under the heading "Why Sabotage Philadelphia?" "Why is America's chief delegate to the United Nations, Warren R. Austin, opposed to Philadelphia as the permanent site of the United Nations Headquarters?" Mr. Stern asked. "It is useless to pretend he is neutral. . . . Mr. President, you ought to have a heart-to-heart talk with Chief Delegate Austin and put him back on the track." But there was no scorch in Mr. Stern's invective. It sounded as if he had his mind on the strike.[1]

The man who got deepest under the skin of the Philadelphia journalists was not, however, Mr. Austin but James Watson Gerard, an old New Yorker who was Woodrow Wilson's Ambassador to Germany. Mr. Gerard, who was born in 1867 and has a long memory, made a speech to some United Nations delegates at an unofficial luncheon given by Thomas B. Watson, of the International Business Machines Company. In it he served up the old wheeze about Philadelphia people walking in their sleep. "Above all, don't go to Philadelphia," the venerable gentleman advised the delegates. "When you're not dreaming your time away in that somnambulant city, you'll spend half your time going back to New York." Somebody should do an exhaustive book on the endemic insult, or wounding local illusion, a form of taunt that evidently retains its sting for centuries. On the coast of Durham there is a town called West Hartlepool, near which, during the Napoleonic wars, a brig was wrecked. The only survivor to make his way ashore was a pet monkey, whom his master had dressed in a military jacket. The local militia, encountering this uniformed invader who couldn't speak English, either shot or hanged him, according to how the story is told, and if you walk in the streets of West Hartlepool today and yell, "Who killed the monkey?" people will come running and throw rocks at you. The sleepwalking gag is apparently Philadelphia's monkey story.

"Until an ignoramus called James W. Gerard poked his snout into the proceedings, the friendly rivalry among American cities for the honor of being known as world capital was carried on without rancor and without resort to the low drivel of the ham actor of another day," the *Inquirer's* Mr. Cummings mildly remonstrated. "No one ever questioned the right of New York to do everything decently within its power to have the permanent headquarters of the United Nations established in or near that city. . . . It was precisely because Philadelphia seemed on

[1]Mr. Stern not long afterward sold the paper to the Bulletin, which suspended its publication. So there is no more Record. Philadelphia, population three million, now has one morning and two evening papers, one of which, the Daily News, is completely overshadowed by its competitor.

the verge of making a sale on the merits of the goods exposed to view that something in the nature of panic seized the burghers of the city on the Hudson. . . . Gerard's contribution to the intercity competition . . . was . . . a silly, stupid, nonsensical warning to shun Philadelphia. . . . Neither Ed Hopkinson nor any other member of the Philadelphia committee urged the delegates to shun New York because the subways stink or because, among the natives, the height of ambition is to have a keyholer like Winchell report that, helplessly drunk, you were rolled by a blonde in the Boob Room. [Winchell's Philadelphia outlet is the *Inquirer* itself.] Rudeness, crudeness (one delegate was shot in a delicatessen), insolence, and highway robbery in the form of excessive prices, these were the hallmarks of hospitality in New York and vicinity. The thing to do was to revive the trick of the old-fashioned traveling salesman—run down the goods of your competitor. And use the bottom-of-the-bag joke of the ham actor—'Spent two weeks in Philadelphia last Sunday.' "

A slightly thicker-skinned columnist named Paul Jones, of the *Bulletin*, wrote, "We don't deny it's a durable joke, but we believe everybody's had enough wear out of it to justify throwing it away or giving it to the radio comedians in fee simple. Still, let us be honest and aboveboard about this thing. New York has certain attractions which Philadelphia cannot match. . . . Take Forty-second Street, famous in song and story. What have you got? A row of burlesque palaces [Mr. Jones evidently has not been here since the O'Brien administration], grind houses, inferior gin mills, and sucker traps, most of which would be run out of any small town by even a moderately honest chief of police. It gives you pause to reflect that the most elevated and ethical form of entertainment to be found in the vicinity of Times Square is a flea museum. . . . Gentlemen of the U.N., let us face the facts. We can offer you no flea museum. . . . Apart from a small tract on the east side of Fifth, and two sections of the Avenue itself, one uptown and one downtown, as well as part of Greenwich Village, New York is strictly a low-budget B production."

Then Mr. Jones displayed that unwilling objectivity which marks the Philadelphian as an American of a distinct species, doomed to failure because he is capable of self-appraisal. "The question may arise," he wrote, "if New York is a B production outside its glittering center, what is Philadelphia? The answer is easy. It is nothing . . . nothing but a collection of houses in which people live and mind their own business." That is the kind of honesty that would cost a columnist his job in Chicago or Los Angeles or Santa Barbara or Des Moines. It made me sorry that poor old Philadelphia had to be left waiting at the church again. I'd rather it had been one of those other places.

[This is more of a mixed-pickles story than most; a review of several newspaper frailties instead of an essay on one.]

Mr. Capone and Other Primates

If Al Capone had died fifteen years ago, the event would have rated more space than a World Series, and I suppose it is a sign of having reached my particular age that I was astonished at the restraint with which most papers handled the news of his death in Miami Beach, of the long haul home to Chicago, and, at last, ten days later, of his burial. Now that the final returns are apparently all in and the feature writers have had the opportunity to recapitulate, I find that I have before me only a handful of snippings which twenty years ago would hardly have done justice to the passing of an understudy of a member of Capone's bodyguard. At no point, from Miami to the grave, did Capone make the first page of the *Times*, and the *Herald Tribune* wrote him off with brisk detachment, as if he had been a former United States senator from Kansas. The *Mirror* gave him a modest obituary, beginning, "Al Capone's death last night wrote 'finis' to a career which rocketed through the beery and boozy 'twenties' with the flash and fury of a machine-gun barrage . . ." The piece ran less than a column. The *News* handled him even more soberly, although at slightly more length. No doubt his send-off wasn't helped any by the fact that he died on a Saturday evening. The afternoon papers didn't get a crack at the story until Monday, and by that time it was thirty-six hours old.

The *comptes rendus* in the Chicago newspapers betrayed embarrassment, as if the town had a new public-relations policy and wanted to forget the crudities of the Coolidge-Hoover years. The Chicago *Sunday Tribune* managed its whole Capone obit without once mentioning Jake Lingle, the *Tribune* police reporter whose erasure in 1930 by Capone's business associates brought to light the information that Lingle had accepted sixty thousand dollars in bribes from the underworld. "In the days of his [Capone's] power there were fantastic tales about him," the *Tribune* memorialist wrote, far away in both time and space. "Dozens of murders were attributed to him and his gang: murders for which no one was ever tried. There were many accusations, most of which no one troubled to deny, that he and his cohorts practiced bribery of public officials and policemen on a large scale."

The only paper I have seen that gave the invalid thug's decease the kind of treatment I had always assumed it would receive was the *Journal-American*. While the hearse from Miami was trundling North, the *Journal* ran a series of six articles called "The Life Story of Al Capone," written by Leon Racht, a reporter who had just finished a crusade against dirty books. (You get to do everything on a Hearst paper.) Mr. Racht's opening story appeared on the first page of the *Journal* below a wirephoto from Miami Beach showing four men and three trees standing in front of Capone's house, and was preceded by the italicized announcement " 'Scarface Al' Capone is dead and with him one of the most amazing eras in American criminal history. This is the first article in the life story of the master racketeer whose army of gunmen and their bullets wrote such a bloody chronicle that the world stood shocked and his name became a by-word for infamy." The use of the word "army" made me wonder. Did it mean as big as the First Army, the Third Army, or the Salvation Army? But it also reassured me, for the first Capone obits had made me fear that hyperbole was now confined to the sports pages and that I would never again see the kind of souped-up crime writing that helped gin make the twenties memorable.

"The incredible era that was Al Capone's was at once the reign of the bloodiest arch-criminal in the hierarchy of American crime and society's most shameful blot," Mr. Racht began, underneath the italics. Stepping up the era so swiftly from "amazing" to "incredible" left the biographer, I noticed with some apprehension, no topping adjective in his kit but "impossible." The first installment of Mr. Racht's effort at historical reconstruction

They marched the offender, now struggling, across the room, lifted him to the sill and dropped him out. . . ."

Mr. Racht's final installment wound up with a statement that his whole amazingly incredible, and slightly slobbering, series had been presented as a tract to keep people from getting the idea that Capone was "a legendary Robin Hood, an Horatio Alger hero in reverse." It rather took the fun out of the baseball-bat scene for me. Back in 1929, fellows used to write Racht's kind of stuff without rationalizing.

In contrast to the *Journal-American's* clean-books crusader, Robert J. Casey, who did a series of three pieces on Capone for the Chicago *Herald-American*, the Hearst afternoon paper out there, seemed tired. "It is difficult to realize," Casey wrote, "that most of the thousands of folks who in one way or another had truck with Al Capone are now dead as he is, not a few of them respectable consumers of his dubious hootch who now lie under conventional slabs—a smaller percentage of his aides and associates who died suitably in gutters to replenish the police records of a harried Chicago. . . . Essentially he was a large, unpleasant stupe who, by a suspension of the law of averages and an acquaintance with the more helpful sort of politicians, achieved wealth, international publicity, and, at the end of his fruitful life, a three-column obituary. . . . In addition to that his hootch —and you may take that on the testimony of experts who sacrificed good stomachs in the research—was pretty bad."

Casey, I am told, was brought out of retirement from writing about the underworld to compose his unenthusiastic valedictory because his byline was once closely associated with the subject. He was one of Chicago's best crime reporters back in the days when the Republican machine ran the city through vicars like Capone, but he has covered a lot of more serious stories since the end of that crass time and he evidently couldn't recapture the mood.

A Chicago *Daily News* columnist named Edwin A. Lahey contributed the only thoughtful observation on Capone I happened to see. (Most of the commentators contented themselves with platitudes about "the end of an era.") Lahey observed that, while Capone had been a creation of the Republican machine of Cook County all right, "a political organization doesn't last long without support of the voters, and we were a pretty cynical lot of people back in the 1920s. Everyone had a share of the blame for Capone."

My daily inspection of the papers leads me to believe that we still have a few oily remnants of cynicism lying around, as when I come across an item to the effect that Senator McKellar has dug up a witness to testify before a congressional committee that certain T.V.A. employees were obviously Communists because they were seen reading a review of "The Grapes of Wrath." ("A red," the fruitgrower says in a memorable passage of "The Grapes," "is any son-of-a-bitch that wants thirty cents an hour when we're paying twenty-five.")[2] Nor am I reassured when the *Mirror* runs a cartoon like the one it ran not long ago, in which all people opposed to the adoption of the ten-cent fare were labeled Reds. (The Steinbeck quotation also has its application here.) Then, too, I begin to suspect, as I flounder through a bale of clippings forwarded to me by a Los Angeles student of the so-called Black Dahlia murder, that West Coast editors have not been entirely aboveboard in the way they have peddled this dubious case to their readers. The victim of the crime, as even most readers of Eastern papers know by now, was a young woman neither black nor flowerlike. She left a notebook containing the names and addresses of seventy-five men with whom she was acquainted, and I gather that the California journalists considered it essential to interview every one of them. During the early stages of the investigation, which, as I write, is still rolling on, "revelations" were promised of a "lewd photograph ring," the police were called upon to list all "sex perverts" in California, and at least five zanies, none of whom could possibly have killed the lady, confessed doing so and their babblings were conscientiously printed—and so on, a new titillation in every edition. The tide of nonsense about the case has only lapped at our East Coast tabloids, but it has at least given us a new adjective to describe a particular kind of crime—"dahlia-like." This was the contribution of a writer on the *News* and, judging by the story

[2] *This sentence of Steinbeck's is the Rosetta stone of American newspaper language. By its use the reader may quickly arrive at the true sense of any story about labor.*

it was used in, it refers to a murder committed by a man who writes on his victim's torso with a lipstick.

It is only when I come upon a story such as the one I found in the *Times*, *Herald Tribune*, and *PM* a couple of weeks ago that I regain my faith in the high destiny of American journalism. Man's heart, it appears, still beats warm for his animal brethren, and a city editor still responds infallibly to the stimulus of a report (or perhaps of a tip from a press agent for the A.S.P.C.A.) that an escaped monkey is at large in the metropolis. And such reports still come to city editors on cold mornings when it's not a fit day out for man nor monkey. To cover this particular story, reporters from the three papers mentioned, and perhaps from others which I have not seen, were dispatched to the Bush Terminal piers in Brooklyn, where they had been told an escaped monkey was hiding out. Each took a look. Each wrote a piece. The *Times* man said the monkey's name was The Mugg. *PM*'s reporter said it was Oscar. The *Herald Tribune* man contented himself with referring to the beast as the No. 1 monkey. (There were originally three monkeys at large, but Nos. 2 and 3, to use the *Tribune*'s system of nomenclature, had been recaptured and had since died.)

"The Mugg detests Mankind," the *Times* man began, telling, much in the manner of the *Journal-American*'s Mr. Racht, what was in the mind of an individual he had had no opportunity to talk to. "Yesterday he brooded in the enshadowed girders under the roof of Pier 5 on the Bush Docks in Brooklyn. He shivered in the winter blast and his protruding eyes glittered with loathing for the longshore crews and other men who labored on the windswept concrete, fifty feet below. Since The Mugg and his childhood jungle chum, The Migg, escaped from their monkey cages on the pier last April while in transit from India's warm Deccan plains to the Trefflich Bird & Animal Company at 215 Fulton St., Men [capitalization by the *Times* reporter] have bedevilled and made mock of them. Worst of all, they were the death of The Migg and of Juliet, a sister rhesus from the Deccan."

The *Times* man did not say who told him the name of the monkey he was after or of the two deceased monkeys, nor did he explain how he knew that they had been acquainted in a jungle, or, as he suggests in the same sentence, on some plains. Such oversights, however, are permissible in the newspaper business when an author is giving a story what is known as the light touch; they are the feature writer's prerogative. "On Dec. 6," the *Times* reporter continued, "Juliet developed a hacking cough. The Men seized her and three days later she died in the ASPCA shelter on Avenue A, a pneumonia victim. The Mugg and The Migg wept in the girders." The story didn't tell how The Mugg and The Migg, five miles away at least from the A.S.P.C.A. shelter, learned that the female monkey had died, and I was further confused when a zoologist of my acquaintance informed me that monkeys don't weep in sorrow. "Now," the *Times* reporter went on, "The Mugg is alone, and his hate and his brooding are magnificent, and The Men stare up at him and wait. . . . But The Mugg is valiant, and huddled in the girder shadows, he defies them and dreams warm dreams of the Deccan's lush greenness, and of The Migg—and of poor little Juliet." A reporter who can tell what a monkey is dreaming about by looking at him has a future as a Washington correspondent.

Arnold Blom, the *PM* man, found that Oscar (or The Mugg) was not a gloomy character but "a smartie-pants." He also wrote that Oscar's playmate (the *Times* man's The Migg, the *Trib* man's No. 2 monkey) was "a dimwit," and thereafter he referred to him as Dimwit. He gave the female monkey no name at all— probably an example of male chauvinism—and he made no attempt to explore the monkey dream world. "Only Oscar, the intellectual, is left," Mr. Blom wrote, possibly in an effort to point up the superior viability of the *PM*-type reader. Oscar and The Mugg do not come through in the *Times* and *PM* stories as the same individual. The two accounts differ like interpretations by Arthur Krock and Max Lerner of the same European statesman.

The *Tribune* man opened his story with the declaration "Once there were three wise monkeys loose on the Bush Terminal Docks in Brooklyn," and I feared for a moment that he was going to call them See-No-Evil, Hear-No-Evil, and Speak-No-Evil, but he didn't. He kept them on an animal level throughout and didn't repeat any of their conversation. That is the trouble with a monkey story: either you fake it and it is a fake or you don't and it is dull. Maybe it is dull anyway.

Post Scriptum: A few days after the Bush Terminal excitement, the *Herald Tribune* printed a monkey story from Japan under this heading:

10 HUNGRY MONKEYS KEEP
TOKYO SUBURB ON GUARD

The story said that the ten monkeys had been "living well" for years off handouts from the villagers of Okutama but that now, because of hard times, the villagers had no food to give and the monkeys were "pretty angry about it," so they stole food. (Two problematical factors would seem to be involved here: a Japanese monkey's standard of living, and whether stealing food is an index of anger or of appetite.) "Monkeys are not indigenous to Japan," the story ended, "and no one knows where these came from." Trefflich's, most likely.

[*The begetter of this one was
a particularly trumpery bit of Krockery on
the Times editorial page.*]

Back to Before Van Buren

My usual preoccupation with the news columns of our daily newspapers does not preclude an occasional dash into the editorial pages for a quick shot of heavy thought, which I gulp on my way from the book reviews to the horse-race charts. A nip of Old Heptisax or Old Arthur Krock customarily sets me up in much the same way as a peg of bourbon, giving me a comfortable, although perhaps unfounded, feeling of lucid omniscience. A few recent swigs, however, have forced me to the reluctant conclusion that somebody has been tampering with the bottle.

Mr. Krock, for example, wrote a column in the *Times* not long ago deploring the fact that there are 2,300,000 Civil Service employees on the federal pay roll—the result, he said, of "a social economy, paternally formed by government, that reached its high point under the New Deal." Their number, he mourned, could not be materially reduced because Civil Service legislation limits their working hours to forty a week. "Since the average cost of these civil servants is about $2,800 a year," Mr. Krock wrote, "the proposed elimination of 800,000 [he did not say by whom it was proposed] would save $2,240,800,000 annually. But this pertinent question is raised . . . 'Will Congress amend or repeal the laws governing wages and working conditions which would permit the government to get enough more time and work out of the remaining employes to do the job required?'" Indignant at the baseness of the 1,500,000 employees who might decline, unless encouraged by special legislation, to do the work of 2,300,000, I got out my pencil to estimate at how small a sacrifice to themselves these loafers could save the Republic that

$2,240,800,000 annually. I found that they could do it easily if they would all work sixty-one hours and eighteen minutes a week. That old radical, President Martin Van Buren, set a sixty-hour week for federal employees shortly before the country repudiated him, in the election of 1840. I am glad that Mr. Krock has got around to urging that the mandate of the electorate be carried out.

Mr. Krock's piece appeared at about the same time as an editorial in the *World-Telegram* (it looked to me like one of the Scripps-Howard national handouts, written in Washington and forwarded to all the trading posts) in which Philip Murray, of the C.I.O., who had said that corporations were making a lot of money, was demolished with this statement: "The national income in 1946 was 164 billion dollars. . . . The corporations got 12 billion dollars, or less than one-thirteenth, in net profits after tax payments." These figures are substantially correct, except that at least nine-tenths of those billions were income *before* tax payments, and corporation profits before tax payments were twenty-six billions, which is nearer one-seventh than one-thirteenth.

A few days later the wave of arithmetical nebulosity overwhelmed Heptisax—the editorial-page nom de plume that cloaks the *Herald Tribune's* Rodney Gilbert in anonymity—catching up with him in the midst of a keen over the corpse of economic liberty in New York City. "Dark as the national picture is, Union Square still has its Gotham under control," wrote Mr. Gilbert, who lives in New Jersey. "It still has both public opinion and politics solidly behind its five-cent fare. It still has that capitalistic vampire, the landlord, where he belongs. Even if he happens to be a widow with five kids, living in the cellar and dining on oatmeal, so that the tenants above can live in statutory comfort at Federally dictated bargain rentals. . . ." I wondered briefly how long it would take a parade of all New York City's cellar-dwelling widow-landlords with five oatmeal-fed children to pass a given point, but what really struck me was Mr. Gilbert's apparent willingness to have the sugar scraped off the tots' cereal. The retention of the five-cent fare, entailing a rise of more than twenty points in the real-estate tax rate—or so some experts claim—would mean a cost of twenty dollars annually to the owner of a house assessed at ten thousand dollars. (I assume that Mr. Gilbert didn't mean that five-bairned landlords snuffle oatmeal in the basements of buildings like River House.) If the children have to take the subway to high school, their transportation costs their widowed mother fifty cents a day; a rise in subway fare would make it a dollar, a difference of a hundred dollars for a school year of two hundred days. If they also use the subway week ends or evenings, and if the widow herself travels occasionally, the ten-cent fare might cost the family as much as two hundred dollars a year—a net loss of $180.

I cite these two examples not because they are important in themselves but because they reflect the late Arthur Brisbane's sublime, half-educated confidence that his readers were totally ignorant—a point of view which was the great man's chief legacy to American journalism. While it is to be expected in the Hearst papers, where it originated, its intrusion into the supposedly more respectable realms of journalism is a kind of tip-off to what I sadly suspect is the editorial fashion of the day—to treat the customer as a chump.

If my suspicion is correct, one of the least fashionable journalists of the time is Virgil Thomson, the accomplished music critic of the *Herald Tribune*, who also happens to be a good reporter. Working in a field in which the average practitioner considers it quite in order to make a dogmatic statement out of what can only be a subjective impression, Thomson sometimes exposes cause and effect in music as reasonably as Thucydides wrote on war or Pierce Egan on the London prize ring. Thomson's piece about a violinist named Tossy Spivakovsky has stayed in my mind for a considerable time as an excellent example of the right way to report a story. Spivakovsky takes an unorthodox grip on the bow "by bending his thumb clean round the nut and flexing the other fingers over it at the outer joints," Thomson wrote. "In this position he has the full weight of his forearm available for bow pressure. . . . Hence the nobility. . . . Hence also the unusual force. . . . This strong but insensitive bow position, which lacks the cushion usually provided by a relaxed first finger, deprives him of two major expressive devices, the long light bow, and the short light, or bouncing, bow. He is obliged, in legato playing, to alleviate the bad acoustical effects of excessive arm

weight by drawing his bow too fast across the strings." This exposition enables the non-fiddling member of the audience to
understand why Spivakovsky sounds as he does. It is the simple
and decisive detail, clearly stated, that tells the story—the story
of a concert, or any story. Of course nobody can bring it off
every time. "Drawing moonbeams and magic from a wooden
box"—I quote from one of Mr. Thomson's colleagues, writing
about Elman—is a good example of my idea of how not to do it.
It reminds me of "Patton's tanks went crashing and dashing
along."

Two recent stories about musicians had sufficient news interest to get on the front pages, but each had to wait for Mr.
Thomson, in his Sunday column, to write it really well. One was
the resignation of Artur Rodzinski as conductor of the Philhar-
monic-Symphony because, he said, of interference with his direction by Arthur Judson, who is the orchestra's manager and head
of Columbia Concerts, Inc., a musical-talent agency. The members of the orchestra's board of directors were reported to have
implied, among other things, that Mr. Rodzinski had resigned
because he had found a better job in Chicago. "The contention
that he resigned merely because a better job was offered him is
not credible, because there is no better job," Mr. Thomson
wrote, with a reasonableness impossible to refute. "Arthur Judson is unsuited by the nature and magnitude of his business interests to manage with the necessary self-effacement a major
intellectual institution doing business with his other interests."
This is as clear as a statement that the manager of a large number of prizefighters would be unsuited for the post of match-
maker at Madison Square Garden, where he might employ too
many of his own clients. (As a matter of fact, the sports writers
occasionally do give the impression that there is a certain analogy
there.)

Serge Koussevitzky, the conductor of the Boston Symphony,
supplied the *Herald Tribune* critic with his second opportunity
to cut patterns for the boys on the outside pages. Koussevitzky
asked for a court injunction to prevent a man named Moses
Smith from publishing his biography of the conductor. "Mr.
Koussevitzky is not the only first-class conductor in the world,
though he is one of the best," Mr. Thomson wrote. "Only he

himself, apparently, hasting fearfully toward Parnassus, though his throne there has long been reserved, and involved, no doubt, in a publicity apotheosis that has already begun, would see any value in posing before an already worshiping universe without the customary habiliment of one human weakness." Koussevitzky's lawsuit, Mr. Thomson went on, added just that element to the picture of himself that the composer wanted to create.

Perhaps nothing in connection with newspapers has saddened me more lately than the fact that Rube Goldberg, the *Sun's* editorial cartoonist, was away on vacation when the Supreme Court upheld the contempt-of-court judgment against John L. Lewis and the United Mine Workers. During Mr. Goldberg's absence the *Sun* substituted a series of photographs of "The Powers in the Present Congress," which were not entirely lacking in graphic humor but weren't as good as Rube would have been. Talburt, the cartoonist in the *World-Telegram*, drew a picture of Mr. Lewis, dressed in a royal robe and labeled "Old King Coal," being hit on the head with a large gavel labeled "Supreme Court Decision." Batchelor, in the *News*, came up with just a head of Mr. Lewis wearing a crown labeled "King Coal" (the boys had ample stocks of that pun lying around) and a plaster across the bridge of his nose. The plaster was labeled "$10,000 Fine," and at the bottom of the drawing was a scroll with the legend "Supreme Court Plaster" (none of the others seemed to have that one in his kitbox). Packer, in the *Mirror*, drew a picture of two ambulance attendants carrying Lewis, portrayed as a fat boy wearing a football suit, off a gridiron on a stretcher. Lewis was saying, "What's the score?" and one of the attendants was answering, "7 to 2," which *Mirror* readers may or may not have considered self-explanatory. Burris Jenkins, Jr.'s, cartoon in the *Journal-American* used up the most black ink, as usual. He showed Uncle Sam spanking a little boy whose backside was marked "John L. Lewis" while a crowd of other brats, carrying a sign reading "Reckless Labor Leadership," looked on. Dollar signs were flying from the seat of Lewis's pants, suggesting how painful the spanking was, and around Lewis's head were exclamation points, making it clear that he had been taken by surprise. Looking at Jenkins' drawing, I felt pretty good about the advance of the newspaper cartoon since Daumier's time.

The three winning news photographs in the eighth annual contest conducted by *Editor & Publisher*, the newspaper trade magazine, showed (1) a woman plunging to her death in the Winecoff Hotel fire in Atlanta. (2) A shot of a striker being clubbed. (3) A man sliding from a ledge of the Empire State Building to commit suicide.

To complete this nosegay of exhibits bearing on the development of American journalism, I should like to submit a few examples of McCormickiana, forwarded to me by a volunteer *Tribune* watcher in Chicago. One is a cover of "Books," the Chicago *Tribune's* Sunday literary supplement, on which are printed a number of small color reproductions of paintings by an illustrator named Sessions. The subjects of the paintings are identified as "(from top right, reading counterclockwise,) Socrates, Demosthenes, Roger Bacon, Dante, Joan of Arc, Columbus, Mary Queen of Scots, Sir Walter Raleigh, Galileo, John Bunyan, Algernon Sidney, Warren Hastings, La Fayette, Madame Roland, and Capt. Alfred Dreyfus." At the end of this stellar, counter-clockwise gallery are two additional, somewhat larger paintings—one of Rear Admiral Husband E. Kimmel and the other of Lieutenant General Walter C. Short. Of these, the *Tribune*, in a big block of type cut into its artistic tableau, says: "The scapegoat is a more constantly recurring character in history than the hero. To the long list of those who have won this unenviable fame, the names of Adm. Kimmel and Gen. Short must now be added. They were the commanders upon whom blame was fixed for the Pearl Harbor disaster."

Next I present a news story from the *Tribune* of February 27, headed "Balloons Carry Tribune History Toward S. Pole." It bears the date line "Aboard Navy Icebreaker Burton Island, Feb. 26," and begins, "Somewhere over the Antarctic continent two helium filled balloons carrying a printed chronology describing the highlights in the history of THE CHICAGO TRIBUNE during the last 100 years were floating toward the south pole tonight. . . . In addition to THE TRIBUNE history, the weather balloons had tied to them a copy of the New York Daily News dated last Dec. 18. They also carried a credo bearing the signature of Col.

Robert R. McCormick, editor and publisher of The Tribune, stating that the function of a modern newspaper, among other issues, includes furnishing 'that check upon the government which no constitution has ever been able to provide.' . . . Navy Capt. George Kosko, aerological officer and chief of the polar expedition's science section, said the balloons carrying The Tribune souvenirs today conceivably might be caught in counter-clockwise currents above the continent and then blown over the pole into Africa. . . . Kosko explained that the balloons should stay up from four days to a week. During that time, he esti-mated, they could cover thousands of miles."

My third, and last, example is taken from a radio address de-livered by Colonel McCormick himself and published in full, naturally, in the *Tribune*. "If New York were destroyed," he said, "with it would be destroyed all the subversive elements in our country."

Three of my Chicago correspondents sent me clippings of a piece that Colonel McCormick himself wrote about New York in May.

The headline says:

COL. M'CORMICK
FINDS NEW YORK
MEDIOCRE CITY

SNOBS ON PARK AV., WITH
POOR IN SLUMS

Then the colonel gives New York the Philadelphia treatment, hauling out what the fellow on the *Inquirer* called a moth-eaten gag.

"A week in New York is a long time," he writes, "but it gave me some very distinct impressions."

The head and the lead are the funniest parts, but the last para-graph isn't bad.

"They [the New York airports] also are obstructed by New York smoke and frequently by ocean fogs. Not long ago, an Atlantic transport had to come all the way to Chicago to find landing weather."

What Are Chances?

What Are Chances?

The nearest I've come to summarizing what I think about the present plight of American newspapers is published in the March number of the *Alumni Magazine* of Dartmouth College. The *Magazine*, during several issues, conducted a symposium, limited to alumni, on Public Opinion in Democracy. The March number contained three articles on newspapers: one by me; one by my classmate at both Dartmouth and Columbia, Claude Jagger, '24, then an Associated Press big shot and associate director of the American Press Institute at Columbia, now a publicity man in Hawaii; and one by Carl D. Groat, '11, editor of the Cincinnati *Post*. Jagger and Groat, who were wrong, took a favorable view of newspapers.

In my piece, which will follow shortly, I concentrated on what I conceive to be the essential point: the diminishing number of newspapers and their concentration in the hands of a group of wealthy individuals who share the same point of view. Other problems, in my opinion, are subordinate. Professional standards will develop when newspapering is made a profession instead of a form of employment. Meanwhile states might set up Newspaper Commissions, like Racing Commissions, which would set down writers for lying and rule off habitual offenders.

Nearly all large publishers of the present generation, the only free and responsible practitioners of journalism, inherited their newspapers. Try to imagine the future of medicine, law, or pedagogy if their absolute control were vested in the legal heirs of men who had bought practices in 1890—even when the heirs lacked any special training. A group of eminences in any intellectual calling, writing, medicine, the church, or even the

highest levels of the Army, might be expected to have a higher
average intelligence quotient than the same number of men
picked at random in the subway. But there would be no
reason to expect such a result from testing a collection of publishers. They have had to display no intelligence in order to
arrive. I was mildly amused, when Ogden Reid died a short
while back, to read the obit in the *Times*, more fulsome than
the one in Reid's own *Herald Tribune*, which was a glorification
of the right of succession. The Reids, the *Times* man said, had
had a chance to sell their *Tribune* to Frank Munsey when the
latter had the *Herald*. But, having a sense of their hereditary
responsibility, they had bought the *Herald* from the self-made
Munsey instead. It was a departure from the line that the *Times*
had plugged during the lifetime of the self-made Adolph Ochs,
who left the paper to his heirs. The present generation of publishers has muted the rags-to-riches theme, like the present generation of Rockefellers.

The remedial measures I suggest in my *Alumni Magazine* piece
have been knocked out of time in advance by one of the provi-
sions of the Taft-Hartley Act. This confirms me in the idea that
they had great merit and that a large number of other people
had been thinking about them. Nothing is more feared by the
true sponsors of that Act than the development of a strong, truly
free press. The Act, however, precludes the growth of a strong
labor press, or of an endowed press indifferent to the profit
motive. That is one of the reasons the Act will be repealed. The
electorate puts a crowd of monkeys in to provide cheap pork
chops, and they strangle freedom of the press.

A Free Press?

I think almost everybody will grant that if candidates for the United States Senate were required to possess ten million dollars, and for the House one million, the year-in-year-out level of conservatism of those two bodies might be expected to rise sharply. We could still be said to have a freely elected Congress: anybody with ten million dollars (or one, if he tailored his ambition to fit his means) would be free to try to get himself nominated, and the rest of us would be free to vote for our favorite millionaires or even to abstain from voting. (This last right would mark our continued superiority over states where people are compelled to vote for the government slate.)

In the same sense, we have a free press today. (I am thinking of big-city and middling-city publishers as members of an upper and lower house of American opinion.) Anybody in the ten-million-dollar category is free to try to buy or found a paper in a great city like New York or Chicago, and anybody with around a million (plus a lot of sporting blood) is free to try it in a place of mediocre size like Worcester, Mass. As to us, we are free to buy a paper or not, as we wish.[1]

---

[1] "A Free and Responsible Press" says, "Although there is no such thing as a going price for a great city newspaper, it is safe to assume that it would cost somewhere between five and ten million dollars to build a new metropolitan daily to success. The investment required for a new newspaper in a medium-sized city is estimated at three-quarters of a million to several million."

Earl L. Vance, in an article in the Virginia Quarterly Review (summer 1945) cited in "Survival of a Free, Competitive Press," a publication of the Senate Committee on Small Businesses, says, "Even small-newspaper publishing is big business. Time magazine recently reported sale of the Massillon,

In a highly interesting book, "The First Freedom," Morris Ernst has told the story of the increasing concentration of news outlets in the hands of a few people. There are less newspapers today than in 1909, and less owners in relation to the total number of papers. In 1909 there were 2,600; today 1,750. Ernst refrains from any reflection on the quality of the ownership; he says merely that it is dangerous that so much power should be held by so few individuals. I will go one timid step further than Ernst and suggest that these individuals, because of their economic position, form an atypical group and share an atypical outlook.

The newspaper owner is a rather large employer of labor. I don't want to bore you with statistics, but one figure that I remember unhappily is 2,867, the number of us who lost jobs when the Pulitzers sold the World for salvage in 1931. He is nowadays forced to deal with unions in all departments of his enterprise, and is as unlikely as any other employer to be on their side. As owner of a large and profitable business, he is opposed to government intervention in his affairs beyond the maintenance of the subsidy extended to all newspapers through second-class-mail rates. As an owner of valuable real estate, he is more interested in keeping the tax rate down than in any other local issue. (Newspaper crusades for municipal "reform" are almost invariably tax-paring expeditions.) A planned economy is abhorrent to him, and since every other nation in the world above the rank of Transjordania has now gone in for some form of economic planning, the publisher has become our number-one xenophobe. His "preference" for Socialist Britain over Communist Russia is only an inverse expression of relative dislike. It is based on the hope that continued financial intervention in

Ohio, Independent (circulation 11,858) for 'around $400,000,' the Spartanburg, S.C., Herald (17,351) and Journal (8678) for $750,000—all smaller dailies. In contrast, William Allen White paid only $3,000 for the Emporia Gazette in 1892. A metropolitan daily now represents an investment of many millions. Scripps-Howard in 1923 paid $6,000,000 for the same newspaper that had been offered in 1892 for $51,000; the Philadelphia Inquirer sold for $18,000,000 in 1930; the Kansas City Star for $11,000,000 in 1926."

I hadn't seen either of these publications before I wrote my Alumni Magazine article; I cite them here to show I wasn't dreaming my figures.

Britain may prove more effectual than the 1919 military intervention in Russia. Because of publishers' wealth, they do not have to be slugged over the head by "anti-democratic organizations" to force them into using their properties to form public opinion the N.A.M. approves. The gesture would be as redundant as twisting a nymphomaniac's arm to get her into bed.[2] I am delighted that I do not have to insinuate that they consciously allow their output to be shaped by their personal interests. Psychoanalytical after-dinner talk has furnished us with a lovely word for what they do: they rationalize. And once a man has convinced himself that what is good for him is good for the herd of his inferiors, he enjoys the best of two worlds simultaneously, and can shake hands with Bertie McCormick, the owner of the Chicago *Tribune*.

The profit system, while it insures the predominant conservative coloration of our press, also guarantees that there will always be a certain amount of dissidence. The American press has never been monolithic, like that of an authoritarian state. One reason is that there is always important money to be made in journalism by standing up for the underdog (demagogically or honestly, so long as the technique is good). The underdog is numerous and prolific—another name for him is circulation. His wife buys girdles and baking powder and Literary Guild selec-

[2] "A Free and Responsible Press," that result of the collaboration of thirteen bigwigs, which I again cite lest you think I am flippant, says:

"The agencies of mass communication are big business, and their owners are big businessmen. . . . The press is a large employer of labor. . . . The newspapers alone have more than 150,000 employes. The press is connected with other big businesses through the advertising of these businesses, upon which it depends for the major part of its revenue. The owners of the press, like the owners of other big businesses, are bank directors, bank borrowers, and heavy taxpayers in the upper brackets.

"As William Allen White put it: 'Too often the publisher of an American newspaper has made his money in some other calling than journalism. He is a rich man seeking power and prestige. . . . And they all get the unconscious arrogance of conscious wealth.'

"Another highly respected editor, Erwin D. Canham of the Christian Science Monitor, thinks upper-bracket ownership and its big-business character important enough to stand at the head of his list of the 'shortcomings of today's American newspapers.' "

"A Free and Responsible Press" was published after the appearance of my article.

tions, and the advertiser has to reach her. Newspapers as they
become successful and move to the right leave room for new-
comers to the left. Marshall Field's Chicago *Sun*, for example,
has acquired 400,000 readers in five years, simply because the
Tribune, formerly alone in the Chicago morning field, had gone
so far to the right. The fact that the *Tribune's* circulation has
not been much affected indicates that the 400,000 had previous
to 1941 been availing themselves of their freedom not to buy a
newspaper. (Field himself illustrates another, less dependable,
but nevertheless appreciable, favorable factor in the history of
the American press—the occasional occurrence of that economic
sport, the maverick millionaire.) E. W. Scripps was the outstanding practitioner of the trade of founding newspapers to
stand up for the common man. He made a tremendous success
of it, owning about twenty of them when he died. The first
James Gordon Bennett's *Herald* and Joseph Pulitzer's *World*, in
the eighties and nineties, to say nothing of the Scripps-Howard
World-Telegram in 1927, won their niche in New York as left-
of-centre newspapers and then bogged down in profits.

Another factor favorable to freedom of the press, in a minor
way, is the circumstance that publishers sometimes allow a certain latitude to employees in departments in which they have no
direct interest—movies, for instance, if the publisher is not keeping a movie actress, or horse shows, if his wife does not own a
horse. Musical and theatrical criticism is less rigorously con-
trolled than it is in Russia.

The process by which the American press is pretty steadily
revivified, and as steadily dies (newspapers are like cells in the
body, some dying as others develop), was well described in 1911
by a young man named Joseph Medill Patterson, then an officer
of the Chicago *Tribune*, who was destined himself to found an
enormously successful paper, the *Daily News* of New York, and
then within his own lifetime pilot it over the course he had fore-
shadowed. The quotation is from a play, "The Fourth Estate,"
which Patterson wrote in his young discontent.

"Newspapers start when their owners are poor, and take the
part of the people, and so they build up a large circulation, and,
as a result, advertising. That makes them rich, and they begin,

most naturally, to associate with other rich men—they play golf with one, and drink whisky with another, and their son marries the daughter of a third. They forget all about the people, and then their circulation dries up, then their advertising, and then their paper becomes decadent."

Patterson was not "poor" when he came to New York eight years later to start the *News;* he had the McCormick-Patterson *Tribune* fortune behind him, and at his side Max Annenberg, a high-priced journalistic condottiere who had already helped the *Tribune* win a pitched battle with Hearst in its own territory. But he was starting his paper from scratch, and he did it in the old dependable way, by taking up for the Common Man—and sticking with him until 1940, by which time the successful-man contagion got him and he threw his arms around unregenerated Cousin Bertie's neck. The *Tribune* in Chicago and the *News* in New York have formed a solid front ever since. Patterson was uninfluenced by golf, whisky, or social ambitions (he was a parsimonious, unsociable man who cherished an illusion that he had already hit the social peak). I think it is rather the complex of age, great wealth, a swelled head, and the necessity to believe in the Heaven-decreed righteousness of a system which has permitted one to possess such power that turns a publisher's head. The whisky, weddings, yachts, horse shows, and the rest (golf no longer sounds so imposing as it did in 1911) are symptoms rather than causes.

Unfortunately, circulations do not "dry up" quickly, nor advertising fall away overnight. Reading a newspaper is a habit which holds on for a considerable time. So the erstwhile for-the-people newspaper continues to make money for a while after it changes its course. With the New York *Herald* this phase lasted half a century. It would, moreover, be difficult to fix the exact hour or day at which the change takes place: it is usually gradual, and perceptible to those working on the paper before it becomes apparent to the outside public. At any given moment there are more profitable newspapers in being than new ones trying to come up, so the general tone of the press is predominantly, and I fear increasingly, reactionary. (In New York, for example, of nine daily papers—there were thirteen when I came up to college—seven are in the black and complacent, while only one, *PM*, which has not yet climbed out of the red, is fighting the good fight. A ninth, the *Post*, has so recently made the financial grade that it doesn't quite seem to know whether it is for the status quo or agin it.) The difference between newspaper publishers' opinions and those of the public is so frequently expressed at the polls that it is unnecessary to insist on it here.

Don't get me wrong, though. I don't think that the battle is futile. I remember when I was a freshman, in 1920, listening to a lecture by Professor Mecklin in a survey course called, I think, Citizenship, in which he told how most of the newspapers had misrepresented the great steel strike of 1919. The only one that had told the truth, he said, as I remember it, was the old *World*. (I have heard since that the St. Louis *Post-Dispatch* was good, too, but he didn't mention it.) It was the first time that I really believed that newspapers lied about that sort of thing. I had heard of Upton Sinclair's book "The Brass Check," but I hadn't wanted to read it because I had heard he was a "Bolshevik." I came up to college when I was just under sixteen, and the family environment was not exactly radical. But my reaction was that I wanted someday to work for the *World*, or for some other paper that *would* tell the truth. The *World* did a damned good job, on the strikes and on the Ku Klux Klan and on prohibition and prison camps (in Florida, not Silesia), and even though the second-generation Pulitzers let it grow namby-pamby and then dropped it in terror when they had had a losing year and were down to their last sixteen million, it had not lived in vain.

I think that anybody who talks often with people about newspapers nowadays must be impressed by the growing distrust of the information they contain. There is less a disposition to accept what they say than to try to estimate the probable truth on the basis of what they say, like aiming a rifle that you know has a deviation to the right. Even a report in a Hearst newspaper can be of considerable aid in arriving at a deduction if you know enough about (a) Hearst policy, (b) the degree of abjectness of the correspondent signing the report.[3]

[3]*Albert Camus, the brilliant and versatile young French novelist, playwright, and critic, who is also editor of Combat, a Paris daily, once had an idea for establishing a "control newspaper" that would come out one hour after the others with estimates of the percentage of truth in each of their*

Every now and then I write a piece for the *New Yorker* under the heading of the Wayward Press (a title for the department invented by the late Robert Benchley when he started it early in the *New Yorker's* history). In this I concern myself not with big general thoughts about Trends (my boss wouldn't stand for such), but with the treatment of specific stories by the daily (chiefly New York) press. I am a damned sight kinder about newspapers than Wolcott Gibbs is about the theatre, but while nobody accuses him of sedition when he raps a play, I get letters calling me a little pal of Stalin when I sneer at the New York *Sun*. This reflects a pitch that newspaper publishers make to the effect that they are part of the great American heritage with a right to travel wrapped in the folds of the flag like a boll weevil in a cotton boll. Neither theatrical producers nor book publishers, apparently, partake of this sacred character. I get a lot more letters from people who are under the delusion that I can Do Something About It All. These reflect a general malaise on the part of the newspaper-reading public, which I do think will have some effect, though not, God knows, through me.

I believe that labor unions, citizens' organizations, and possibly political parties yet unborn are going to back daily papers. These will represent definite, undisguised points of view, and will serve as controls on the large profit-making papers expressing definite, ill-disguised points of view. The Labor Party's *Daily Herald*, in England, has been of inestimable value in checking the blather of the Beaverbrook-Kemsley-Rothermere newspapers of huge circulation. When one cannot get the truth from any one paper (and I do not say that it is an easy thing, even with the

---

stories, and with interpretations of how the stories were slanted. The way he explained it, it sounded possible. He said, "We'd have complete dossiers on the interests, policies, and idiosyncrasies of the owners. Then we'd have a dossier on every journalist in the world. The interests, prejudices, and quirks of the owner would equal Z. The prejudices, quirks, and private interests of the journalist, Y. Z times Y would give you X, the probable amount of truth in the story." He was going to make up his dossiers on reporters by getting journalists he trusted to appraise men they had worked with. "I would have a card-index system," he said. "Very simple. We would keep the dossiers up to date as best we could, of course. But do people really want to know how much truth there is in what they read? Would they buy the control paper? That's the most difficult problem."

best will in the world, for any one paper to tell all the truth), it is valuable to read two with opposite policies to get an idea of what is really happening. I cannot believe that labor leaders are so stupid they will let the other side monopolize the press indefinitely.

I also hope that we will live to see the endowed newspaper, devoted to the pursuit of daily truth as Dartmouth is to that of knowledge. I do not suppose that any reader of the *Magazine* believes that the test of a college is the ability to earn a profit on operations (with the corollary that making the profit would soon become the chief preoccupation of its officers). I think that a good newspaper is as truly an educational institution as a college, so I don't see why *it* should have to stake its survival on attracting advertisers of ball-point pens and tickets to Hollywood peep shows. And I think that private endowment would offer greater possibilities for a free press than state ownership (this is based on the chauvinistic idea that a place like Dartmouth can do a better job than a state university under the thumb of a Huey Long or Gene Talmadge). The hardest trick, of course, would be getting the chief donor of the endowment (perhaps a repentant tabloid publisher) to (a) croak, or (b) sign a legally binding agreement never to stick his face in the editorial rooms. The best kind of an endowment for a newspaper would be one made up of several large and many small or medium-sized gifts (the Dartmouth pattern again). Personally, I would rather leave my money for a newspaper than for a cathedral, a gymnasium, or even a home for streetwalkers with fallen arches, but I have seldom been able to assemble more than $4.17 at one time.[4]

A provision of the Taft-Hartley Act (Section 304), aimed primarily at labor-union newspapers, prohibits any non-profit

[4]Professor Michael E. Choukas, of the Dartmouth faculty, summing up after the last article of the Public Opinion in a Democracy series, commented: "Mr. Liebling's 'endowed newspaper' would probably be free from direct pressure, but it would be unable to avoid the indirect efforts of the propagandists." I think that Professor Choukas, a sociologist who has specialized in the study of propaganda, has developed an exaggerated respect for the opposition. Albert Camus's plan for the "control newspaper," which I have briefly described in another footnote, is an example of the ingenuity a good newspaperman can bring to bear, and men like Vic Bernstein, Paul Sifton, and Edmond Taylor in this country (to cite only a few—there are

publication from publishing political news or opinion. This would, of course, also stop any endowed newspaper.

It will also, I believe, outlaw or severely limit the *Christian Science Monitor*, published by the Church of Christ, Scientist, and several hundred church and diocesan publications, a circumstance which Mr. Taft will surely regret before he is much older.

Non-profit publications supported by corporate funds will also be barred from writing about politics, according to the senatorial author of the Act in a debate on June 6, but newspapers, although corporations, will be allowed to continue as usual because: "They get their money from advertising." This is a curious qualification of freedom of the press; only mediums of bally-hoo will be allowed to express an opinion. Senator Taft has not yet explained whether a newspaper will be stopped from discussing politics until its advertising begins to support it—in some cases a period of several years. Mr. Howard's *Telegram*, for example, would not have been allowed to peep about politics from the time he bought it, in 1927, until 1932, when, by virtue of an assist from the Pulitzer brothers, it began to pay. Even at that, the disastrous Ohio statesman has not explained

---

hundreds of others) would certainly bring into the ring with them more perspicacity than anybody the National Association of Manufacturers could hire. A man who thinks he can fool other men is always a little a fool himself. His assumption that he can do it presupposes a foolish vanity—like that of the recidivist con man who spends most of his life in jail. His contempt for the truth marks him as a bit sub-human. Professor Choukas did not mention my hopes for strong labor papers.

The professor's own remedy for the dilemma, however, is worthy of citation. I hope somebody makes a good hard try at it.

"I frankly do not believe that any indirect assault would have much effect as a check against those who deliberately set out to mislead us," he wrote. "A direct attack could be launched against them by a privately endowed, independent agency whose main task would consist of compiling a list of all the propaganda groups in the country, analyzing their techniques, discovering their goals, and releasing the available information to government officials, to men responsible for our channels of communication, to men who measure public opinion, to colleges and universities, and to those pathetically few groups in the country who have undertaken to fight the battle of Democracy in a positive manner.

"This I feel should be done before our crisis reaches climactic proportions —before the next depression."

whether such a newspaper will be considered profitable until it has paid off all its debts. He has not said, either, whether old-established papers will be enjoined from writing about politics if they start to lose money and have to draw on corporate funds to keep going. How much grace will they receive before being ruled "non-profit" publications: five minutes? five months? five years?

This provision, from a long-range view perhaps the most important in the bill, received virtually no publicity in the regular daily press, which may have seen in it an aid to its own continued monopoly. I never read anything about it myself until President Truman mentioned it in his veto message. It was the old story of the correspondents at London asking an outside power to crack down on their competitors. The foremost enemies of freedom of the press are its chief beneficiaries. The newspaper publishers, those avowed great enemies of government regulation of the press, have now tacitly supported government regulation of an important part of it. They favored the Taft-Hartley Bill almost unanimously. I am against government-owned newspapers and government interference with privately owned ones. But monopoly invites regulation, and when a large city has only one newspaper, the paper becomes as much a public utility as the gas company. The publishers' hope for continued independence lies in keeping the way open for the rise of new newspapers. By sealing off the potential sources of new papers, the Taft-Hartley Act would insure the eventual regulation of those that remain.

It might be argued, of course, that publishers, despite their talk, have no interest in freedom of the press beyond their freedom to make as much money as possible. I do not believe this. I think they just act that way.

I recently read an inane attack upon President Truman, whose conduct during the final struggle over the Taft-Hartley Act has been irreproachable. Whoever it was that was smearing him said he will be remembered as the President who went to a ball game while Congress was passing the Act over his veto. What else could the poor man have done? I myself would have preferred to go to the races, but that is a matter of taste, and anyway the Maryland tracks weren't operating at the time and he would have had to go all the way to Delaware Park to see any.

What really burned my bottom was reading every day about the collection of leading newspaper publishers who were on a round-the-world junket in a Pan-American Airways plane, with menus prepared by a famous chef so they wouldn't get airsick and a beautiful stewardess picked by somebody else so their eyes wouldn't get tired. They would pause for a few hours at each airport for another reception by the local headmen, while the hastily assembled local peasantry cheered and did dances for the funny Americans.

The publishers could have done more than the President, at that stage, to block the great legislative assault upon the liberties of the press. But they didn't.

Somehow, thinking about them, I couldn't stop myself from remembering a story Major General Terry Allen had told me in North Africa, about a profane old cavalry colonel inspecting an unsatisfactory troop in Texas, when Terry was a junior officer.

"Old Tommy looked at them," Terry said, "and he yelled: 'If the good, just God should look down from Heaven today and see you, He would hit you over the head with a stocking full of rocks!' "

Only Terry didn't say rocks.

Last ad, Liebling—The *Herald Tribune* today (July 11) carries a front-page story by Tom Twitty, saying that the Department of Justice holds that Section 304 applies to *all* newspapers published by corporations, which means *all* newspapers.

God didn't need to hit the publishers with that stocking. They hit themselves with it.

Reading List

Reading List

When trout fishermen continually buy books on how to tie feathers into vaguely insectile shapes and semi-occasional wine drinkers load their bookshelves with works on vintage years, can one presume to savor that massive product of the multiple human intellect, the American press, without a light course of collateral reading?

The word bibliography implies inclusiveness, for which reason I shun it. But here are a few books, pamphlets, and articles that will help the habitual newspaper reader to understand what the habitual newspaper writer is habitually writing. You can't tell the players without a scorecard.

RECENT PUBLICATIONS

The First Freedom, by Morris Ernst (Macmillan, 1946).
  Provides useful factual framework of discussion.

Survival of a Free, Competitive Press: The Small Newspaper, Democracy's Grass Roots. 80th Congress, 1st Session: Senate Committee Print No. 17. (Subtitled "Report of the Chairman to the Members of the Committee of the Special Committee to Study Problems of American Small Business" Jan. 2, 1947. Government Printing Office, Washington.)
  This seventy-two-page pamphlet contains, by reason of the type used and the method of setting it, as much printed matter as an ordinary book. It may be obtained only by writing to the

secretary of the Special Committee, et cetera, because it is not
on sale. It should be, of course.

It includes, in addition to information about concentration
of newspaper ownership and capital requirements for the aspiring
newspaper owner, material on the difficulties of would-be independent publishers in obtaining newsprint, printing machinery,
and syndicate features. Much of this material was made available
to the committee only through that body's exercise of the
power of subpoena. The pamphlet also contains details of the
government subsidy to all publishers through second-class mail
rates and some suggestions for changes.

The chairman, Senator James E. Murray of Montana, may
have been stimulated in his efforts by the fact that all but
one of the dailies in his state are owned and operated by that
fountainhead of liberal journalism, the Anaconda Copper Company.

A Free and Responsible Press. Report of the Commission on
Freedom of the Press, with a foreword by Robert
M. Hutchins (University of Chicago Press, 1947).
There isn't anything much in this that isn't in the Senate
pamphlet, and there is a lot in the pamphlet that isn't contained
in *A Free and Responsible Press.* But if you are disposed to
believe a thesis more readily when it is solemnly stated and
impressively sponsored, then *A Free and Responsible Press* is
the book for you. (Thirteen Professional Big Minds signed the
Report, thirteen, count them! Many of them Yale Men! With
Four Foreign Advisers, including Jacques Maritain and Hu Shih,
former Chinese Ambassador to the United States—A $215,000
Production.)

Public Opinion in a Democracy. May be obtained from the
Dartmouth *Alumni Magazine,* Hanover, N.H., for
twenty-five cents.
Pamphlet containing nine essays by Dartmouth men now
compelled to earn a living, all about the state of mass communications. A couple of the essays are remarkable; a couple of the
others are dead wrong. One of the pieces, which falls into
neither category, is already in your possession if you own this

book. The *Alumni Magazine*, however, will allow you no discount from the fixed price of twenty-five cents on this account. Authors' fees for this publication totaled $225, unless some other contributor got more or less than I did, and the difference between that and $215,000 should be a lesson to Henry R. Luce, who bankrolled *A Free and Responsible Press*.

Our Fair City, edited by Robert S. Allen (Vanguard Press, 1947).
   This collection of reports on seventeen different American cities by seventeen authors, mostly newspapermen or ex-newspapermen, does not deal primarily with the press, but virtually every chapter takes note of the unheroic role played by the local papers. The book places the newspaper in its relation to other factors in American municipal life, as the Tidewater Pool Group in the American Museum of Natural History shows the jellyfish in symbiosis with other marine things. The newspaper is not an isolated entity, but is a commensal of other corporations, devourer of small fry it can attack with impunity (gunmen, streetwalkers, "radicals"), sham warrior like the blowfish in the face of larger creatures.

My Quest for Freedom, by John M. Mecklin (Scribner's, 1945).
   An honest, tortured book. Chapter VI touches on the press.

LESS RECENT

The End of the World, by more than a score of staff members (Harper, 1931).
   Record of three days that shook the newspaper world.

The World, The Flesh and Messrs. Pulitzer, by James W. Barrett (Vanguard Press, 1931).
   Post-mortem that teaches much of the essence of newspapering.

Freedom of the Press, by George Seldes (World Publishing, 1942); *Lords of the Press*, by George Seldes (Julian Messner, 1938).

Seldes is strident, like a man shouting into a telephone in a
dream, one of those dreams in which one simply can't raise
the operator, although the house is on fire and a monstrous he-
goat is about to thrust a red-hot poker in one's ear. He is about
as subtle as a house falling in, and he makes too much of the
failure of newspapers to print exactly what George Seldes would
have printed if he had been managing editor. But he is a useful
citizen.

In Fact, his four-page weekly, which he calls "An Antidote
for Falsehood in the Daily Press" ($2 a year), is a fine little
gadfly, representing an enormous effort for one man and his
wife. It is difficult to catch the press in a heinous fraud every
week, and I get the impression that some numbers of In Fact
have more buzz than sting. But if newspapers find it incon-
venient to suspend on days when they have no news, it must
be equally awkward for a weekly to mail its subscribers postcards
with the message "Sorry—no infamy this week."

I think he too often treats errors as lies, and lies as the effect
of a deliberate and universal conspiracy of the devils in human
form known to him as publishers, but since we have Kent
Cooper and Dean Carl W. Ackerman of the Columbia School
of Journalism to tell us constantly that the American press is
perfect, it is nice to have George around to tell us that it ain't.

The Brass Check, A Study of American Journalism, by Upton
      Sinclair.
    The only copy I could find in a search of Fourth Avenue book-
stores is a paper-bound item, published by the author at Pasa-
dena, California, and undated. The first edition, I am pretty
sure, came out in 1920.

We are now in a period like that which followed the last war,
and much of The Brass Check seems now to have a pertinence
it had lost ten or fifteen years ago. Viking recently published
a new edition of The Jungle, Sinclair's old exposé of the packing
industry, and I should think that The Brass Check would be an
even better bet today. I read it for the first time last spring, and
so am not influenced by any ancient, boyish admiration. Sinclair
was no newspaperman, although he has proved himself, on
occasion, a good reporter. The Brass Check is full of the author's

preoccupation with himself; he even felt that the publication of the book might prove personally dangerous. He is still whole. He also thought that the book might be smothered by the press's refusal to review it. But as I remember, it had a considerable impact even though it missed me. The times gentled. Viewed in retrospect from 1925, *The Brass Check* might well have seemed too lurid. In 1935 the reader might have thought it merely an interesting historical exhibit. But in the National Association of Manufacturers' all-time-high year of 1947, *The Brass Check* seems as fresh as today's newspaper.

Collected Edition of Heywood Broun, compiled by Heywood Hale Broun (Harcourt, Brace & Co., 1941).

Particularly the sections, listed in the Table of Contents, on Journalism, Justice, and Labor. Broun was a great man, and it is a great pity that he couldn't have lived to sweat through all this. I wonder what form his brand-new Catholicism would have taken with the years; I remember what he used to do to suits. Having observed him for years on race tracks, where he bet everything over 50 to 1, I could understand the reason for his conversion. If there was one chance in a million of a life after death, Broun had to have a two-dollar ticket.

UNRECENT PUBLICATIONS

Martin Chuzzlewit, by Charles Dickens (Chapman and Hall, London, 1844). Chapters XVI and XVII.

Monographie de la Presse Parisienne, Honoré de Balzac, précedée de l'Histoire Véridique du Canard, par Gérard de Werval (Aubry, Paris, 1943).

I don't know the year in which Balzac wrote this monograph, but to read it now is like listening to a sermon on the text "*Plus ça change . . .*" et cetera. The 1943 edition, done under the German Occupation by a publisher with his tongue in his cheek, provided a pat commentary on the collaborationist press. From the jacket: "Janin said to us the other day during an attack

of frankness—'Do you know why I have lasted for twenty years?
—Because I changed my opinions every fortnight.' "

Letters from Ireland, from the *Political Register,* William Cob-
        bett, (London, 1834). Reprinted in *Cobbett's
        Rural Rides,* edited by G. D. H. and Margaret
        Cole (Peter Davies, London, 1930).

I throw this in as an example of how good reporting, and
journalistic writing, can be.